Anna Förster

Teaching Networks How to Learn

Anna Förster

Teaching Networks How to Learn

Data Dissemination in Wireless Sensor Networks with Reinforcement Learning

Südwestdeutscher Verlag für Hochschulschriften

Impressum/Imprint (nur für Deutschland/ only for Germany)
Bibliografische Information der Deutschen Nationalbibliothek: Die Deutsche Nationalbibliothek verzeichnet diese Publikation in der Deutschen Nationalbibliografie; detaillierte bibliografische Daten sind im Internet über http://dnb.d-nb.de abrufbar.
Alle in diesem Buch genannten Marken und Produktnamen unterliegen warenzeichen-, marken- oder patentrechtlichem Schutz bzw. sind Warenzeichen oder eingetragene Warenzeichen der jeweiligen Inhaber. Die Wiedergabe von Marken, Produktnamen, Gebrauchsnamen, Handelsnamen, Warenbezeichnungen u.s.w. in diesem Werk berechtigt auch ohne besondere Kennzeichnung nicht zu der Annahme, dass solche Namen im Sinne der Warenzeichen- und Markenschutzgesetzgebung als frei zu betrachten wären und daher von jedermann benutzt werden dürften.

Verlag: Südwestdeutscher Verlag für Hochschulschriften Aktiengesellschaft & Co. KG
Dudweiler Landstr. 99, 66123 Saarbrücken, Deutschland
Telefon +49 681 37 20 271-1, Telefax +49 681 37 20 271-0, Email: info@svh-verlag.de
Zugl.: Lugano, USI, Diss., 2009

Herstellung in Deutschland:
Schaltungsdienst Lange o.H.G., Zehrensdorfer Str. 11, D-12277 Berlin
Books on Demand GmbH, Gutenbergring 53, D-22848 Norderstedt
Reha GmbH, Dudweiler Landstr. 99, D- 66123 Saarbrücken
ISBN: 978-3-8381-0936-7

Imprint (only for USA, GB)
Bibliographic information published by the Deutsche Nationalbibliothek: The Deutsche Nationalbibliothek lists this publication in the Deutsche Nationalbibliografie; detailed bibliographic data are available in the Internet at http://dnb.d-nb.de.
Any brand names and product names mentioned in this book are subject to trademark, brand or patent protection and are trademarks or registered trademarks of their respective holders. The use of brand names, product names, common names, trade names, product descriptions etc. even without
a particular marking in this works is in no way to be construed to mean that such names may be regarded as unrestricted in respect of trademark and brand protection legislation and could thus be used by anyone.

Publisher:
Südwestdeutscher Verlag für Hochschulschriften Aktiengesellschaft & Co. KG
Dudweiler Landstr. 99, 66123 Saarbrücken, Germany
Phone +49 681 37 20 271-1, Fax +49 681 37 20 271-0, Email: info@svh-verlag.de

Copyright © 2008 Südwestdeutscher Verlag für Hochschulschriften Aktiengesellschaft & Co. KG and licensors
All rights reserved. Saarbrücken 2008

Produced in USA and UK by:
Lightning Source Inc., 1246 Heil Quaker Blvd., La Vergne, TN 37086, USA
Lightning Source UK Ltd., Chapter House, Pitfield, Kiln Farm, Milton Keynes, MK11 3LW, GB
BookSurge, 7290 B. Investment Drive, North Charleston, SC 29418, USA
ISBN: 978-3-8381-0936-7

To Alexander

Abstract

Wireless sensor networks (WSNs) are a fast developing research area with many new exciting applications arising, ranging from micro climate and environmental monitoring through health and structural monitoring to interplanetary communications. At the same time researchers have invested a lot of time and effort into developing high performance energy efficient and reliable communication protocols to meet the growing challenges of WSN applications and deployments. However, some major problems still remain: for example programming, planning and deploying sensor networks, energy efficient communication, and dependability under harsh environmental conditions.

Routing and clustering for wireless sensor networks play a significant role for reliable and energy efficient data dissemination. Although these research areas have attracted a lot of interest lately, there is still no general holistic approach that is able to meet the requirements and challenges of many different applications and network scenarios, like various network sizes and topologies, multiple mobile data sinks, or node failures. The current state-of-the-art is rich in specialized routing and clustering protocols, which concentrate on one or a few of the above problems, but perform poorly under slightly different network conditions.

The main goal of this thesis is to demonstrate that machine learning is a practical approach to a range of complex distributed problems in WSNs. Showing this will open up new paths for development at all levels of the communication stack. To achieve our goal we contribute a robust, energy-efficient, and flexible data dissemination framework consisting of a routing protocol called FROMS and a clustering protocol called CLIQUE. Both protocols are based on Q-Learning, a reinforcement learning technique, and exhibit vital properties such as robustness against mobility, node and link failures, fast recovery after failures, very low control overhead and a wide variety of supported network scenarios and applications. Both protocols are fully distributed and have minimal communication overhead. Additionally, CLIQUE gives a distributed solution to the recently emerged novel paradigm of non-uniform data dissemination, where the size of the clusters in a network grows with increasing distance from the data sinks.

We evaluate the protocols analytically and experimentally under a realistic simulation environment and on real hardware. Thus, we show not only that machine learning is applicable to real-world wireless sensor networks, but that it also achieves significantly better performance in terms of energy spent, network lifetime, load spreading, and delivery rate under various network conditions, when compared to other state-of-the-art routing and clustering approaches. This thesis is one of the rare attempts to compare two routing protocols in terms of communication overhead and delivery rate on real hardware.

We believe that this thesis successfully proves that machine learning is a feasible approach for solving various hard problems in wireless sensor networks, paving the way to further applications, protocols and optimizations, which will inherently improve the performance of wireless sensor networks.

Acknowledgements

I would like to thank my advisor Amy Murphy for introducing me into the research area of wireless sensor networks, for her help and support during all phases of this thesis and mainly for the many long and fruitful discussions, which always inspired and motivated me. I am grateful for all the time she dedicated to me and my work despite the long geographic distance between us and her family duties. She became a good friend and I hope this relationship will last after the end of this thesis too.

I had many helpful and interesting discussions with all the other dissertation committee members. To Jochen Schiller goes my very special thank for supporting my hardware studies with advice and material and to his whole research group at FU Berlin for the help and support in implementing the protocols on hardware. In fact, the main implementation work was conducted during the research stay of Kirsten Terfloth in Lugano in June 2007.

I would like also to thank G. K. Venayagamoorthy from the Missouri University of Science and Technology and his student R. V. Kulkarni for the joint work on the survey of computational intelligence techniques for wireless sensor networks, parts of which are used in this thesis. Further I would like to thank the professors and Ph.D. students at the University of Lugano for their friendship and support: especially our dean Mehdi Jazayeri, Antonio Carzaniga, Jochen Wuttke, Cyrus Hall, Paolo Bonzini and all the others with whom I shared work and life for four years.

I am also very grateful to my parents Radmila Stoyanova and Alexey Egorov for showing me the way to computer science and research, for supporting my interests and goals, for paving my way up to here and for pushing me always to give more than the best out of me.

However, the most I am grateful to my husband Alexander Förster: he supported me in all phases of my dissertation, motivating me to continue and not to give up, even during frustrating periods. My discussions with him inspired a lot of the work presented here and often showed me the right direction as it seemed lost. He provided me with invaluable feedback about the theoretical aspects of this work and was always willing to help me in the programming and debugging phases. Further we worked together on the optimal cluster analysis presented at the end of this dissertation. Last but not least, he took care of our little son Max while mum was working on her thesis. Thank you for everything.

Contents

Contents		x
1 Introduction		**1**
1.1	Contributions	3
1.2	Dissertation overview	5
2 Target WSN Application Scenario		**7**
3 Related Research Efforts		**17**
3.1	Energy-efficient multicast routing in WSNs	17
	3.1.1 Point-to-point routing in WSNs	18
	3.1.2 Multicast routing in WSNs	20
	3.1.3 Sink mobility in WSNs	23
	3.1.4 Failure recovery for routing in WSNs	24
	3.1.5 Routing cost metrics for WSNs	25
	3.1.6 Routing in WSNs: Summary	27
3.2	Energy-efficient clustering for WSNs	27
	3.2.1 Random protocols	29
	3.2.2 1-hop grid clustering	29
	3.2.3 K-hop clustering	30
	3.2.4 Location and tree based clustering	31
	3.2.5 Infrastructure supported clustering	31
	3.2.6 Non-uniform clustering in WSNs	32
	3.2.7 Centralized clustering	33
	3.2.8 In-cluster data aggregation and clustering	34

		3.2.9	Optimal clustering analysis	34
		3.2.10	Clustering in WSNs: Summary	35
	3.3	Machine learning for WSNs		36
		3.3.1	Neural Networks	38
		3.3.2	Support Vector Machines	41
		3.3.3	Decision trees and case-based reasoning	43
		3.3.4	Reinforcement learning	43
		3.3.5	Swarm Intelligence	49
		3.3.6	Genetic algorithms	55
		3.3.7	Heuristic Search	58
		3.3.8	Fuzzy logic	60
		3.3.9	Summary	63
	3.4	Concluding remarks		66

4 Methodology and Solution Path 67

	4.1	Background on Q-Learning		68
	4.2	Evaluating wireless sensor networks		73
		4.2.1	Evaluation through simulation	73
		4.2.2	Evaluation on real hardware	86
		4.2.3	Theoretical analyses	87
		4.2.4	Identified evaluation methodology	88
	4.3	Concluding remarks		91

5 FROMS: Routing to Multiple Mobile Sinks in WSNs 93

	5.1	Protocol intuition		94
	5.2	Routing data to multiple sinks with Q-Learning		96
		5.2.1	Problem definition	97
		5.2.2	Multicast Routing with Q-Learning	97
	5.3	Theoretical analysis of FROMS		101
		5.3.1	Worst-case complexity and convergence	101
		5.3.2	Correctness of FROMS	106
		5.3.3	Memory and processing requirements	108
	5.4	Protocol implementation details and parameters		108

	5.4.1	Sink announcement	109
	5.4.2	Feedback implementation	109
	5.4.3	Data management	110
	5.4.4	Route storage reducing heuristics	114
	5.4.5	Loop management	115
	5.4.6	Mobility management	115
	5.4.7	Node failures	117
	5.4.8	Cost metrics	117
	5.4.9	Exploration strategies	121
	5.4.10	Summary	123
5.5	Stand-alone evaluation of FROMS	123
	5.5.1	Memory and processing requirements (hardware testbed)	125
	5.5.2	Route storage heuristics (simulation)	127
	5.5.3	Exploration strategies (simulation)	128
	5.5.4	Cost functions (simulation)	130
5.6	Comparative evaluation of FROMS	133
	5.6.1	Multi-source multi-sink routing (simulation)	134
	5.6.2	Multi-source multi-sink routing (hardware testbed)	139
	5.6.3	Recovery after failure (simulation)	141
	5.6.4	Sink mobility (simulation)	144
5.7	Concluding remarks	146

6 CLIQUE: Role-free Clustering for WSNs   149

6.1	Grid-based cluster membership computation	151
6.2	Finding the cluster head with Q-Learning	154
	6.2.1	Discussion of key properties and convergence of CLIQUE	158
	6.2.2	Sink mobility	160
6.3	Comparative evaluation of CLIQUE	162
	6.3.1	Uniform clustering evaluation	164
	6.3.2	Non-uniform clustering evaluation	169
6.4	Optimal cluster sizes	170
	6.4.1	Defining the optimal cluster	172
	6.4.2	Finding the optimal cluster	175

   6.4.3 Optimal clustering summary and rules 182
 6.5 Concluding remarks 183

7 Conclusions   **185**

Acronyms   **187**

Bibliography   **189**

Chapter 1

Introduction

The beginning of wireless sensor networks (WSNs) is commonly associated with the SmartDust [97] project from 1998, when the vision of large autonomous sensor networks for monitoring various environmental and industrial fields was born. Since then a lot of research has been conducted and many different sensor network hardware platforms have emerged. The price of individual sensors has been constantly decreasing, while their memory, processing and sensory abilities have been growing. At the same time their application scenarios have been also expanding. Researchers and practitioners from many scientific and industrial areas have leveraged the achievements of the wireless sensor networks community and have installed hundreds of sensor networks. These deployments range from scientific monitoring applications of active volcanos [199], glaciers [126] and permafrost [182], through agricultural monitoring [113], military and rescue applications[3, 36] to the futuristic vision of the InterPlaNetary Internet [2, 122], designed to connect highly heterogeneous devices like satellites, Mars and Moon rovers, sensor networks, space shuttles, and common handheld devices and laptops into one holistic network.

The growing number of applications for WSNs and especially their heterogeneous requirements and properties demand new communication protocols and architectures. The WSN community has put a lot of effort in developing energy efficient, reliable and fast communication services for various applications and network scenarios. However, many topics like deployment and tuning of sensor networks, programming and debugging, and energy-efficiency of data dissemination are still considered major challenges [156].

Especially the area of data dissemination – routing and clustering – for WSNs has attracted a lot of research in the latest years, and developed many different protocols, for various application scenarios, and data traffic schedules. However, lately this area is attracting a lot of criticism: application scenarios are too restricted or not even carefully described, experimental setups are unrealistic, and simulation environments are too abstract [152]. And despite the overwhelming number of routing protocols and variations, there are still unsolved challenges, the most important being energy efficiency in various application scenarios and traffics, and tolerance against failures and mobility. Additionally, the problem of sending data to multiple, possibly mobile sinks via optimal paths (multicast) has not been solved efficiently yet. The same problems arise also in clustering algorithms, where current state-of-the-art solutions need complex algorithms to agree on cluster head roles, usually incurring significant communication overhead, not related to the real data traffic.

There are also other challenging problems in WSNs such as distributed medium access, localization, link management, optimal positioning and coverage etc. We believe that these complex distributed problems, including routing and clustering, can be efficiently and elegantly solved with machine learning techniques. Machine learning and some related computational intelligence algorithms exhibit vital problems like distributed autonomous behavior and adaptability to changing environments, which make them highly applicable to WSNs. However, WSN practitioners seem reluctant to use these algorithms in their applications. The main reason for this is that machine learning techniques have higher memory and processing requirements than traditional approaches in WSNs. In addition, there have been no conclusive studies or applications of machine learning to complex distributed problems in WSNs and the real dimensions of their requirements remain unclear.

The main goal of this thesis is to demonstrate that machine learning is a practical approach to a range of complex distributed problems in WSNs. Showing this will open up new paths for development at all levels of the communication stack. To achieve our goal we contribute a robust, energy-efficient, and flexible data dissemination framework consisting of a routing protocol called FROMS and a clustering protocol called CLIQUE.

Both protocols are based on Q-Learning, a reinforcement learning technique, and exhibit vital properties such as robustness against mobility, node and link failures, fast recovery after failures, very low control overhead, and a wide variety of supported network scenarios and applications. Both protocols are fully distributed and have minimal communication overhead. Additionally, CLIQUE gives a distributed solution to the recently emerged novel paradigm of non-uniform data dissemination, where the size of the clusters in a network grows with increasing distance from the data sinks. Unlike other routing, clustering, or generally data dissemination protocols, the designed framework needs to cope innately with mobility and failures and to be able to efficiently manage multiple sources and multiple destinations. It needs to provide WSN developers and practitioners with a highly flexible, intuitively parametrizable tool. Additionally and most importantly, the real world applicability of the framework needs to be proven by implementing and evaluating the protocols on a state-of-the-art sensor network hardware platform.

1.1 Contributions

As stated above, the main goal of this thesis is to show the real world applicability of machine learning techniques and algorithms to complex distributed problems in wireless sensor networks. To reach our goal we approach the problem of energy efficient, robust multicast data dissemination for large deployments of wireless sensor networks. Our primary contributions are:

- A novel multicast routing protocol called FROMS (Feedback ROuting to Multiple Sinks), extensively evaluated in theory, simulation, and hardware. FROMS is compared to three other state-of-the-art routing protocols and shows superior performance compared to all of them in terms of energy expenditure, delivery rate, network lifetime, and mobility and failure management. This thesis presents one of the few attempts to directly compare two routing protocols in terms of communication overhead and delivery rate on a real sensor network hardware platform under the same network conditions.

- A novel role-free and overhead-free clustering approach called CLIQUE, extensively evaluated in theory and simulation. This protocol is particularly interesting, because it presents the novel concept of self-organized role-free clustering for WSNs. Instead of assigning the role of cluster heads to some nodes, the nodes themselves decide on a per-packet basis whether to act as such or to route the data further to better suited neighbors. The protocol is based again on Q-Learning and compared to a traditional clustering algorithm, is able to achieve approximately 25% longer network lifetimes and to spread the energy expenditure among the nodes in the network.

The obtained results from evaluating FROMS and CLIQUE are highly promising and clearly show that machine learning can be successfully applied to various difficult distributed problems in WSNs, such as medium access, neighborhood management, localization, or fault recognition. The experiences gathered while designing, implementing and evaluating both protocols pave the way to further research and development in WSNs. This will inherently improve the performance of WSNs, ease their development and deployment, and broaden their application areas.

In addition to novel protocol design and implementation, this dissertation offers further complementary contributions:

- A theoretical study of optimal cluster sizes for WSNs in terms of incurred communication overhead. Beside the extensive research body on clustering in WSNs, there have been only few efforts on identifying the optimal size of clusters or the optimal position of the cluster heads inside the clusters. Here, we step back from any clustering protocols in particular and conduct an experimental study on optimal clusters in terms of incurred communication overhead.

- An extensive survey and evaluation of machine learning and computational intelligence techniques for various applications in wireless sensor networks. For each application in WSNs, it identifies the best suited ML algorithms, and for each surveyed ML technique it identifies its WSN-related properties and requirements. This work is intended to be used also by other researchers as a guide to optimizing their own protocols and algorithms and to selecting the best suited ML techniques.

- A broad assessment of current evaluation practices and methodologies for routing and clustering protocols in WSNs. This study includes 30 late-stage or final versions of communication protocols. It surveys their evaluation platforms, network models, and evaluation metrics and derives a general credible state-of-the-art evaluation methodology. Again, this work can be used by other researchers when designing and planning their protocols' evaluations: in simulation, on real hardware or in theory.

1.2 Dissertation overview

We concentrate first on the targeted application scenario, its properties and requirements in Chapter 2, thus giving the context for the rest of the work. Then we present an extensive survey on related work in routing and clustering for WSNs, and our guide and survey to machine learning and computational intelligence techniques for various applications in WSNs in Chapter 3. Chapter 4 identifies the solution approach for the data dissemination protocols and presents the assessment of state-of-the-art evaluation methodologies for routing and clustering in WSNs. It also identifies our own evaluation methodology, required network models, and protocols for comparative studies.

Chapter 5 describes the design, implementation and evaluation of FROMS, our multicast routing protocol. Chapter 6 presents our clustering algorithm CLIQUE, its implementation and evaluation details. Further, it presents our experimental study on optimal cluster sizes and parameters. Chapter 7 summarizes the results and contributions of this thesis and presents our vision of further research topics and challenges for wireless sensor networks.

Chapter 2
Target WSN Application Scenario

Real deployments of wireless sensor networks usually implement one of three general applications: periodic reporting, event detection, and database-like storage. Periodic reporting is by far the most used and simplest application scenario: at regular intervals the sensors sample the environment, store the sensed data, and send it further to the base station(s). Actuators are often directly connected with those sensor networks, for example automatic irrigation systems or alarm systems. This scenario is used in most monitoring applications for agriculture [113, 129], microclimate [21, 126, 182] and habitat surveillance [19, 135, 181], military operations [3], and disaster relief [36]. The main property of periodic reporting applications is the predictability of the data traffic and volume.

In contrast, in event detection applications [199, 201] nodes sense the environment and evaluate the data immediately for its usefulness. If useful data (an event) is detected, the data is transmitted to the base station(s). The data traffic can hardly be predicted: events usually occur randomly and the resulting data traffic is bursty. However, a small amount of data has to be propagated for route management and liveness checks even in case no events are detected.

The third group of sensor networks applications, database-like storage systems [121], are very similar to event-based systems. All of the sensory data (regular sampling or events) is stored locally on the nodes. Base stations search for interesting data and retrieve it from the nodes directly. The main challenge in these applications is to store the data in a smart way, so that searching and retrieving can be fast.

In this work we consider periodic reporting scenarios, since they make up the major part of current and future WSN deployments. More precisely, we consider sample applications such as:

- Disaster relief and military operations [3, 36]. Sensors are deployed randomly over large areas in a non-planned manner. They deliver vital data about the environment or detect events such as military enemies or survivors in a disaster area. The nodes are usually static, while the data consumers are for example rescue workers who move with handheld devices around the disaster area. Maintenance of the network after deployment is usually impossible.

- Environmental monitoring and surveillance [19, 20, 21, 113, 126, 129, 135, 181, 182, 199]. These deployments exhibit mainly the same properties as disaster relief and military applications. However, networks are usually planned in advance and continuos monitoring of the environment is performed. Often actuators are deployed together with the sensor network, such as automatic irrigation systems.

- The InterPlaNetary Internet [2, 122]. These networks include highly heterogeneous devices such as satellites in orbit around Earth, Moon and Mars, space stations, Moon and Mars habitats, handheld devices for astronauts, autonomous robots, robotic swarms, and sensor networks. While each of these components has its own main mission, their secondary goal is to form a fully connected network and to guarantee reliable communication. Sensor networks are a significant part of this scenario, to be deployed in multiple areas to deliver vital environmental data and to support communications in regions with insufficient satellite coverage.

Although these scenarios are very different in their nature and goals, they share a lot of properties. In the next paragraphs we derive the properties of the application scenario for routing and clustering protocols to be considered in this dissertation, called here for simplicity the data dissemination protocols.

1. *Network size.* During disaster monitoring and recovery it is usually impossible to plan the network and its topology in advance. Thus, the main application requirement for the data dissemination protocols is to be able to cope with *randomly deployed* networks with random links, varying density and unknown reliability and quality. The same requirement holds for military applications and for the InterPlaNetary Internet, where the requirement has been defined: "...multiple sensor networks consisting of ten to one hundred nodes may be deployed in inaccessible locations on Moon/Mars to obtain scientific data" [122]. The number of nodes in environmental monitoring spans a wide range too. In different deployments of SensorScope [20] the number of nodes reached from 20 to 100. Deployments for precision agriculture [113, 129] use 100 to 150 nodes. Volcano monitoring [199] or glacier monitoring [126, 182] need to cope with extremely hostile environments and current deployments have been usually in the range of 10 to 15 nodes. However, these numbers are expected to rise in the next years and larger deployments are already planned [182].

   Thus, we conclude that the number of nodes is unknown and can vary from only several nodes to hundreds or even thousands randomly organized into a multi-hop topology.

2. *Energy restrictions.* One of the main challenges of wireless sensor networks are the highly restricted power reserves of the sensor nodes. The sensor nodes typically have on-board low capacity batteries, which are used for sensing, processing and communication. However, the primary power consumer is the radio [6, 112], which drains the node's battery quickly for active listening of the wireless medium and data transmission. In addition, many WSN deployments need to run unattended over weeks or even months and batteries cannot be replaced. This is the case, for example, for disaster relief operations [3] or for sensor networks as part of the InterPlaNetary Internet [2, 122]. On the other hand, failing of some sensor nodes might disconnect the network and stop data delivery. This event if often referred to as network death. Thus, one of the major design goals and requirements for data dissemination protocols is the efficient

use of energy reserves and network life prolongation through on-board optimization and node-wide balancing of communication overhead.

3. *Node failures.* Node failures are a direct consequence of the limited energy availability on the nodes. With dwindling battery reserves, the node's behavior becomes first very unreliable in terms of communication and then the node fails completely. In unattended environments the node will never recover. However, in agricultural monitoring [113, 129] exchange of batteries is possible and the node will re-enter the network. Node failure or restart can happen also for other reasons, for example because of loose contacts, defect hardware or bad environmental conditions. A data dissemination framework needs to cope well with all these events and to guarantee continuous data delivery during the full network lifetime. It also needs to accommodate new nodes to make efficient use of all network resources.

4. *Sink mobility.* Sensor nodes in all our sample applications are usually simple, static entities. Current deployments often plan only one fixed base station. However, this approach has various drawbacks: the base station is a single point of failure and other data consumers in the sensor network have to retrieve the data directly from the base station. The second argument is often considered an inconvenience rather than a real risk. However, imagine a disaster relief scenario as described in [36], where a sensor network has been deployed to observe the environment, estimate risks and discover people. The rescue workers are equipped with wireless handheld devices, which usually are able to communicate with the base station (the emergency habitat). In the "normal" situation they can get sensory data from it directly. However, what happens when they move around and their handheld devices go out of range of the base station? Usually no functioning infrastructure is available to ensure communication. In such cases the sensor network itself can take over the communication among the sensor network, the base station and the rescue workers. The consequence for data dissemination protocols is that multiple mobile sinks are present in the network.

Nearly the same situation arises in other application scenarios. In the InterPlaNetary Internet [2, 122] the requirements are mostly the same as for disaster relief. There, communication between mobile entities (robots or humans) and the rest of the network is crucial and needs to be reliable under all conditions. Imagine a situation where human explorers of Mars are working outside the habitat and lose communication to it. In such a case, any other communication-enabled devices (sensor networks, robots, satellites) need to take over and to re-connect the network.

For environmental monitoring the need of mobile sinks is not that urgent, but it would be helpful to unobtrusively replace the base station in case of failure or to receive the data directly from the sensor network in case the used device has no access to the base station.

Thus, the data dissemination protocols need to support mobile sinks and to be able to route data between heterogenous devices considering non-uniform costs of the links.

5. *Data generation, delivery and traffic.* Usually there are many different data types available in a sensor network, e.g. temperature, humidity, light, gas concentration, acceleration. Sinks need to be able to choose between different data types, data sensing intervals, reporting intervals, compression parameters, etc. The sensing and reporting can be continuos or temporary. The achievable throughput of a network depends mostly on the Medium ACcess (MAC) protocol in use. The contribution of the data dissemination protocols to managing data traffic is to generate as few packets as possible. This lowers the overall latency, and increases the delivery rate and reliability. At the same time, sinks' requirements on data quality need to be met (see next point).

We assume that a suitable MAC protocol is used and the volume of data traffic can be anything between few readings from a single node to a single sink to all nodes reporting to several sinks.

6. *Quality of service requirements.* In addition to the data requirements above, the sinks have also quality of service requirements. Different applications

have different requirements. For example, disaster relief operations [3] need reliable minimum delay delivery of sensory data for ensuring fast response. On the other hand, they allow data compression and aggregation, since the network is often deployed very densely to ensure full coverage and data readings from neighboring nodes can be compressed or aggregated. In contrast, agricultural monitoring [113] is a delay-tolerant application where efficient energy use and long network lifetimes are more important to keep maintenance effort and costs low. Data aggregation or compression are possible too.

Micro-climate monitoring differs from the above by its high delay tolerance, but tight requirements on reliability of delivery of non-compressed raw data readings. Monitoring of areas such as glaciers [126, 182] or volcanos [199] is very costly and requires high effort of planning and deploying. The high cost of these applications makes it impossible to densely deploy the network for redundancy of sensing. The sensor network usually gathers data about previously non-observable phenomena, which helps researchers understand the dynamics of these environments and needs to be gathered on the base stations without any loss. On the other hand, as already stated, these applications are highly delay tolerant and compression can be used to reduce communication overhead if data quality does not suffer.

One of the main properties of the InterPlaNetary Internet [2, 122] is its two-fold mission: gathering sensory information and serving as communication infrastructure in emergency cases. The first mission is in fact micro-climate monitoring, with the same requirements as above. However, the second mission changes the requirements significantly. Communication services become first priority in case of emergencies and require minimal delay and high reliability. Compression can be used in some cases, for example for voice or video transmissions.

In summary, the data dissemination framework designed in this thesis needs not only to support all of these quality of services requirements, but to be able to switch between them quickly and efficiently. The most important requirements are support of compression and aggregation of data, minimum delay, minimum energy expenditure, and high reliability (delivery rate).

7. *Non-uniform data requirement.* In addition to the above typical wireless sensor network quality of service and data requirements, we explore the the relatively novel concept of *non-uniform data dissemination*. For example, in a disaster recovery scenario sinks are rescue workers, moving through the disaster area and receiving information about their environment like temperature or toxic gas concentration. They may require highly accurate information close to their present location (i.e. raw sensor readings), and only approximate information (i.e. computed mean sensor readings) about distant locations. In other words, the allowed aggregation rate is proportional to the distance between the worker and the data source. Other non-uniform quality requirements are also possible, like incorporating movement direction to require accurate information in the direction of movement and less accuracy in the movement wake, or adjusting accuracy depending on the density of workers in a particular area. Other possible parameters are setting the point of highest data quality to some other position than the worker's or setting two points of interest.

Additionally, there are some other important design criteria concerning the quality and the credibility of the conducted work. Unlike the requirements outlined above, which arise directly from the described deployments and applications, the design criteria and their fulfillment are important for practitioners in the area and other researchers. They guarantee the real world applicability of the implemented communication protocols.

- *Simplicity.* The protocols must be easy to understand and implement in order to be feasible for real-world deployments.

- *Memory and processing requirements.* The implementation must fit comfortably onto a typical sensor node, leaving space for other protocols and applications.

- *Flexibility.* The protocol must be easily adaptable to different applications and optimization goals.

- *Scalability.* The implemented protocols must be scalable in terms of network size, number of sources, and number of sinks.

In order to design and implement the data dissemination protocols, we need to make some assumptions about the rest of the communication stack:

1. *Sink announcements (data requests).* We assume that sinks announce themselves via a network-wide broadcast in which they state their optimization goal, clustering and data requirements. A sink initiates this process by sending out a sink announcement packet to all nodes in its range. Each of the receiving nodes updates the information in this packet and re-broadcasts it to its neighbors and so on. For example, hops to the individual sinks can be easily propagated this way. The sink initiates the process by sending a packet with hop count 0 (hops to itself), its direct neighbors update this information to $0+1$, their neighbors to $0+1+1$ etc. Propagating sink announcements is a very common approach in WSNs.

2. *Data aggregation and compression functions.* The above outlined application requirements implicitly allow for in-network data aggregation or compression. Typically this is done by dividing the nodes in the network into groups called clusters, and aggregating the data from each cluster before sending it to the base stations. A single node is selected to be the cluster head and to take care of aggregating the data of its cluster. There are mainly two mechanisms for performing the data aggregation [41]: tree-based or centralized. The first method implies that data is aggregated on the way to the cluster head. The second approach gathers the full sensory data of the cluster on the cluster head and aggregates it there before sending a single data packet to the base stations. In our work we assume either of the methods can be used. Additionally compression can be used instead of aggregation. However, the exact data aggregation or compression functions are out of scope of this dissertation. We assume that they are simple

and do not have any additional processing or memory requirements. Thus, any sensor nodes can serve as cluster heads.

3. *MAC layer.* Data dissemination protocols (routing and clustering) rely heavily on the lower layer protocols' performance. We consider a simple broadcast-enabled MAC protocol without re-transmissions and without delivery guarantee, basically any sensor network MAC protocol.

4. *Neighborhood management.* Often separate neighborhood or link management protocols are used, which measure the link quality of a node's neighbors and prohibit the use of unreliable neighbors. We do not assume any neighborhood management protocol - the neighbors' reliability and quality need to be managed by the routing and clustering protocols directly, in order to be able to manage failures and mobility in an efficient and holistic way.

This chapter presented and analyzed the most important application requirements for this thesis. In summary, our data dissemination framework needs to cope with different network sizes, multiple mobile sinks, failing nodes, restricted energy reserves, various data and quality of service requirements, and the novel concept of non-uniform data quality.

Our first intuition is that the data dissemination framework needs to be divided into clustering and routing. Network clustering will take care of data aggregation and compression, where applicable, and routing will conduct the data delivery to the base stations. Additionally, a machine learning algorithm seems a good choice for solving the above problems in an autonomous, self-organized, and energy-efficient way. In the next Chapter 3 we will explore related efforts on solving the routing and clustering problems. We discuss their properties, advantages and disadvantages. We also offer an extensive survey of machine learning and its related discipline computational intelligence for various applications in wireless sensor networks.

16

Chapter 3
Related Research Efforts

The targeted scenario described in the previous chapter exhibits two main challenges: routing to multiple sinks with managing failures and mobility, and energy-efficient, low-overhead, possibly non-uniform clustering. In the following we will discuss each of them individually, explain why it is hard to solve them and outline related efforts for meeting them. The goal of this survey is to identify the approaches and algorithms used by researchers to solve different problems of our application scenario and to discuss them in the context of our own requirements (see Chapter 2).

Additionally we present a survey on machine learning (ML) and computational intelligence (CI) applications in wireless sensor networks. Our first intuition is that this class of algorithms is highly suitable to meet all of the challenges of the presented application scenario. However, we need to understand how each of these algorithms performs in the context of wireless sensor networks in order to identify the best suited technique for this thesis.

3.1 Energy-efficient multicast routing in WSNs

While a large body of different routing protocols has emerged in the last years, there is still no general and well-performing routing protocol for WSNs. Real deployments often decide for a simple, already implemented routing protocol based on hops like MintRoute [202] for TinyOS. However, they often also change the protocol according to their needs [19, 113, 199], for example by using a different neighborhood management protocol or a custom cost metric. Thus, the resulting protocols are highly specialized and optimized solutions for the targeted network rather than a standard protocol for a broad variety of scenarios.

In this chapter we give an overview of state-of-the-art routing protocols. First, we summarize traditional point-to-point routing algorithms before proceeding with multicast approaches for WSNs. Then we deepen our survey in terms of sink mobility, failure management and various routing cost metrics.

3.1.1 Point-to-point routing in WSNs

There are many different routing protocols and techniques for WSNs and several surveys have tried to classify and summarize them [3, 4, 9]. Many routing protocols have emerged from routing protocols for Mobile Ad Hoc Networks (MANETs). They build a full routing path table at all nodes and each node keeps the full route to each possible destination. The main disadvantage of such an approach is that route information needs to be propagated throughout the network (from the source to the destination and back). Second, a complicated route repair procedure needs to be started in case of topology changes or failures to re-build the routes. Some protocols take an abstraction step of dividing the route into segments, where only segments need to be repaired [193]. MANET-based protocols have been implemented for WSNs with some changes (in this case, multi-path routing), like AOMDV [83] based on AODV [144]. However, the main disadvantages remain.

A popular routing technique designed especially for energy-restricted unreliable wireless sensor networks is content-based networking [35]. It is a routing framework where data is sent from the source to the destinations based on interests expressed by the destinations to receive a particular pattern of data. Such an approach is relevant for sensor networks as it is data driven as opposed to address driven. This has been demonstrated in [77] where the authors use a distance vector protocol to construct a tree from the source node to an interested sink.

Another instantiation of content-based networking for sensor networks is Directed Diffusion [88, 170] where routes from the source to the destinations are established on-demand based on interests that are flooded through the network. This flooding establishes gradients for data to follow from multiple sources to the sinks. As the source sends low-rate data samples, the routes where data first arrives are reinforced by the sinks.

Directed Diffusion motivated many other routing protocols. Rumor routing [30] and its successor, Zonal rumor routing [17] limit the initial interest propagation phase by routing the interests to the specified zones in the network only. For this, the nodes need to know who is producing what kind of data. When a node produces data, it generates a long-lived agent, which traverses the network and informs other nodes of the available information.

GRE-DD [117] and LMMER [13] are also extensions of Directed Diffusion. They consider the remaining battery level of neighbors when selecting the gradient to the sink. However, they do not dynamically change the gradient, even if a node exhausts its energy. Instead, they must wait until the subsequent sink flooding to update the battery level and the route. A similar approach is described in [162], where each node knows the "heights" of its neighbors (number of hops to the sink). If the battery level of some node drops below a threshold, it increases its height and propagates this new information to its neighbors.

MintRoute [202] from TinyOS[1] is a similar hop-based routing approach, which additionally incorporates a neighborhood management protocol. It selects the next hops based on link quality and hops to the sink.

Location-based (or geographic) network routing is based on the location-awareness of the nodes. All nodes of the network are able to obtain either their exact coordinates by a GPS receiver or their relative locations by incoming signal strengths from their neighboring nodes. For example, GEAR [215] is an improvement over Directed Diffusion, where interests are routed to their destinations via a location-based heuristic. Thus, flooding of the interests is restricted and energy is saved.

A traditional geographic routing protocol is GPSR [99], which selects next hops based on their progress to the destination. In case the routing is stuck (a node is reached with no progress to the sink), a special face routing procedure

---

[1] www.tinyos.org

is started to route the packet around the void region. The main disadvantage of geographic routing protocols is the length of the selected routes, especially in case of void regions. An effort to overcome this problem is presented in [60], where a landmark-assisted geographic routing protocol is described. Here, in a pre-processing phase the nodes exchange information about their location and the full global topology is reconstructed at each of the nodes. However, topology information is abstracted and the network is divided into tiles. Thus, node failures and low mobility can be handled without full-network broadcasts of the events. Special landmarks are used for routing the packets through the tiles. Unfortunately the work is not evaluated in terms of overhead or spent energy and no comparison to existing works is given.

Another problem with traditional geographic routing schemes is their preference of long unreliable hops. In case no separate link protocol is used, geographic routing selects next hops only based on their progress to the sink - thus, mostly long lossy connections. An extensive study of this problem and a comparison of various other location-based metrics on simulation and real hardware is presented in [219]. Traditional greedy strategies are compared with blacklisting highly unreliable neighbors, selecting only the most reliable neighbors and using the product of geographic progress and reception rate for identifying the next hop. The study shows the last product-based metric results in highest end-to-end delivery rate.

3.1.2 Multicast routing in WSNs

Let us consider the sample topology from Figure 3.1. It shows a small network with two sinks and one source. After the proposed sink announcement from Chapter 2, all of the nodes in the network have some initial routing information, e.g. hops to the individual sinks. For example, node S (the source) has three neighbors and routes through each of them to both sinks. According to its information, the best next hops to take include neighbor A for sink P and neighbor C for sink Q. From the local perspective of the source it looks like the route costs $(3+3)$ hops or 5, if the first hop is shared via a broadcast message (the dotted route in the figure).

3.1 Energy-efficient multicast routing in WSNs

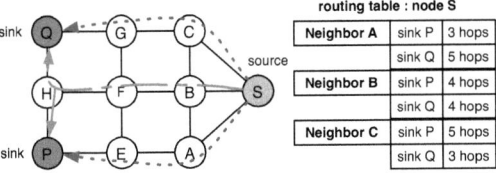

Figure 3.1. A sample topology with 2 sinks, the main routes to them from source S and its initial routing table.

However, looking *globally* at the network graph we immediately see that the route through nodes B, F, H and then to the sinks (the middle route in the figure) costs only 4 hops - even in this small network there is possible saving of 20% compared to the locally best route. Additionally, the remaining energies on the nodes can be considered. Finding the globally optimal route is what we call the *multicast challenge*.

There are different approaches of how to solve the multicast challenge. Many traditional multicast routing protocols come again from the MANET environment, for example MAODV [144], LAM [94], AMRIS [203], ADMR [93], and RBM [43]. They build on-demand a multicast tree in the network via exchanging control packets. However, this approach requires large overhead for building and maintaining the tree, especially in case of mobility and failures. There are some recent works using swarm intelligence [51, 167], but again the overhead from sending ants is unbearable for wireless sensor networks (see the discussion of swarm intelligence in Section 3.3.5). Other researchers also report about substantial problems and challenges when implementing MANET multicast routing protocols for sensor networks, like the implementation of ADMR on MicaZ motes [37].

Mesh-based algorithms for MANETs maintain an overlay structure for forwarding data to all receivers. They proved to be very efficient in high mobility scenarios, but cause great communication overhead for constructing and maintaining the mesh and thus cannot be successfully applied to WSNs. Such protocols are for example ODMPR [115], CAMP [68], PUMA [191], AMRoute [207], and PAST-DM [74].

From the wireless sensor networks community there are two main groups of research efforts in the area of multicast routing: geographic based and "fake multicast". GMR [160] and MSTEAM [66] are both geographic based multicast routing protocols. These approaches do not need any control packet exchange to build the multicast tree. In fact, they greedily take next hops to reach the sinks. However, having geographic information in large, randomly deployed sensor networks is unrealistic or too costly, and thus alternatives have to be found. Another disadvantage of geographic protocols is the so called face routing, which is used to route data around face (void) regions. This takes a much longer route than necessary and is not able to learn from its previous experience, like previous routing around the same void area.

Another approach for WSNs for multicasting is what we call "fake multicast": unicast protocols, which are slightly optimized for multicast routing. Such protocols just build paths from a source to each of the sinks without really considering sharing of paths or finding globally optimal ones - a simple example is Directed Diffusion [170], which can easily support multiple sinks. Another work [42] concentrates on sharing of paths from multiple sources to multiple sinks by locally sharing next hops with the same costs. However, the main assumption of [42] is that packets from different sources can be aggregated, which makes the work a tree-based clustering approach rather than a traditional routing algorithm. Additionally, the definition of the routing cost function leads to routing oscillations in the beginning, causing a lot of additional communication overhead.

Other researchers [216] formulate the problem of routing to multiple sinks in a different manner: it finds the optimal data rates of all data sources and best sink node to route to. In particular, this means that each source routes its data to the next sink only and all sinks cooperate to reconstruct the data field. Similarly, [45, 102, 139] present solutions to the optimal sink placement problem in a WSN. A study on the multicast capacity of certain networks is presented in [164].

Again, there are some mesh or overlay routing protocols, which successfully handle multiple mobile sinks. They are presented in the following section.

3.1.3 Sink mobility in WSNs

Some routing protocols assume that the mobility pattern of the sinks is known a-priori at the sensor nodes. One such protocol is the spatiotemporal mobicast routing algorithm in [82]. This protocol is rather an overlay routing protocol, which decides *when* to forward the data through a geographic routing protocol to which neighbors. In this way it guarantees spatiotemporal delivery of needed data to needed regions. The work was further developed in [40], which is able to better handle void areas. IDDA [205] is following a similar idea, where the mobile sink uses a directional antenna to wake up nodes in its next location. Nodes in the predetermined area use gradients as in Directed Diffusion to send data to the node next to the sink's future location, thus preparing data for the sink and waiting for the sink there.

TTDD [120] is a layered routing protocol, developed especially for high mobility scenarios. The authors concentrate on efficient delivery to multiple mobile sinks through building a routing overlay. The network is clustered into cells and mobile sinks flood their requests in the local cell only. Thus, the overlay is always aware of the current position of the sinks and routes the data to them. This approach proved to be very effective in high mobility scenarios. However, the nodes building the overlay (a cell structure) drain their power quickly and the overlay has to be rebuilt with high communication overhead. That is why the protocol is better suited for event-detecting sensor networks with only sporadic traffic rather than continuous monitoring. Other overlay-based routing protocols are ODMPR [115], CAMP [68], PUMA [191], AMRoute [207] and PAST-DM [74].

SEAD [103] optimizes routing from single source to multiple mobile sinks. Each sink selects an "access sensor node", to which data from the source is routed. A tree is built based on a geographic location heuristic between the source and all access nodes. When the sink moves away, a path between its current nearest neighbor and the access node is maintained, so that it is not necessary to rebuild the tree. If the sink moves too far away, a new access node is selected and the tree is rebuilt, but only with high communication overhead. The approach shows very good results compared to Directed Diffusion [170] or TTDD [120] in terms of dissipated energy for data packets. However, no extensive evaluation of the control overhead under mobile sinks is presented, which is expected to be high. A further refinement of SEAD is DEED [104], which introduces delay constrains on the multicast routes.

Multiple mobile sinks are the target scenario for DST [86]. A shared routing tree is constructed by the first (master) sink and shared by next slave sinks. Unlike SEAD [120], the whole tree is dynamically updated when sinks move away from their access sensor nodes. The approach shows slightly better results than SEAD in high mobility single-sink scenarios and the same performance as SEAD in multiple-sink settings.

An analytical evaluation of virtual infrastructure routing protocols (TTDD [120], SEAD [103] and others) is presented in [78].

3.1.4 Failure recovery for routing in WSNs

One of the main routing challenges is managing link and node failures. Failures have been widely considered in routing for WSNs and different approaches have been taken. The most important design criterion is to be able to register a failure and to update the available next hops easily.

Failure recovery is closely related to and in fact part of link quality management. Here, two different techniques exist: pro-active beacons and passive refreshment of routes. The first technique is used by nearly all management protocols and by nearly all geographic routing protocols [66, 99, 160]. Here, the nodes exchange small non-data related packets (beacons) to refresh their information about their 1-hop neighbors. Usually, the RSSI (Received Signal Strength Indication) level of the radio signal and data reception rate are used to calculate the link quality. Failure recovery is incorporated automatically in these algorithms by assigning very low quality to failed links (non responding nodes), and thus signaling the problem to higher layers. The main disadvantage of separate link management protocols is their unawareness of the requirements of the higher layers. For example, many link management protocols supply the

3.1 Energy-efficient multicast routing in WSNs

higher layers with a list of "good" neighbors or a list of the n-best neighbors. In the first case, the routing protocol is unable to choose the best neighbor because of lack of knowledge, in the second case it might miss a good neighbor, which has a good quality, but resides on place $n+1$ of the quality-sorted list.

The second recovery technique, passive refreshment of routes, is applied often by hop-based routing protocols like Directed Diffusion [170], which do not make use of any separate link management. Here, the sinks (or any other leading nodes) refresh the routing information at regular intervals by a full-network broadcast of a simple control packet, called the sink announcement or data interest. Note that we use the same sink announcement in our scenario (see Chapter 2), since this is an energy-efficient and general approach to inform nodes in the network about the sinks' requirements. However, sending such an announcement too often, for example to keep routes up-to-date, is not efficient and dramatically increases the data traffic in the network. A similar technique is also used by all MANET-like routing protocols, where control packets are exchanged at regular intervals to refresh routes.

3.1.5 Routing cost metrics for WSNs

Location-based (geographic) routing is probably one of the largest families of routing protocols. Here, *progress to sink* is used as routing cost metric and next hops are selected accordingly [66, 99, 160].

A metric coming from MANET routing protocols is *end-to-end latency*, as used for example in the original two-phase pull version of Directed Diffusion [170]. Here, the sources start delivering data at low rates over many possible routes. Thus, the sink observes from where the data arrives first and reinforces this route, which becomes the main route for data delivery at higher rates.

In homogenous WSNs the *number of hops* is highly related to latency and has been used extensively as a routing metric [162, 170]. Hops are a simplified version of latency and can often be used interchangeably with it. Both metrics have several advantages over location awareness: they are cheaper to acquire and they automatically build minimum hop/latency (shortest path) routes without void areas. On one side this leads to shorter, very energy-efficient routes.

However, these routes are quickly depleted and the network could become disconnected.

Therefore, other research efforts additionally take the node's *residual energy* into account. Such approaches work in one of two ways: considering strictly localized information where only the neighbors' remaining energy is given [13, 117, 175, 193, 215], or full global information where all remaining power levels for all nodes are known at the base station [92]. Considering the remaining energy on the 1-hop neighbors has the advantage of being fully localized and thus very energy-efficient, but does not guarantee that the nodes on the remaining path to the destinations have high energy reserves. On the other hand, global information helps identifying truly optimal routes, but has a large communication overhead.

A widely used cost metric for estimating the quality of links and neighbors is the *RSSI level* of received packets, assuming that high RSSI values come from nearby, reliable neighbors and the other way around. However, some researchers [193] use this metric also with the opposite assumption – low RSSI indicates a far away neighbor – and use it to select neighbors which are possibly further away and thus closer to the destination. However, such a metric suffers from the same disadvantages as geographic routing - the connection link to the farthest neighbor is usually very error-prone, which results in many retransmissions or a high packet loss rate. Another use of RSSI is the computation of the distance between the sender and the receiver and is often used by clustering approaches (see Section 3.2).

A current effort to improve connectivity in wireless sensor networks has led to a new cost metric, the *connectivity importance value* [141]. A node is considered important if after failing it will disconnect part of the network. Thus, routes are taken which avoid important nodes to avoid disintegration of the network. Unfortunately, these values cannot be computed in a distributed manner, since full topology information is needed on all of the nodes in the network. The values also need to be re-calculated after node failures, reflecting the new topology. This becomes a communication challenge especially towards the end of the network lifetime when nodes start to fail quickly one after another.

3.1.6 Routing in WSNs: Summary

There is a huge research body on routing protocols for WSNs, based on various assumptions, cost metrics and network scenarios. Simple techniques like MintRoute [202] or Directed Diffusion [170] are usually preferred. However, in the context of our application requirements from Chapter 2 they do not efficiently manage multiple sinks, node failures or mobility. Other efforts concentrate specifically on one of these challenges, but none of them gives a general, flexible and robust solution to all of them simultaneously.

Thus, the goal of this dissertation is to design and implement a general solution to all of these problems. However, unlike the solutions presented here which need a substantial increase in processing, memory or communication overhead to handle each of the described challenges one by one, our solution needs to be universal and self-consistent.

3.2 Energy-efficient clustering for WSNs

Clustering in wireless sensor networks is the process of dividing the nodes of the WSN into groups. Each group agrees on a central node, called the cluster head, which is responsible for gathering the sensory data of all group members, aggregating it and sending it to the base station(s). Clustering and data aggregation have proved to be powerful techniques to minimize energy expenditure in wireless sensor networks, while at the same time keeping some minimal quality of the delivered data.

While simple and straightforward, this approach hides important and hard to solve issues. In particular, the selection of cluster heads is critical: randomly selected heads do not cover the sensors well and cause non-balanced intra-cluster communication overhead. Deterministic selection based on ID, remaining energy, or other metrics, requires either global information about the network to compute the optimal clustering, or k-hops neighborhood information at all nodes. The announcement of cluster heads causes non-data related communication overhead, and failures of cluster heads cause a whole cluster to fail or have to repair.

CLUSTER HEADS	CLUSTER FORM	# HOPS IN CLUSTER	TAXONOMY
random nodes LEACH [149], [32], [70], [92], TEEN [123], APTEEN [124], [209]	random form LEACH [149], [32], [70], [92], TEEN [123], APTEEN [124], [209] *LNCA [206]**	1 hop, var. trans. power LEACH [149], [32], [70], [92], TEEN [123], APTEEN [124], [209]	RANDOM PROTOCOLS
min/max distance from other CHs [7], BP [8], UCCP [11], TRC[15], [38], EDC [39], FLOC [48], PC [69], [80], [120], [138], LNCA [206], HEED [211], [214]	quasi-circular [7], BP [8], UCCP [11], TRC[15], [38], EDC [39], FLOC [48], PC [69], [80], [120], [138], HEED [211], [214]	1, fixed trans. power BP [8], UCCP [11], PC [69], [120], HEED [211]	1-HOP GRID CLUSTERING
		parameter k [7], TRC[15], [38], EDC [39], FLOC [48], [80], [120], [138], LNCA [206], [214]	k-HOP CLUSTERING
location-based *[120]**, GROUP [213]	exact (squares, hexagons, etc.) *[120]**, GROUP [213]	any possible [16], [38], [58], [67], [70], [89], [174], [188], [196], GROUP [213]	LOCATION AND TREE BASED CLUSTERING
tree-based [16], [67]	geographically limited [16], [67], [89], [196]		
pre-deployed [89], [174], [196]			INFRASTRUCTURE SUPPORTED CLUSTERING
random [38], [58], [70], [188]	non-uniform [38], [58], [70], [174], [188]		NON-UNIFORM CLUSTERING

* exceptions from the taxonomy

Figure 3.2. Classification of state-of-the-art clustering protocols and their main properties.

This survey is not intended to be exhaustive or complete. We have, however, identified six main families of protocols: random, 1-hop grid, k-hop, location-based, infrastructure-supported and non-uniform clustering protocols. There is also the additional family of centralized protocols, which we discuss shortly. The main properties of all protocol families and our taxonomy are summarized in Figure 3.2. Note that some of the protocols are marked as exceptions, because their properties differ in some small way from most of the other protocols of the same family. We discuss these exceptions in detail together with the related works next.

3.2 Energy-efficient clustering for WSNs

After presenting state-of-the-art clustering protocols, we continue with a short summary of data aggregation techniques and conclude the survey with related efforts on optimal clustering techniques and theoretical studies.

3.2.1 Random protocols

Many clustering protocols are improvements or modifications of LEACH [149], in which network nodes choose to be cluster heads based on an a a-priori probability. Self-elected cluster heads flood a cluster head role assignment message to their neighbors, which in turn identify and select the nearest cluster head. In the original LEACH protocol, the probability corresponds to the number of desired cluster heads in the network. Additional metrics such as remaining node energy can also be used to change the clustering properties [32, 70, 92, 209].

Random-clustering algorithms perform well and have two important advantages. First, they are very simple, and second, they avoid rounds of control messages to converge on a single cluster head in a cluster, since the cluster heads are randomly selected. However, their greatest disadvantage is the unpredictability of the sizes and shapes of the clusters. Cluster heads can be anywhere in the network. Sometimes data from half of the network, while other times only a few data readings will be aggregated. Another disadvantage is that these algorithms assume one-hop communication (however, nodes are allowed to vary their transmission power) and in a multi-hop network they perform poorly with significant control overhead (see Figure 3.2).

TEEN [123] and APTEEN [124] are built over LEACH and further minimize the number of transmitted packets by introducing thresholds on the gathered sensory data: if the threshold is not exceeded, the node does not inject a new data packet into the network. However, the clustering protocol is the same as LEACH.

3.2.2 1-hop grid clustering

Assuming full network 1-hop connectivity as in LEACH is not reasonable in all scenarios, therefore multi-hop topologies need to be addressed. Two different families of protocols have evolved over time: 1-hop grid and k-hop fixed transmission power clustering algorithms. Representatives of the 1-hop grid clustering protocols are HEED [211], BP [8], Passive Clustering (PC) [69], and others [38, 214]. These protocols require the cluster head in any cluster to be able to communicate to its neighboring cluster heads in one hop, thus building a virtual grid. Consequently, they assume very dense networks. The control overhead for agreeing on cluster heads is significant. The shape of the resulting clusters is semi-circular and the size is bounded by the communication radius of the nodes. For these algorithms it is important to keep the number of clusters as low as possible and often the *optimal clustering* is defined as the one which minimizes the number of clusters while meeting the 1-hop grid communication requirement.

Some 1-hop grid clustering approaches are location-based [120]. Here the size of the cells is selected such that communication from cluster heads to neighboring cluster heads is guaranteed.

3.2.3 K-hop clustering

The second family of protocols, including FLOC [48], EDC [39] and others [11, 15, 80, 138], extend the size of the clusters to multiple hops between cluster members and cluster heads, thus also eliminating the virtual grid of the 1-hop grid clustering (see above). Again, they first randomly assign cluster head roles to some nodes in the network and then "grow" clusters around them. In case a node cannot find a cluster head at most k hops away, it becomes a "forced" cluster head [15]. Others [7, 138] use k-hop neighborhood information to optimize clusters and cluster heads: for example selecting the lowest ID as the cluster head. The protocol described in [11] uses optimization techniques from operations research to find a well-balanced cluster head. As for 1-hop grid algorithms, the number of clusters should be minimized, such that most of the clusters are exactly k-hops wide.

In LNCA [206] nodes first exchange information about their data readings, then, according to similarity of data, form k-hop clusters. As such, it is one of the rare efforts to match the size and shape of clusters to the gathered sensory data:

nodes form clusters only if their data is similar and can be aggregated with no or little data loss. From the cluster shapes perspective the algorithm is a traditional k-hop clustering, but with random cluster sizes because of the similarity of data requirement (see Figure 3.2).

3.2.4 Location and tree based clustering

Geographic, or location-based clustering protocols have well defined cluster sizes and shapes, which are usually parameters. GROUP [213] builds a location-based grid with quadrants of tunable size. This grid is laid over the network and nodes next to the grid's crossing points become cluster heads. However, cluster head selection raises some issues: several broadcasts are needed for the nodes to converge on one cluster head in each round and each round needs a network-wide broadcast of the next clustering grid center.

Another geographic-based clustering approach is applied in [67] to multi-resolution in-network storage of data for WSNs. In this case a hash function is used to map the cluster head roles to network locations: the nearest nodes to those locations become cluster heads and store aggregated data for further reference. The organization of the network is rather a tree than cluster-based: when searching for data, the request travels through the tree and aggregated data stored at the vertices are used for routing the request down to the leaf with the required non-aggregated data. Another tree-based approach is presented in [16], where first a spanning tree over the whole network is computed. Each node stores how many children its own sub-tree contains. The protocol traverses all of the nodes and selects some of the nodes as cluster heads for their corresponding sub-trees.

3.2.5 Infrastructure supported clustering

Some clustering approaches assume a pre-existing backbone of powerful nodes throughout the network. The challenge here is to assign sensor nodes to these powerful nodes or cluster heads such that the load for the nodes and for the cluster heads is balanced. Such an approach is taken for example in [89], where a special metric called "business" of parent nodes is introduced. Sensors select their cluster heads such that the processing and communication load of all cluster heads is balanced.

A similar problem is discussed in [196], where the nodes need to be associated with a powerful application node such that the overall network lifetime is maximized. Unlike many other clustering approaches this work assumes that once associated with a cluster head, nodes never change their membership.

3.2.6 Non-uniform clustering in WSNs

Last but not least is the research field of non-uniform data dissemination in WSNs. The basic idea is that sinks need accurate information from sensors nearby and less accurate information from nodes far away. Thus, aggregation needs to be done depending on the distance to the sinks. The fisheye [119] technique from computer graphics has similar properties, using distance to determine accuracy. This technique inspired the Fisheye state routing [143], a MANET routing protocol in which nodes exchange routing tables with frequencies dependent on the distances to the routing table entries. However, the non-uniformity there is applied to routing information, not to the data itself.

Similar non-uniform data approaches have been introduced in distributed systems [73, 208]. However, neither of these approaches consider energy or CPU processing and both require global knowledge of the static network, thus making them inappropriate for the wireless sensor network domain.

The idea was first introduced for clustering and aggregation in sensor networks in [188], where a randomized algorithm produces clusters of different sizes depending on the distance to the single base station. The idea was then extended into two different directions: in [58] we presented a pre-study for this thesis, where we use a distributed hop-based approach to define the cluster heads and clusters grow bigger with increasing distance from the base station. However, the size and the shapes of the resulting clusters are again random and communication highly imbalanced. In [174], a centralized approach with Voronoi tesselation or an approximation of it is used to define cluster heads a-priori, so that the network lifetime is maximized. The cluster sizes grow with increasing distance from the single base station and their shapes and sizes are defined by location information. However, global topology knowledge is needed to compute the clustering information.

The latest work on non-uniform or unequal clustering is [38]. It assumes that clusters near to the single base station need to be smaller to preserve energy for routing packets from more distant clusters. It uses a simple LEACH-like selection scheme, where a random set of nodes compete to be cluster heads. Each competing node has its own competing radius, which is increasing with increasing distance from the base station. After the competition phase, only one cluster head remains in each competing radius and all nodes adjust their power levels to reach the closest cluster head. Packets are routed only through cluster heads, thus quickly draining their batteries. Like any other random clustering protocol, the work in [38] produces random clusters with larger clusters far away from the base station. However, load is not balanced well and cluster heads drain their batteries too fast.

A very similar clustering approach is presented in [70]. However, instead of having competing random cluster heads, nodes exchange their residual energies with all neighbors in their cluster radius. The cluster radius grows with increasing distance from the base station and the node with maximum residual energy is selected to act as cluster head. Communication with the base station is direct from any cluster head.

3.2.7 Centralized clustering

There are many clustering algorithms that require full network topology and/or remaining energy information to centrally compute optimal clusters (e.g. [5, 127]). At each round they disseminate the cluster information to all nodes. These protocols can clearly build any clusters with any properties. However, such approaches do not scale and do not consider fundamental network issues such as failures and asymmetric links.

3.2.8 In-cluster data aggregation and clustering

One major goal of clustering is to allow in-network pre-processing (aggregation or compression), assuming that cluster heads (and other intermediate nodes) collect multiple data packets and relay only one aggregated/compressed packet. The survey in [41] identifies three different aggregation techniques: tree aggregation, centralized pre-processing and gossiping. The first refers to the case in which data is processed and aggregated at each hop. Thus, the task of aggregation is not limited to the cluster head, but is spread over many nodes in the cluster. This is a great advantage especially in multi-hop clusters. The second refers to a LEACH-like clustering and aggregation scheme in which the data of the whole cluster is gathered on one central node (cluster head) and pre-processed there. If the cluster is multiple hops wide, however, this aggregation scheme has a greater communication overhead compared to a tree-based one. On the other hand, data processing itself is more precise, since all raw data readings are available. The third aggregation technique describes the case where no clusters are maintained: instead, nodes exchange (gossip) some of their data readings with other nodes, typically randomly.

3.2.9 Optimal clustering analysis

Figure 3.3 illustrates the clusters built by some representative clustering protocols in a sample topology. Looking at them we can easily see advantages or disadvantages in terms of size and shape of the clusters, number of nodes per cluster etc. However, this is a subjective view and depends highly on the given particular network. The question about what is the optimal clustering remains unanswered: which is the cluster with a size and shape such that communication overhead for routing data from nodes to base station(s) is minimal?

Some research works take a step back and analytically evaluate clustering techniques in terms of their optimality. In a very recent effort [194], the author shows that the hop diameter of the optimal cluster grows with increasing size of the network. In this work a simple network scenario is used with fixed node density, one base station and unit disk graph communication model where a

3.2 Energy-efficient clustering for WSNs

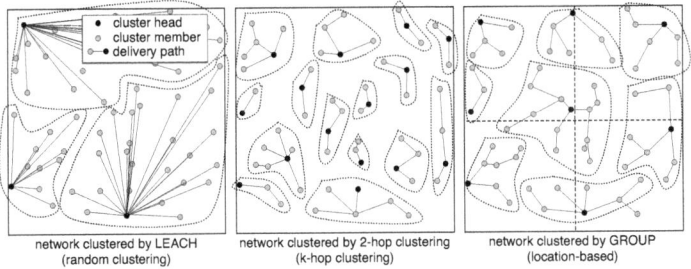

Figure 3.3. Sample clusters, as built by some state-of-the-art protocols.

node spends energy only when transmitting a packet, not when receiving it. Another similar work [206] comes to the conclusion that a 2-hop cluster radius is optimal for all practical networks up to 3000 nodes. Here, the authors use multi-hop routing through normal sensors to reach the base station instead of cluster heads only.

3.2.10 Clustering in WSNs: Summary

In this section we presented part of the wide variety of clustering protocols for WSNs together with some efforts on finding the optimal clustering scenario. Clustering together with data aggregation has been shown to inherently decrease the communication overhead in WSNs, to save energy and to improve delivery rate. However, there are some major challenges not yet efficiently met. Given the application and design requirements from Chapter 2, the first challenge of clustering protocols is the process of cluster head selection. In case the cluster heads are pre-known (powerful specialized nodes) their cost and deployment planning are a big disadvantage and the network is hardly scalable. In case the network is homogeneous and any node can serve as a cluster head and aggregator, substantial overhead is needed for agreement on cluster heads. Simple, low-overhead agreement schemes are nevertheless possible, but lead to highly unbalanced clusters and communication load of the nodes.

Another major challenge is management of node failures and mobility. Special failure detection and repair mechanisms are needed to handle these situations and result in high non-data related communication and processing overhead, high packet loss and long delay. Last but not least an overwhelming part of the clustering approaches rely on a *single* base station and cannot be extended to serve more than one of them.

We use clustering in this thesis to meet the challenges of data dissemination in large networks. Our goal when designing the clustering protocol is to solve efficiently all of the above described problems. Our clustering protocol needs to overcome the communication overhead of cluster head selection, to be robust against node failures, to support multiple mobile sinks, and to use energy in an efficient and balanced way. In addition, it needs to support non-uniform data requirements.

3.3 Machine learning for WSNs

Our first intuition for solving the routing and clustering challenges in our application scenario is to apply artificial intelligence techniques. In this section we explore the various available machine learning (ML) and computational intelligence (CI) approaches, which have been successfully applied to a wide variety of problems in WSNs. Our goal is to better understand their properties and requirements, their application areas, and to identify the best suited approach for our scenario.

The major applications already addressed by ML and CI in WSNs techniques are:

- *Sensor Fusion and Data Mining.* Sensor fusion is the process of combining data derived from multiple sources such that either the resulting information is in some sense better than would be possible with individual sources, or the communication overhead of sending individual sensor readings to the base station is reduced. This includes computation of data models (data mining), which help the sensors or the base station to differentiate between expected and unexpected data or faulty and valid sensor readings.

- *Energy Aware Routing and Clustering.* Economic usage of energy is important in WSNs, because replacing or recharging the batteries on the nodes may be impractical, expensive or dangerous. In many applications, network life expectancy of a few months or years is desired. Here we introduce routing and clustering protocols based on machine learning in addition to those presented in Sections 3.1 and 3.2.

- *Scheduling and Medium Access Protocols.* Sensor nodes are very power-restricted and are usually expected to perform unattended over months or even years. Thus, it is very important to first identify the largest power consumers and then to minimize their consumption. It is well known [6, 112] that the primary power consumer on any sensor node is the radio. Thus the MAC protocol becomes the crucial instrument to minimize energy expenditure in sensor networks. The MAC protocol sits on top of the physical layer and controls the radio. It schedules and manages its sleeping and idle phases, trying to minimize or to avoid collisions, overhearing and idle times. In the latest years, many efforts have been made to design the ultimate MAC protocol, which minimizes the energy spent for message transmission. A summary of state-of-the-art MAC protocols is presented in [112].

- *Design and Deployment.* WSNs are used in vastly diversified applications ranging from monitoring a biological system through tissue implanted sensors to monitoring forest fire through air-dropped sensors. In some applications, they need to be placed accurately at predetermined locations, whereas in others such positioning is unnecessary or impractical. Sensor network design aims at determining the type, amount and location of measuring devices that need to be placed in an environment in order to get complete knowledge of its condition. On the other hand, sensor network deployment copes with hardware and software installation and primary testing.

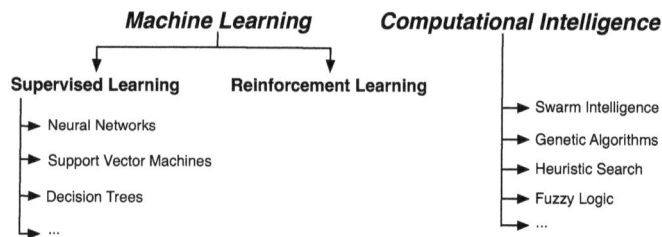

Figure 3.4. Taxonomy of Machine Learning and Computational Intelligence, compiled from [44, 59, 131].

- *Localization.* Node localization refers to determining the locations of all deployed sensors. Location information is used to detect and record events, or to route packets using geographic-aware routing (see Section 3.1). Besides, location itself is often the data that needs to be sensed. An overview of localization systems for WSNs is presented in [28].

Some recent surveys give an overview of applications of machine learning and computational intelligence for wireless sensor networks [9, 49, 62, 91, 108, 146, 171]. A general taxonomy of the applied techniques and algorithms is given in Figure 3.4. We follow this taxonomy to present the individual algorithms and their applications below. However, this study is not intended to be exhaustive or complete. Instead, we summarize the most promising or relevant efforts for our target scenario and explore their properties and requirements.

3.3.1 Neural Networks

Artificial neural networks (or just neural networks - NNs) are mathematical models of some function $F : X \to Y$. Their initial inspiration comes from biological networks of neurons. They consist of simple nodes or neurons, interconnected with each other. Simple functions are usually associated with each node (like addition) and weights are assigned to the connections between the nodes. Data is flowing from the input through the whole network, using the connections be-

3.3 Machine learning for WSNs

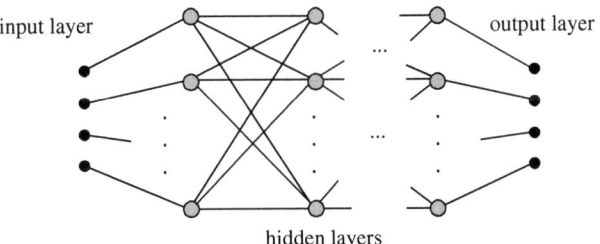

Figure 3.5. A generic layered architecture of an artificial neural network with input, hidden and output layers. Copyright [155].

tween the nodes and arriving at the output neurons. Figure 3.5 gives an example of a simple neural network. The most important property of neural networks is their ability to *learn* - the weights between the neurons are the real computational power and have to be adjusted such that the output is exactly the mapped function. For learning or *training* of neural networks, a set of training data is needed, where possible inputs are already mapped to the needed output. For example, in the case of a classification problem of hand-written numbers, different pictures (input) are classified as numbers (output).

More information about neural networks and how to train them can be found in [14, 155].

Sensor Fusion and Data Mining. Neural networks are a feasible solution to centralized problems like sensor fusion and data mining. The authors in [150] concentrate on the problem of class-imbalanced data for sensor-based intrusion detection. In their learning protocol, they first gather some real sensor data, send the data to a base station, which learns a classification model and sends the model back to the sensors. The goal is to minimize communication overhead since the sensors report only positive (intrusion detected) samples to the base station. The approach uses a neural network on the base station to learn the classification model and is fully centralized.

A different data mining problem has been addressed by [25, 26]. In this work, the authors present a neural network-based approach for checking sensor data integrity or automatic sensor calibration. The main feature of the protocol is the used neural network, a competitive learning NN (CLNN). This NN is an unsupervised learning agent, able to learn data online from a continuous, non-labeled data stream (sensor readings). After the learning phase, the agent is able to differentiate between N different clusters (N is fixed and known before starting the learning process) and thus to recognize faulty sensor readings. The authors combine the learning method with a clustering approach to minimize the communication cost. Each sensor sends its readings first to a local cluster head, where the CLNN is trained, the data is classified and filtered and eventually sent to the base station. The algorithm is semi-distributed, since in theory each sensor node could have its own learning agent. However, the learning phase will be very long (only own sensor readings available) and the input set is restricted. The clustered approach taken by the authors is the best way to go, such that a trade-off is found between communication overhead and optimality of learning.

The main objective of [61] is to detect biological and mechanical faults in a sensor-monitored greenhouse environment. The authors train two different neural networks to classify biological faults (stressed plants) and mechanical faults (sensor or actuator faults). As input they use sensory data from the environment, both current and historical. The data has to be gathered on a centralized sink for processing.

Energy Aware Routing and Clustering. Neural networks have been widely applied in WSNs. SIR [18] is an energy-efficient routing protocol, which assigns a neural network to each node in the network. The nodes use beacons to find out the quality of links to their neighbors and the information is fed into the NN to learn the quality of the links. Routing is performed based on a modified Dijkstra shortest-path algorithm from a source to a single sink using the learnt link quality. The protocol performs well compared to Directed Diffusion [170], but results in a high beacon overhead. Additionally, the implementation of a neural network on each of the nodes has high memory requirements and might

3.3 Machine learning for WSNs   41

be hard on memory-restricted sensor hardware.

Scheduling and Medium Access Protocols. A centralized neural network has been applied to solve the optimal TDMA scheduling for a WSN in [168]. However, a centralized computation of schedules does not take into account link asymmetry, link and node failures, mobility etc. Additionally, it incurs high communication overhead to dissipate the schedules to the nodes.

Summary. It can be concluded that neural networks are a good solution for learning network-wide data models, which are not expected to change very fast. Examples are models of faulty data, self-calibration etc. On the other side, both the nature of NNs and the results achieved by the works presented in this section show that they are impractical for distributed tasks like routing and scheduling. Further feasible application areas for neural networks are optimal sensor and sink placement, localization etc.

3.3.2 Support Vector Machines

Support vector machines (SVM) are a supervised learning method used for classification. The input data is viewed as a set of vectors in an N-dimensional space and the output of the SVM is a separating hyperplane between both sets, which maximizes the difference between the hyperplane and each of the sets (the margin between the sets). For computing this hyperplane two parallel hyperplanes are constructed on each side of the separating one and "pushed against" the data sets. Figure 3.6 presents a simple example with two data sets (classes) in a 2-dimensional space. The two parallel hyperplanes on each side of the separating hyperplane together with the data samples they include are called the support vectors.

Localization. A solution to the localization problem with support vector machines has been proposed in [1]. Given $n + m$ nodes in the network, where the positions of n nodes are known and of m nodes unknown, and given the RSSI signal strength between any pair of nodes, the positions of the un-localized nodes have to be recovered. The authors first train a SVM for classifying nodes

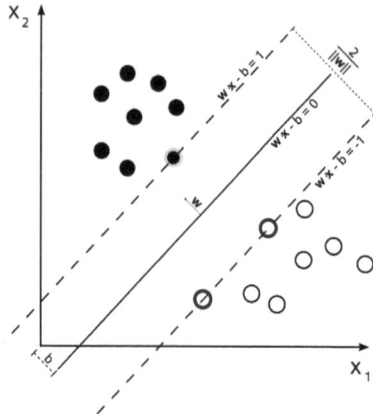

Figure 3.6. Separating hyperplane and margins for a SVM trained with samples from two classes. Samples on the margin are called the support vectors. *source:www.wikipedia.org*

depending on their distance to each other, then match the output of the SVM to the positions of the nodes. The algorithm is fully centralized, which is a consequence of using a support vector machine. Other researchers have also used SVMs for localization in WSNs [98, 189].

Summary. Similarly to other supervised learning approaches, support vector machines are memory and processing intensive and need centralized gathering of the input data. They are well suited for data mining problems like sensor fusion. Additionally, they are suitable for localization, since it is usually done only once right after deployment. Other centralized problems like optimal sensor placement are further possible applications.

3.3.3 Decision trees and case-based reasoning

These two similar techniques are based on the idea of classifying items into ever smaller clusters, like classifying an orange first as fruit, then as a citrus fruit, then as an orange. These data mining algorithms are easy to understand, relatively fast to train and very fast to execute. They require that the items to classify are attribute-value pairs. For example, an orange can have attribute-value pairs *color = orange, shape = sphere*. There are two main algorithms for creating the decision tree: ID3 and the its successor C4.5 [131]. Basically, they need to answer the question *"which attribute to check at the root of the tree, which next?"* A formal description can be found in [131].

Energy Aware Routing and Clustering. An application to link quality classification in WSNs is presented in [197]. The authors use simple rules to classify links into good and bad, based on the RSSI level of received packets, buffer sizes, etc. The computation is done centrally on the base station and the data model is disseminated to all nodes in the network.

Summary. Decision trees and case-base reasoning are feasible techniques for small size localized problems on individual sensor nodes or larger data sets on a centralized base station. They are simple to implement and deploy, but do not lead to optimal results.

3.3.4 Reinforcement learning

Reinforcement learning (RL) [96, 179] is biologically inspired, where the learning agent acquires its knowledge by actively exploring its environment. At each step, it selects some possible action and receives a reward from the environment for this specific action. Note that the *best* possible action at some state is never known a-priori. Consequently, the agent has to try many different actions and sequences of actions and learns from its experiences. A simple example is a mouse or a robot learning to move in a maze environment (Figure 3.7). At each step it can select one action from a pool of available actions according to its current view of the environment and previously acquired knowledge, it fulfills

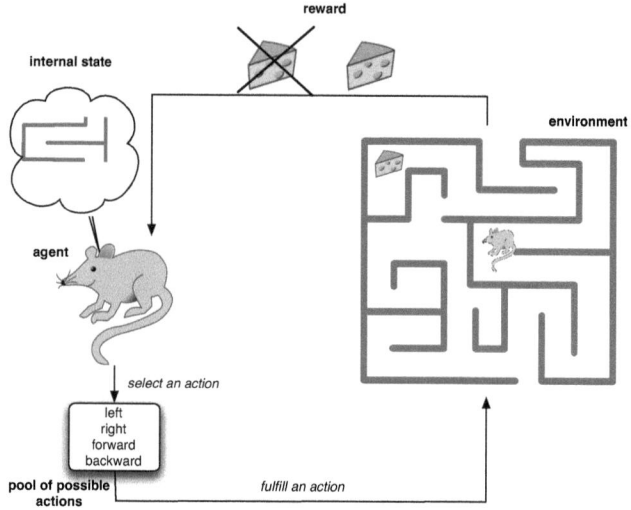

Figure 3.7. General reinforcement learning model. The agent selects one action according to its current internal state (current view of the environment and previous knowledge), fulfills this action and observes a reward.

---

this action and observes a reward from the environment. Usually the reward is negative when the goal if not reached yet (e.g. the cheese is not found) or positive when it is reached.

RL is well suited for distributed problems, like routing. It has medium requirements for memory and rather low computation needs at the individual nodes. This arises from the need of keeping many different possible actions and their values. It needs some time to converge, but it is easy to implement, highly flexible to topology changes and achieves optimal results. The most widely used reinforcement learning algorithm is Q-Learning, which assigns a Q-Value to each possible action representing their goodness or quality. After learning, the best Q-Values mirror the optimal actions.

3.3 Machine learning for WSNs

Energy Aware Routing and Clustering. One of the fundamental and earliest works in packet routing using machine learning is Q-Routing [29]. The authors describe a very simple, Q-Learning based algorithm, which learns the best paths considering the least latency to the destinations. Possible actions are next hops at the nodes, and a Q-Value is assigned to each pair (*sink, neighbor*) representing the time which a packet needs through this neighbor to reach the sink. Simulations proved the algorithm to be efficient under high network loads and to perform also well under changing network topologies. Although the approach was developed for wired, packet-switched networks, it inspired a lot of works in the wireless ad hoc and WSN communities, because it is fully distributed. A recent implementation on Crossbow motes [47] has demonstrated its practicality.

Many other routing protocols have been inspired from Q-Routing [10, 23, 79, 109, 141, 166, 212, 222]. The main difference between them is the used cost metric for routing. Delivery time is used in [109, 176], maximum compression paths are learnt in [23, 79, 212], and geographic-based routing is implemented in [10, 166]. A novel cost metric is used by [141], where the routing protocol learns to avoid "important" nodes: nodes, which after failing might disconnect the network. Neighboring nodes exchange information about their importance (computed locally at the nodes based on full topology information) and the best routes (with least important nodes on them) are learnt. A more general cost function is defined in [222], where any combination of number of hops, delay, and remaining energy on the nodes can be applied.

Another difference between the above approaches is the used reinforcement learning algorithm. The authors of [109] use dual reinforcement learning, which gives rewards not only for previous actions, but also to next ones. Thus, learning converges faster and the protocol shows better performance. Q-Learning is used by [10, 166, 212, 222]

Team-partitioned, opaque-transition reinforcement learning (TPOT-RL) has been developed for simulated robotic soccer [177] and applied to packet routing [176]. It allows a team of independent learning agents to collaboratively learn a shared task, like soccer playing. It differs from traditional RL in its value function, which is partitioned among the agents and each agent learns only the part of it directly relevant to its localized actions. Also, the environment is *opaque* to the agents, which means that they have no information about the next possible actions of their mates or their goodness.

A formal definition of RL in a distributed environment and a learning algorithm is given in [56]. It presents a reinforcement learning algorithm, designed especially for solving the point-to-point routing problem in MANETs. Collaborative RL (CRL) is greatly based on Q-Learning, but uses also a decay function (similar to pheromone evaporation in ACO, see further Section 3.3.5) to better meet the properties of ad-hoc networks.

An additional contribution of [79] beside the Q-Learning routing protocol is the automatic learning of the optimal values of the parameters of the algorithm with a Bayesian exploration strategy. The paper presents an idea which can be applied to all other RL-based algorithms, which need parameter pre-setting and should be further explored and refined.

The setting of [195] is similar to those presented above: many source nodes are sending data to a single base station. The algorithm takes into account the aggregation ratio, the residual energy on the nodes, the hop cost to the base station and the link reliability between the nodes. The algorithm runs in learning episodes. The learning agents are again the nodes and Q-Values are assigned to each possible next hop at each node. During each episode, the current Q-Values are used to route a packet to the base station. At each hop, the full hop information is appended to the packet (residual energy, rewards, etc.). Rewards are generated at the base station. When the base station has enough such packets (undefined how many), it calculates the Q-Values offline for the nodes in the network and disseminates them via a network-wide broadcast.

Although all of the above studies show promising results from applying various reinforcement learning algorithms to routing in WSNs, none of them has reached the state of a mature communication protocol with implementation and evaluation in a realistic simulation and real hardware environment. Their evaluations are rather preliminary and concentrate on a few of their properties, leaving out important questions about overhead and efficient implementation.

3.3 Machine learning for WSNs

Scheduling and Medium Access Protocols. Actor Critic Algorithm [157] is a early reinforcement learning algorithm, where the policy is detached from the leant action values. In current RL algorithm like Q-Learning the policy is fully dependent on the learnt Q-Values, which represent the current state of the value function. This incurs search overhead when the best Q-Value needs to be found. In actor critic algorithm a separate table (called the *actor*) can be defined together with the value table (called the *critic*) to speed up action selection. This algorithm has been applied for example to point to point communication in sensor networks [140]. The goal of the algorithm is to maximize throughput per total consumed energy in a sensor network, based on node-to-node communication. Given its current buffer size and last channel transmission gain, the node decides the best modulation level and transmit power to maximize the total throughput per consumed energy. For this, the authors use the standard RL algorithm and test their algorithm on a two-node and multinode scenarios. Unfortunately no comparison to other state-of-the-art protocols is presented in order to evaluate the gain of the RL algorithm.

RL-MAC [118] applies reinforcement learning to adjust the sleeping schedule of a MAC protocol in a WSN setting. The MAC protocol is very similar in its idea to the other WSN MAC protocols such as S-MAC or T-MAC. It divides the time into frames and the frames into slots, where each node is allowed to transmit messages only during its own reserved slot. However, unlike other protocols, it changes the duration of the frames and slots according to the current traffic. At the beginning of its reserved slot, the node first transmits some control information, including also a reward for the other nodes. The reward function depends on the number of waiting messages on the nodes and on the number of successfully transmitted messages during the reserved slot. The paper reports higher data throughput and lower energy expenditure compared to S-MAC.

COORD, a distributed reinforcement learning based solution to achieve best coverage in a WSN is presented in [163]. The goal of the algorithm is to cooperatively find a combination of active and sleeping sensor nodes in a sensor network, which is still able to perform full covered sensing of the desired phenomena. For this the authors propose three similar approaches, all based on

Q-Learning. The possible actions are two: transitioning from sleeping to active mode and back. The sensor network is divided into a rectangular grid and the goal is to cover each grid vertex by some sensors, best by exactly one. A Q-Value is assigned to each grid vertex, which represents the number of sensor nodes, currently covering this vertex. In each run of the algorithm, each node evaluates its current Q-Value table with all grid vertices it covers and takes an action. After that, all nodes evaluate again their Q tables and so on.

The other two solutions are very similar and the results they show are also comparable. A comparison to some state-of-the-art approach is not provided and thus the results cannot be properly evaluated. Also, a clear protocol implementation is missing, leaving open many questions about coordination and exchange of Q-Values and the states of the grid vertices. However, the approach is fully distributed and can be run online if needed. Also, it shows a nice modeling work of converting a centralized problem into a distributed one and solving it with RL.

Design and Deployment. The study reported in [71] presents a reinforcement learning based approach for service positioning in MANET. The system is presented as a SMDP (Semi-Markov Decision Process) and the optimal behavior is learned with Q-Learning. The learning agent is situated together with the service provider on one of the hosts in the network and has the ability to move to other hosts. Thus, only one learning agent is present in the system (with more service providers more agents have to be deployed). The system state is given through different query-related parameters, like queries' average hop count, number of neighboring clients, etc. The protocol is designed for MANETs, but can be successfully applied to similar problems in WSNs.

Summary. Reinforcement learning is the most widely used ML technique for distributed problems in MANETs and WSNs such as routing, scheduling, medium access control, service positioning etc. Its most important strengths are the model-free nature and online learning algorithm, but also its flexibility and fast adaptability to changing environments. RL implementations for WSNs incur only minimal communication overhead and achieve optimal results. *Thus, RL should be the first choice when solving distributed problems in WSNs.*

3.3.5 Swarm Intelligence

The term Swarm Intelligence refers to a class of computational intelligence techniques biologically inspired by the behavior of social insects like ants or bees. The main idea is the distributed nature of the algorithms, where individual agents have only very limited memory and computational resources. However, the agents are able to communicate with each other through the shared environment (like ants' pheromone trails) and to cooperatively learn its properties. A good introduction to swarm intelligence for wireless communications is presented in [100]. A more general overview of Swarm Intelligence can be found in [101].

There are two main branches of swarm intelligence: particle swarm optimization (PSO) and ant colony optimization (ACO). The first technique was developed by Kennedy and Eberhart [101] in 1995 and is inspired by bird flocking or fish schooling. It is applicable to problems where the solution can be represented as a point in a search space. Agents are points in the solution space and possess movement speed and direction. Usually a high number of agents is used to represent many different solutions. During learning, agents move around in the solution space and are evaluated at each step according to some fitness function. With time, individual agents accelerate towards other agents with higher fitness in their direct neighborhood, thus forming schools or flocks. Figure 3.8 illustrates the main concept of PSO. The algorithm is extremely resilient to the local minimum problem, because of the high number of agents.

The second technique, Ant Colony Optimization, was first introduced by Marco Dorigo in [53]. A very compresehensive description of the theory and applications of ACO is given in [55]. The algorithm finds near-optimal solutions to various problems, which can be described as graph optimization problems. Ants walk on the edges of the graph, leaving pheromones on their way, which are used to optimize the paths of future ants (Figure 3.9).

Energy Aware Routing and Clustering. Four variants of PSO are proposed for energy aware clustering in [76]. The difference between them are the PSO parameters - initial speed, acceleration, etc. Although PSO is a distributed al-

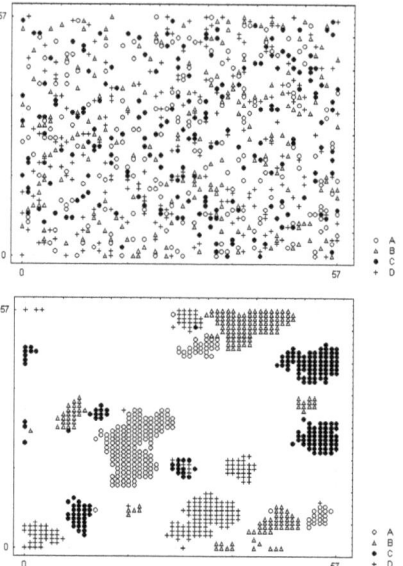

Figure 3.8. Particle swarm intelligence (PSO) in action: particles are initialized at random positions (top) and after learning cluster into groups (bottom) [153]

gorithm, here the algorithm is centralized and run on the base station with full topology information about the network. The algorithm is based on a simple idea that for a group of nodes that lie in a neighborhood, the node closest to the base station becomes the clusterhead. The approach has some drawbacks: Clustering depends solely on the physical distribution of nodes and is centralized. Thus, in case of failures or any topology changes, the new information needs to be gathered at the base station and clustering needs to be re-computed.

A novel clustering approach for WSNs called CRAWL is defined in [22] with the use of soldier ants. Biological soldier ants that have the support of other soldier ants are found to be more aggressive in nature. An ant is observed to exhibit

3.3 Machine learning for WSNs

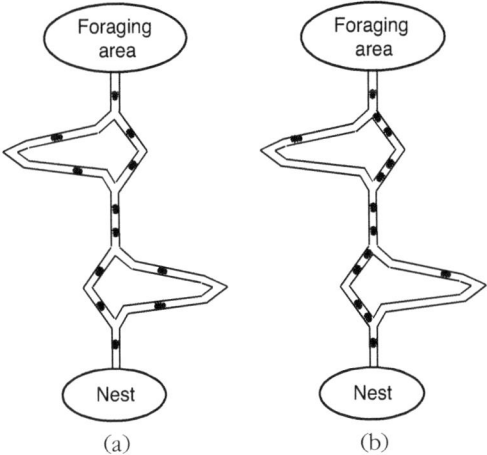

Figure 3.9. The double bridge experiment for finding shortest paths with Ant Colony Optimization. (a) In the beginning of the experiment ants take explore all possible routes. (b) At the end of the experiment most of the ants take the shortest path to the foraging area, while few ants explore other non-optimal routes. Copyright [54].

---

higher eagerness to fight when it is amidst strong ants. This fact inspires the collaborative clustering algorithm for wireless sensor network longevity *(CRAWL)* that possesses good scalability and adaptability features. Here, each node has an *Eagerness* value to serve as a clusterhead, which is computed based on its own remaining battery and the remaining batteries of its neighbors. At regular intervals, each node computes its *Eagerness* value and broadcasts it over the network. The node that has the highest *Eagerness* value decides to act as a clusterhead, and the other nodes accept it. The clusterhead floods the new clustering information, which helps other nodes to readjust their power levels just enough for them to transmit to the clusterhead.

The method assures that only the nodes that have sufficient energy in their reservoir, and have strong neighbors, opt to become clusterheads. The algorithm has a significant communication overhead due to the fact that each node has to flood its *Eagerness* value at regular intervals. In addition, the traffic of packets might flow away from a sink node just because a node in that direction has higher *Eagerness*. Thus, the algorithm is sub-optimal in terms of minimizing energy expenditure of individual nodes, but optimal in terms of making effective use of the energy available to the whole network.

AntNet [50] is an ACO application in communication networks used to find near-optimal routes in a communication graph without global information. The agents are divided into *forward* and *backward* ants. Forward ants are initialized at the data source and sent to all known destinations at regular intervals. They travel through the network graph by *randomly* choosing the next hop and leave pheromones on their way. The more ants have chosen the same path the higher the pheromone level of that path. During their travel, forward ants gather routing information, indicating the arrival time at each node on their way. At destination arrival, the forward ants are transformed into backward ants and use the cashed route they have traveled to traverse the same route again and to update the pheromone tables according to the gathered routing information. Details of this computation can be found in [50, 51]. A decay function is implemented as evaporation of the pheromone levels, indicating which routes are the most freshly used ones. The version of AntNet for MANETs is called AntHocNet [51] and is developed by the some of the authors of AntNet.

AntNet and AntHocNet use both reactive path setup and proactive path maintenance for single source - single sink. However, the approach requires ants to be traveling independent from data packets and even to trace each path twice (forward and backward), which causes a great overhead and is not well suited for energy-restricted WSNs. Nevertheless, the method is fully distributed and is the one best explored and described in the literature for using swarm intelligence in wireless networks.

MANSI [167] (Multicast for Ad Hoc Networks with Swarm Intelligence) is a multicast routing protocol for MANETs, based on swarm intelligence. The protocol is similar to traditional multicast protocols, where a core node initiates the

3.3 Machine learning for WSNs

building of the multicast tree through a forward Join Request Packet and a backward Join Reply Packet. However, nodes different from the core send ants into the network at regular intervals to explore the network for better routes to the core, leaving routing information (pheromones) on their way. This information is later used by following ants for opportunistically selecting their next hops. The approach is similar to AntHocNet [51], however, optimization is applied to multicast instead of unicast routing.

In [132], the authors propose an AntHocNet [51] based approach for routing in a sensor network installed in a building. Its main disadvantage is that the returning ants in the network create unnecessary overhead for a sensor network.

Ant-Based Control [161] is similar to AntNet in many aspects, but also has some important differences. There is only one class of ants, started at regular intervals at the data sources, traversing the network probabilistically and updating the routing tables as they travel to the destinations. Once reaching their destination, the ants are eliminated. The update of the routing tables is thus not based on the trip times to the destination, but rather on the present *lifetime* of the ant, calculated as the delay from its launching node to the present one. Because of its relatively smaller communication overhead (only forward ants), ABC is better suited for energy-restricted scenarios like WSN. However, it is still costly to send ants at regular intervals and the advantages of using it should be carefully evaluated.

UniformAnts [178] presents a simple ant-optimization based technique for finding and maintaining routes in a MANET. Similarly to the original ABC algorithm, it uses only forward ants, updating the probability-based routing tables on the nodes as the ant travels towards the sink. Two different ant types are used, the difference is how the next hop is selected - greedy or uniformly between all options. The method achieves fairly good results and shares the properties of ABC.

Mobile agents are often mistaken for a machine learning or swarm intelligence approach. However, they refer to the usage of simple, small entities (packets), which traverse the system (in our case the network) and deliver fresh information to the system's nodes. In the case of routing, for example, the agents update routing information (paths or next hops) on the nodes [27, 33, 187]. Although very efficient in some applications (like routing in less mobile scenarios), they cannot be classified as a learning nor as a swarm intelligence algorithm. They represent a good optimization to traditional routing approaches in mobile scenarios. However, they also increase the communication cost for sending the agents.

Design and Deployment. PSO has various applications to design and deployment in WSNs. It has been successfully applied to optimal detection coverage in maritime surveillance in [137], to finding optimal sink paths across a sensor field [130] and topological planning for traffic surveillance in [81]. All of the applications use the original PSO algorithm, with different parameters for the particles' speed and acceleration.

Localization. A suitable application area of PSO is also localization in sensor networks. In [72], the base station runs a PSO-based algorithm with centralized information to find the positions of the network nodes. However, PSO is a distributed technique and can be applied also here as such.

Summary. Swarm intelligence is well suited for distributed network scenarios, where mobility and topology changes are of greatest importance, but energy is not limited, like MANETs. Interestingly, PSO has been applied only in a centralized manner, although it is a distributed technique and network nodes could represent individual particles. ACO, on the other hand, has been applied mostly to routing and has proved to be an efficient and flexible algorithm. In the context of energy-restricted WSNs, PSO seems the better choice because of its localized nature and small communication overhead. To the best of our knowledge, there are no PSO applications to routing in WSNs. ACO is better suited for non energy-restricted scenarios like MANETs. All WSNs applications of ACO suffer from the great communication overhead of the traveling ants. However, a different implementation of ACO is also possible, where ants carry data packets and thus minimize exploration overhead.

3.3 Machine learning for WSNs

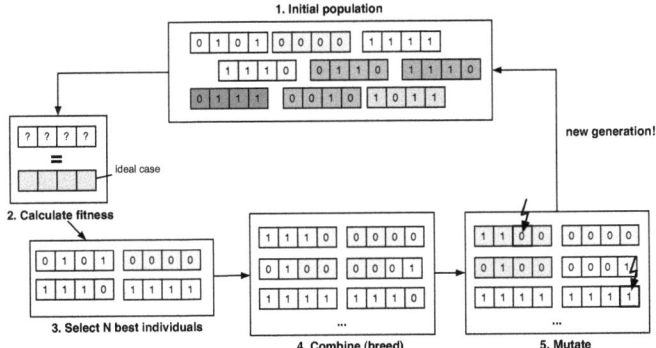

Figure 3.10. General model of genetic algorithms.

3.3.6 Genetic algorithms

The paradigm of genetic algorithms (GA) is based on biological evolution. It describes a system, consisting of *individuals (chromosomes, genes)*, which evolve through *cross-over* (combination of two individuals) and *mutation* (spontaneous change of the properties of one individual). The individuals are organized into *generations* and represent possible solutions to the problem: with time, the properties of the generations change and evolve and the solutions become better in terms of some predefined fitness function. The general model of genetic algorithms is illustrated in Figure 3.10. More information about genetic algorithms can be found for example in [159].

Genetic algorithms are easy to understand and the system easy and fast to define. However, they require centralized computation and converge slowly. Since they keep at least two full generations at any time to be able to compute the next one, they have also high memory requirements. However, their biggest disadvantage is their inflexibility in case of changes of the input: the whole evolution process has to be rerun in order to find a new solution.

Sensor Fusion and Data Mining. The issue of data aggregation for a target detection application is addressed in [204] through mobile agent-based distributed sensor networks wherein a mobile agent selectively visits the sensors and incrementally fuses the appropriate measurement data. GA is used to determine the optimal route for the agent to traverse. Results are compared with those of the popular heuristic algorithms "local closest first" (LCF) and "global closest first" (GCF). The results show that the GA results in routes superior to the ones determined by LCF and GCF in all case studies.

An extension of the study in [204] is presented in [217]. In addition to data acquisition and processing time, this study also includes agent transmission time delay in a route R in the fitness function definition. The paper shows that the quality of the routes determined by *GAgent2* is superior to that determined by LCF. However, in both [204] and [217], the cost of gathering the information on a central unit to compute the optimal path is not considered. This cost does not apply to the distributed algorithms GCF and LCF.

Energy Aware Routing and Clustering. A GA based multi-hop routing technique named *GA-Routing* is proposed in [90] for maximizing network longevity in terms of time to first node death. The proposed GA approach generates aggregation trees, which span all the sensor nodes. Although the best aggregation tree is the most efficient path in the network, continuous use of this path would lead to failure of a few nodes earlier than others. The goal of the study in [90] is to find an aggregation tree, and the number of times a particular tree is used before the next tree comes in force. The spanning trees are modeled as individuals. Simulation results show that GA gives better lifetime than the *single best tree* (SBT) algorithm, and the same lifetime as the cluster based maximum lifetime data aggregation algorithm [46] for small network sizes. However, the algorithm's overhead if not evaluated.

Another application of GA in energy efficient clustering is described in [85]. The proposed GA represents the sensor nodes as bits of chromosomes, cluster-heads as 1 and ordinary nodes as 0. The number of bits in a chromosome is equal to the number of nodes. The fitness of the chromosomes are computed based on the distances between the nodes and the cluster heads, the distance between the cluster heads and the sink and the energy spent to deliver packets to the sink. The results show that the GA approach possesses better energy efficiency than do hierarchical cluster based routing (HCR) and LEACH [149]. However, clustering overhead is not considered.

There are also some other similar ideas based on GAs, where a base station computes the optimal routing, aggregation or clustering scheme for a network based on the information about the topology, remaining energy on the nodes, etc. [84, 127, 183]. Such algorithms are only feasible if the network is expected to have a static topology, perfect communication, symmetric links and constant energy. Under these restrictions, a centrally computed routing or aggregation tree makes sense and is probably easier to implement. However, these properties are in conflict with the nature of WSNs.

Scheduling and Medium Access Protocols. A model based on GA is proposed for sleep scheduling of nodes in a randomly deployed large scale WSN in [169]. Such networks deploy a large number of redundant nodes for better coverage, and how to manage the combination of nodes for a prolonged network operation is a major problem. The scheme proposed in the article divides the network life into rounds. In each round, a set of nodes is kept active and the rest of the nodes are put in sleep mode. It is ensured that the set of active nodes has adequate coverage and connectivity. When some of the active nodes die, blind spots appear. At this time, all nodes are woken up for a decision on the next set of nodes to remain active in the next round. This is clearly a multi-objective optimization problem. The first objective is to minimize the overall energy consumption of the active set, and the second objective is to minimize the number of active nodes. Again, gathering the topology information on a single base station is critical and not feasible in a realistic scenario.

A similar scheduling problem called the active interval scheduling problem in hierarchical WSNs for long-term periodical monitoring is introduced in [95]. In this scenario, nodes are partitioned into clusters with local cluster heads, which dictate active intervals to the nodes. Active intervals need to be coordinated among clusters to avoid intra-cluster interference and minimized to minimize energy expenditure. Again, the proposed algorithm is centralized and does not take into account crucial WSN properties such as failures.

Design and Deployment. A decision support system (DSS) based on GAs is proposed in [34]. The DSS is meant for the use of a process engineer who interacts with it to determine optimal sensor network design. Usually the engineer first defines some measurable quality metrics, selects an initial sensor network design and evaluates it. Depending on the achieved results, she changes the design and re-evaluates it. The DSS presented in [34] automates this process by feeding random network designs into a GA and searching for the best solution according to the defined quality metrics. On one side, this is a valuable tool for WSN designers and speeds up their work. On the other side, their expertise is still crucial, since they need to define the quality metrics and to define how the optimal solution looks like.

Localization. A GA based node localization algorithm *GA-Loc* is presented in [134]. Each of the N non-anchor nodes in the study is assumed to have ability to measure its distance form all its one-hop neighbors. GA estimates the location (x_i, y_i) of node i by minimizing the distance error to the anchor nodes and among all nodes. The algorithm assumes the full distance information is available on a centralized base station. A similar techniques with slightly different fitness functions are used in [125, 221].

Summary. Genetic algorithms have high memory and processing requirements and are very inflexible in case of an environmental change. Nevertheless, they can be used for some centralized problems, where the results need to be disseminated only infrequently to the nodes. Examples are localization in mostly static networks or sensor network design and optimal positioning.

3.3.7 Heuristic Search

Traditional heuristic search methods operate in two steps: planning and plan execution. For example, working with a search tree, they will first calculate the value function (the goodness) of all nodes and then take the best possible path through the tree. This approach cannot be applied in real time scenarios, where agents traverse the search space and have to take their decisions based on locally available data only. Real time heuristic search methods, also called

3.3 Machine learning for WSNs

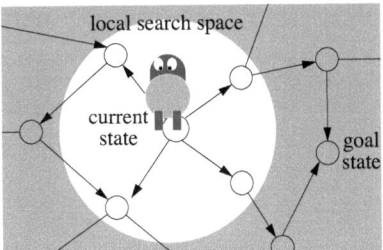

Figure 3.11. Agent-centered search model. Copyright [105]

agent-centered search [105], operate successfully in such environments. The agent evaluates only its current state neighborhood – the states it can reach in the next step only – and executes its next action according to these values. Figure 3.11 illustrates the general model. A simple example is a robot, trying to find its way in an environment full of obstacles and to reach some goal position. It will evaluate its immediate action possibilities (movements) and choose the best one. After this planning/execution step, the robot will re-evaluate its current state and so on. Crucial for the algorithm is the evaluation of the current options of the learning agent. They need to be initialized with a globally known fitness function. Such an algorithm is for example LRTA* (Learning Real Time A*), where the initial values of the states are calculated using a simple heuristic (e.g. the Manhattan distance to the goal). If the used heuristic is admissible (guaranteed to never overestimate the real costs to the goal), the algorithm finds the optimal solution. More information can be found in [105, 106].

Energy Aware Routing and Clustering. Real time heuristic search methods are very well suited for wireless ad-hoc scenarios - the nodes in the network can be modeled as the agent states, the packets as the agents and the information available at the nodes about their one-hop neighbors can be used for evaluating the search neighborhood. LRTA* is applied to routing in ad-hoc networks in [158, 165] with good results. However, the need of a global heuristic limits the applicability of the algorithm in distributed environments.

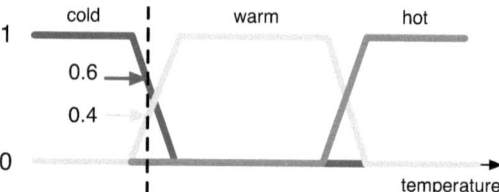

Figure 3.12. Fuzzy logic example. The classification of some variable (temperature) is not binary like cold OR warm, but fuzzy like a little bit cold and little bit warm.

Summary. On the first glance, real time heuristic search might seem very similar to reinforcement learning. However, the used heuristic requires global knowledge about the environment and no exploration of non-optimal routes is ever conducted. In the presence of such a heuristic, like available location information for the neighbors and the sinks, the approach is feasible. On the other hand, reinforcement learning is a better choice because of its ability to learn from previous experience.

3.3.8 Fuzzy logic

Classical set theory allows elements to be either included in a set or not. This is in contrast with human reasoning, which includes a measure of imprecision or uncertainty, which is marked by the use of linguistic variables such as *most, many, frequently, seldom*. This approximate reasoning is modeled by fuzzy logic, which is a multivalued logic that allows intermediate values to be defined between conventional threshold values. Fuzzy systems allow the use of fuzzy sets to draw conclusions and to make decisions. Fuzzy sets differ from classical sets in that they allow an object to be a partial member of a set. For example, a person may be a member of the set *tall* to a degree of 0.8 [218]. Or, as Figure 3.12 shows, the current temperature of a room can be 0.6 cold and 0.4 warm at the same time.

In fuzzy systems, the dynamic behavior of a system is characterized by a set

3.3 Machine learning for WSNs

of linguistic fuzzy rules based on the knowledge of a human expert. Fuzzy rules are of the general form: *if* antecedent(s) *then* consequent(s), or continuing our example from Figure 3.12: *IF* temperature is cold *THEN* turn on the heating. It is important to note that fuzzy rules contain only *IF* statements and no *ELSE* statements. Each of the rules is evaluated individually and independently from each other, since any of them (or all of them) can be true.

Antecedents and consequents of a fuzzy rule form the fuzzy *input space* and fuzzy *output* space respectively. Non-fuzzy inputs (e.g. the current temperature) are mapped to their fuzzy representation (e.g. cold, warm, hot) in the process called fuzzification. Fuzzy logic has been applied successfully in control systems (e.g., control of vehicle subsystem, power systems, home appliances, elevators etc.), digital image processing and pattern recognition.

Energy Aware Routing and Clustering. A novel distributed approach based on fuzzy numbers for energy efficient flooding-based aggregation is proposed in [114]. In this study, each sensor node maintains an estimate of the aggregation value represented as a fuzzy number. Aggregation is done at each node if either a new measurement value is locally available to the node, or if a new value is received from a neighboring node. Based on the estimate, a node decides if a newly measured sensor reading has to be propagated in the network or not. This reduces the number of messages transmitted, and thus reduces the energy spent. The article presents the results of experiments on a network of 12 motes, deployed in an apartment to monitor maximum temperature over 24 hours. The article reports a reduced number of received and transmitted messages leading to a network lifetime of 418 days. Although this network lifetime is impressive, the authors do not give the network lifetime without fuzzification and thus no comparison is possible.

Judicious clusterhead election can reduce the energy consumption and extend the lifetime of the network. A fuzzy logic approach based on remaining energy and location information is proposed for clusterhead election in [75]. The study uses a network model in which all sensor nodes transmit the information about their location and available energy to the base station. The base station takes into account the energy each node has, the number of nodes in the vicinity, and a node's distance from other nodes and determines which nodes should serve as clusterheads. The base station fuzzifies the variables *node energy* and *node concentration* into three levels: *low*, *medium* and *high*, and the variable *node distance from base station* into *close*, *adequate* and *far*. The fuzzy outcome that represents the probability of node being chosen as a clusterhead, is divided into seven levels: *very small*, *small*, *rather small*, *medium*, *rather large*, *large*, and *very large*. The article observes substantial increase in network lifetime in comparison to a network that uses the low energy adaptive clustering hierarchy (LEACH) approach. However, the approach is centralized and incurs substantial overhead for collecting necessary information at the base station and disseminating the cluster head roles.

Scheduling and Medium Access Protocols. A fuzzy logic approach towards secure media access control (*FSMAC*) is presented in [154] for enhanced immunity to collision, unfairness and exhaustion attacks. In collision attacks, attackers transmit packets regardless of status of the medium. These packets collide with data or control packets from the legitimate sensors. In unfairness attacks, adversaries transmit as many packets as possible after sensing that the medium is free. This prevents the legitimate sensors from transmitting their own packets. In exhaustion attacks, adversaries transmit abnormally large number of *ready-to-send* (RTS) packets to normal sensor nodes, thereby exhausting their energy quickly. A node can detect an attack by monitoring abnormally large variations in sensitive parameters: collision rate R_c (number of collisions observed by a node per second), average waiting time T_w (waiting time of a packet in MAC buffer before transmission), and arrival rate R_{RTS} (rate of RTS packets received by a node successfully per second). These variables are represented as fuzzy and the output is again a fuzzy variable representing the probability that an attack was detected. The node stops sending/receiving packets when an attack is detected and goes to sleep for some period of time. After that, the medium state is re-evaluated. Performance of FSMAC is compared with that of CSMA/CA. The results show that FSMAC offers a 25% increase in successful data packet transmission, and 5% less energy consumption per packet. In each type of attack, FSMAC extends first node death time in the network by over 100% as compared to CSMA/CA.

3.3 Machine learning for WSNs

The fuzzy model needs to be disseminated to all nodes in the network. However, it is not expected to change often and the medium evaluation is performed in a distributed manner. On the other side, the extension of the network lifetime is probably due to the enforced sleep mode during an attack.

Design and Deployment. Fuzzy logic has been proposed for deployment in [224]. This techniques assumes that the area to be monitored by a sensor network is divided into a square grid of subareas, each having its own terrain profile and a level of required surveillance (therefore, its own path loss model and required path loss threshold). The proposed technique uses fuzzy logic to determine the number of sensors $n(i)$ necessary to be scattered in a subarea i. For a subarea i, path loss $PL(i)$ and threshold path loss PL_{TH} are normalized on a scale 0 to 10, then divided into overlapping membership functions *low*, *medium* and *high*. The output of the system is de-fuzzified again and gives the number of nodes to be deployed in each area. The article shows that the fuzzy deployment achieves significant improvement in terms of worst case coverage in comparison to uniform deployment.

Summary. Fuzzy logic is well suited for defining and solving complex multi-objective functions. Examples are congestion control, attack discovery, and optimal sensor deployment. The main challenge lies in defining the fuzzy variables and determining the fuzzy rules. Usually this needs to be done offline and manually, and then the fuzzy model to be disseminated to the network nodes. However, this is feasible for problems whose models are not expected to change fast - like the above examples.

3.3.9 Summary of Machine Learning and Computational Intelligence techniques

There are many applications of various machine learning and computational intelligence techniques to WSNs. The main goal of this survey and classification is to compare the suitability and applicability of the different ML approaches to the main topic of this dissertation: routing and clustering. Figure 3.13 summarizes the presented works. The suitability of the different ML and CI approaches is

ML approach	Sensor Fusion/ Data Mining	Routing and Clustering	Scheduling and MAC	Design and Deployment	Localization
Neural Networks	[25], [26], [61], [150]	[18]	[168]		
Support Vector Machines					[1], [98], [189]
Decision Trees		[197]			
Reinforcement Learning		[10], [23], [29], [47], [56], [79], [109], [141], [176], [195], [212], [222]	[118], [140], [163]	[71]	
Swarm Intelligence		[22], [50], [51], [76], [132], [167], [178]		[81], [130], [137]	[72]
Genetic Algorithms	[204], [217]	[46], [84], [85], [90], [127], [183]	[95], [169]	[34]	[125], [134], [221]
Heuristic Search		[158], [165]			
Fuzzy Logic		[75], [114]	[154]	[224]	

Legend: not suited | less suited | medium suited | well suited

Figure 3.13. Summary of ML and CI applications to WSNs. The suitability of the algorithms to each of the surveyed applications in WSNs is shown, together with the surveyed works.

evaluated and the resulting protocols and algorithms for WSNs are cited.

Concerning routing and clustering in WSNs, it can be concluded that there are four well-suited ML and CI techniques and one less suited approach. In general, all of the suited techniques are distributed, simple to implement and have little to medium processing and memory requirements. While Figure 3.13 concentrates on the general applicability of the proposed algorithms, Table 3.1 goes one step further and compares the most suitable of them in terms of their properties: memory and processing requirements, optimality, and flexibility in case of failures.

3.3 Machine learning for WSNs

ML/CI Approach	Comput. requirements	Memory requirements	Flexibility	Optimality	Add. overhead
Reinforcement learning	Low	Medium	High	Optimal	low
Swarm intelligence	Low	Medium	High	Optimal	high
Heuristic search	Low	Medium	Low	Optimal	medium
Fuzzy Logic	Medium	Medium	Low	Near optimal	medium

Table 3.1. Properties of basic Computational Intelligence Paradigms

Fuzzy logic (last approach in Table 3.1) has higher computational requirements because of the offline fuzzification of the objective function. Additionally, the fuzzy rules have to be stored at all nodes and their number grows exponentially with the number of fuzzy values of each of the variables. The dissemination of the fuzzy rules is responsible for the incurred additional communication overhead. The results achieved by fuzzy logic are near-optimal because of the fuzzification process - the exact optimal solution is hard to find. Additionally, in case of changes of the objective function, the fuzzy rules need to be recomputed.

Heuristic search is very similar in its properties to reinforcement learning, see Section 5.4.4. However, it requires a globally known heuristic function, which increases the incurred communication overhead. Assuming the heuristic is admissible, the achieved results are optimal.

Swarm intelligence is a widely used technique for routing in MANETs, where it performs very well under high mobility scenarios. Usually Ant Colony Optimization is used. However, the traveling ants incur high communication overhead throughout the network lifetime.

Reinforcement learning, on the other hand, seems to be the best performing and suitable technique to apply to routing and clustering in WSNs. It achieves optimal results at low processing and medium memory costs and is highly flexible in case of failures or topology changes. The incurred additional communication overhead is minimal.

3.4 Concluding remarks

This chapter presented an extensive survey of state-of-the-art work in routing and clustering for wireless sensor networks and applications of machine learning to various problems in WSNs. A lot of research effort has been invested in these topics, but most of the work presented here suffers from some restrictions. Often the routing or clustering protocol is implemented for a very specific application scenario and cannot be easily applied to other scenarios. Many of the algorithms cannot cope efficiently with node and link failures or mobile sinks. Especially clustering protocols incur a lot of communication overhead for agreeing on the network structure. Last but not least, machine learning based approaches present a theoretically well designed solution, but do not implement a real-world communication protocol nor do they evaluate or compare it to traditional existing ones.

Given the related works presented here with their advantages and disadvantages and the identified suitable machine learning technique, we decide to apply *reinforcement learning* to solve the routing and clustering problem as defined in Chapter 2.

Chapter 4
Methodology and Solution Path

The target scenario, as identified in Chapter 2, is challenging in many aspects: the data dissemination protocol (including routing and clustering) needs to cope with many different applications and requirements, including mobility of sinks and node failures. Additionally, new research directions need to be taken to enable a low-overhead non-uniform clustering. Chapter 3 summarized related efforts in the field together with machine learning and computational intelligence applications to WSNs. It showed that no efficient unified routing or clustering protocol is available for the targeted scenario. However, three general take-aways can be derived:

- Separating routing from clustering has several advantages in comparison to unified protocols: the protocols are easier to parametrize and to plug into various communication stacks, the application scenario is broader and more application requirements can be met, and the definition of the problem and protocol implementation are more memory and processing efficient. Cross-layer optimized communication stacks are well suited for a specific restricted environment or application scenario. However, our goal in this thesis is to design a broadly applicable data dissemination framework and separating routing from clustering is more advantageous.

- Reinforcement learning (RL) is well-suited for solving complex distributed problems like routing in a fully localized manner. We studied the properties and applications of RL to WSNs in Section 3.3 and identified it as the most appropriate algorithm to use in this thesis. Although there are only a few protocols implemented with reinforcement learning and their application scenarios are different than our target scenario, their results are highly promising and the protocols exhibit exactly the desired properties: localized exchange of information, flexibility in case of mobility and node failures, optimal routing solutions, and memory and processing efficient implementation.

- Evaluation methodologies for communication protocols in WSNs have experienced a lot of criticism lately. This is a critical issue when designing new protocols: evaluation needs to be thoroughly planned, so that cross-article comparison is possible and applicability to real hardware systems is shown.

Consequently from above, we turn our attention to Q-Learning, a widely used reinforcement learning technique. We divide our solution into two main parts with the following properties and parameters:

- **Routing to multiple mobile sinks.** Optimal shared multicast routes are desired, taking into account the mobility of the sinks and eventual link and node failures.

- **Non-uniform clustering.** A low-overhead clustering approach is targeted, with parameters defining the uniform or non-uniform cluster sizes based on location information.

In the next section we give an introduction to Q-Learning and its properties and challenges. Later in the chapter we turn our attention to evaluation and analysis techniques usually applied to routing and clustering in WSNs and define our own evaluation methodology.

4.1 Background on Q-Learning

Q-Learning [198] is a widely used reinforcement learning algorithm, able to learn an action-value function without an explicit model of the environment. It

4.1 Background on Q-Learning

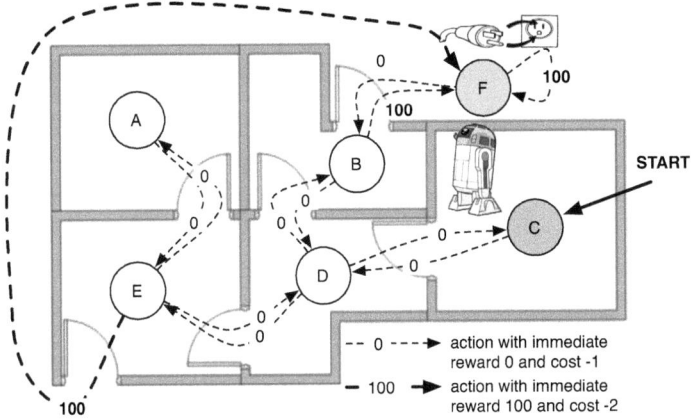

Figure 4.1. An example of Q-Learning application. The robot learns how to move in the unknown environment to find the goal (state F).

manages a pool of possible actions and assigns Q-Values to them. At each step of the algorithm, it selects an action, executes it and observes the achieved reward from the environment. A simple update rule recomputes the new Q-Value based on the old one and the current reward. Thus, after a finite number of steps, the algorithm learns the value-cost function for all actions and is able to select an optimal action in any state. Figure 4.1 gives an example of a Q-Learning application: a robot learning its way in an unknown environment to find the way out of a building. The example is inspired by the online tutorial of Kardi Teknomo [185].

Agent states. The learning agent has a finite set of possible states S and s_t represents the agent's state at time step t. The agent can only be in one of them and they describe its internal state or location in the environment. In our example from Figure 4.1, states are the different rooms in the environment, marked A to F. As in finite state machines, there is a start state (room C in our case) and a goal state (state F outside of the building).

4.1 Background on Q-Learning

Actions. Q-Learning associates a different set of actions A_S to each of the states in S. In our robot environment, the actions are represented by the state transitions, for example, from room D the robot can either move to room B or to room E or to room C.

Immediate rewards. There is an associated immediate reward $r(s_t, a_t)$ with each of the state transitions. In our example, all of the state transitions which do not lead to the goal state have immediate rewards of 0 and the ones leading to the goal state have an immediate reward of 100 (see Figure 4.1). The rewards are scalar and are either given a-priori or calculated online. The rewards can be either seen by the agent before taking a specific action or not. However, in any case, the agent can see only the actions with their associated rewards from its current state. It does not have any global knowledge about the environment, its states and their rewards.

Value function. In contrast to the immediate rewards, which are associated to each action in each state and are easily observable, the value function represents the *expected total accumulated reward*. The goal of the agent is to learn a sequence of actions with a maximum value function, that is, the reward on the taken path is maximized.

Q-Values. To represent the current expected total future reward at any state, a Q-Value is associated to each action and state $Q(s_t, a_t)$. The Q-Value represents the memory of the learning agent in terms of the quality of the action in this particular state. In the beginning Q-Values are usually initialized with zeros, representing the fact that the agent knows nothing. Through trial and experience the agent learns how good was some action, for example, was it a good idea to go to room A from room E. The Q-Values of the actions change through learning and finally represent the absolute value function. After convergence, taking the actions with greatest Q-Values in each state guarantees taking the optimal decision (path).

Action costs. Additionally to the rewards there is also a cost $c(s_t, a_t)$ associated with each action in each state. It is again a scalar value, which represents

4.1 Background on Q-Learning

how costly is this action. In our example, it costs two units of energy to move from room E to the final goal F because the path is much longer. All other actions cost exactly 1 unit of energy. Costs are usually represented as negative numbers, as they decrease the total accumulated reward. Very often the action costs are modeled as part of the immediate reward. In our example from Figure 4.1, we can easily integrate the action costs into the immediate rewards of the actions by subtracting the action costs from the rewards.

Updating a Q-Value. There is a simple rule of updating a Q-Value after each step of the agent:

$$Q(s_{t+1}, a_t) = Q(s_t, a_t) + \gamma(R(s_t, a_t) - Q(s_t, a_t)) \tag{4.1}$$

The new Q-Value of the pair $\{s_{t+1}, a_t\}$ in state s_{t+1} after taking action a_t in state s_t is computed as the sum of the old Q-Value and a correction term. This term consists of the received reward and the old Q-Value. γ is the learning constant - it prevents the Q-Values from changing too fast and thus oscillating. The total received reward is computed as:

$$R(s_t, a_t) = r(s_t, a_t) + c(s_t, a_t) \tag{4.2}$$

Where $r(s_t, a_t)$ is the immediate reward as defined above and $c(s_t, a_t)$ is the cost of taking the action a_t in state s_t. In our example, the cost of all actions but one is 1. Only the transition from room E to the goal F is more costly: 2. In this case, after learning the agent will identify the route C - D - B - F as the optimal policy with maximum accumulated rewards on the way. The alternative path C - D - E - F is more costly and thus not optimal. However, if we change all costs to equal, both routes will be optimal and the agent will have two alternative optimal routes.

Exploration strategy (action selection policy). Learning is performed in episodes - the robot takes actions in its environment and updates the associated Q-Values until reaching the goal state. Then the next episode is started and so on, until the Q-Values do not change any more. The question is how the robot selects the next action to take. Always taking the actions with maximum Q-Value (greedy policy) will result in finding local minimal solutions. In our example, if the robot takes by chance first the route through room E it will continue following it and will never learn that there is another one through room B.

On the other hand, being always random (random policy) will mean not to use the already accumulated experience and to spend too much energy on learning the complete environment. For example, if the robot learns once that going to room A is useless (it needs to go back again), it should avoid taking this action in the future.

These two extreme strategies are called *exploitation* and *exploration* of routes. The problem of combining and weigthing both so that optimal results are achieved as fast as possible has been extensively studied in machine learning [179]. The mostly used strategy is called ϵ-*greedy*: with probability ϵ the agent takes a random action and with probability $1 - \epsilon$ it takes the best available action.

Properties and challenges of Q-Learning. Q-Learning has been shown to converge towards the optimal policy, that is, the Q-Values do not change any more regardless of the route taken, and represent the value function [198]. This is an important property for us, since it guarantees that the optimal route is found and can be easily followed by selecting the maximum Q-Values.

In contrast, how fast Q-Learning converges depends on the problem itself: on the complexity of the environment, on the reward function and on the exploration strategy used. The original work on Q-Learning [198] shows that it converges after each pair of $\{s_t, a_t\}$ has been visited an *infinite* number of times. For our purposes this is not appropriate and one of the major challenges of this dissertation is to design a Q-Learning based communication protocol which is able to converge after some finite number of steps.

Another challenge when using Q-Learning is modeling the environment. In some cases, like the learning robot from Figure 4.1, it is a relatively simple task. However, in our distributed environment with failing and moving nodes, where the topological knowledge is distributed, it will be a major challenge. Additionally, the reward function (in our case the routing costs) cannot be computed a-priori because no global topology information is available.

4.2 Evaluating wireless sensor networks

Next we concentrate on *how* the presented routing and clustering protocols from Chapter 3 were evaluated rather than the results they achieve. The goal is to design an evaluation methodology for our routing and clustering protocols according to state-of-the-art techniques and practices. For this, we concentrate on some of the works presented in Chapter 3, considering their length and the status of the projects. Mostly journal, full conference papers and technical reports have been considered. Additionally, we divide the works into routing and clustering approaches since both classes of protocols exhibit different properties and evaluation requirements.

The protocols we include in our survey are listed in Table 4.1 together with their publication years and venues. The information refers to the latest or the most full known publication of the protocols. We gave names to protocols without own names or acronyms and added a prefix *r-* or *c-* for clarity and better differentiation between *r*outing and *c*lustering protocols. All of the surveyed works are explicitly designed for wireless sensor networks.

Illustrative summaries of the evaluations methodologies of the protocols based on their comparative analyses, evaluation environments, and metrics are presented in Figure 4.2 for clustering protocols and in Figure 4.3 for routing protocols. Next we describe in detail each of the used evaluation environments, simulation, real hardware and theory, with their models, parameters, and metrics and discuss their usage in the surveyed works.

4.2.1 Evaluation through simulation

One of the most widely used evaluation environments is simulation. There are several well-known network simulators with large user and developer communities, like ns-2/ns-3 [173], OMNeT++ [52], QualNet [148], etc. Additionally, MATLAB [128] is often used for coarse-grained (usually packet-level) simula-

protocol name	publication year	publication venue
ROUTING PROTOCOLS		
r-GEAR [215]	2001	Technical report
r-MintRoute [202]	2003	Conference (SenSys)
r-DEED [104]	2005	Journal
r-Directed Diffusion [170]	2005	Book chapter
r-GLIDER [60]	2005	Conference (GLOBECOM)
r-TTDD [120]	2005	Journal
r-DV/DRP [77]	2006	Technical report
r-IDDA [205]	2006	Conference (SenSys)
r-SARA [158]	2006	Journal
r-GMREE [160]	2007	Journal
r-MSTEAM [65]	2007	Technical report
r-MTM (Many-To-Many)* [42]	2007	Conference (EWSN)
r-MTEKC [141]	2008	Journal
r-AOMDV [83]	2008	Conference (ADHOC-NOW)
r-PRR [219]	2008	Journal
r-VCP [12]	2008	Conference (MASS)
CLUSTERING PROTOCOLS		
c-Max-Min [7]	2000	Conference (INFOCOM)
c-GraphCluster* [16]	2001	Conference (INFOCOM)
c-CMLDA [46]	2003	Conference (WCMC)
c-K-CONID [138]	2003	Journal
c-TRC [15]	2003	Conference (INFOCOM)
c-FLOC [48]	2004	Conference (BroadNets)
c-HEED [211]	2004	Journal
c-CLD [32]	2005	Journal
c-LBR [89]	2006	Journal
c-EEPA [214]	2007	Journal
c-EDC [39]	2007	Conference (EWSN)
c-BP [8]	2008	Conference (EWSN)
c-UUCP [11]	2008	Journal
c-UCR [38]	2009	Journal

* Protocol names assigned for better reference

Table 4.1. Routing and clustering protocols included in our survey of evaluation methodologies. The prefix r- or c- differentiates between routing and clustering protocols.

4.2 Evaluating wireless sensor networks

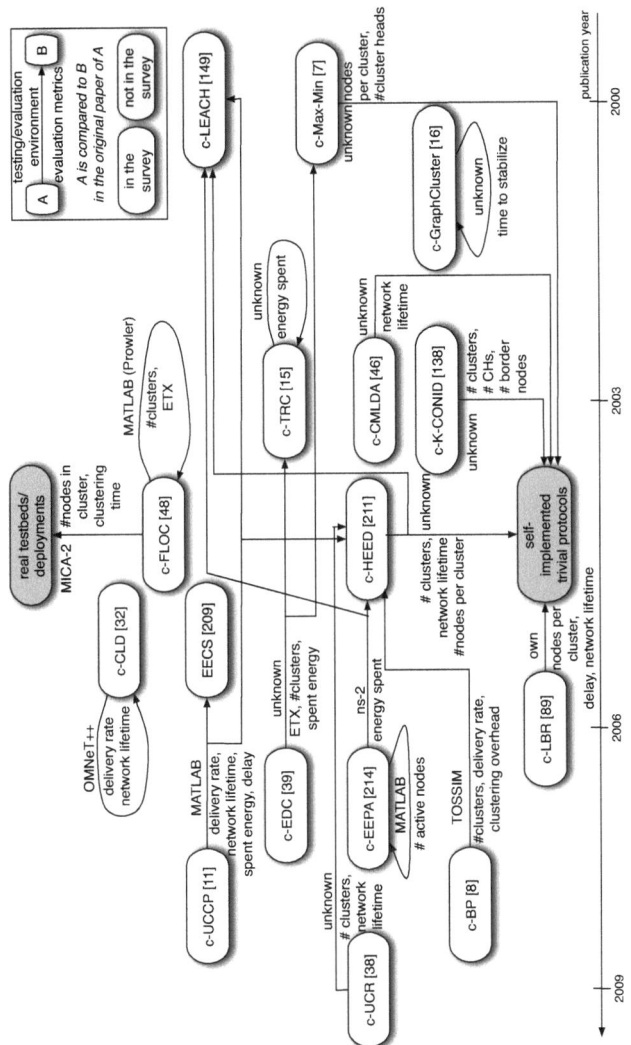

Figure 4.2. Comparison studies of state-of-the-art clustering protocols. For each work, the arrows show to which other clustering protocols the work was compared in the original paper, what was the testing environment (over or right of the arrow), and what were the evaluation metrics (below or left of the arrow).

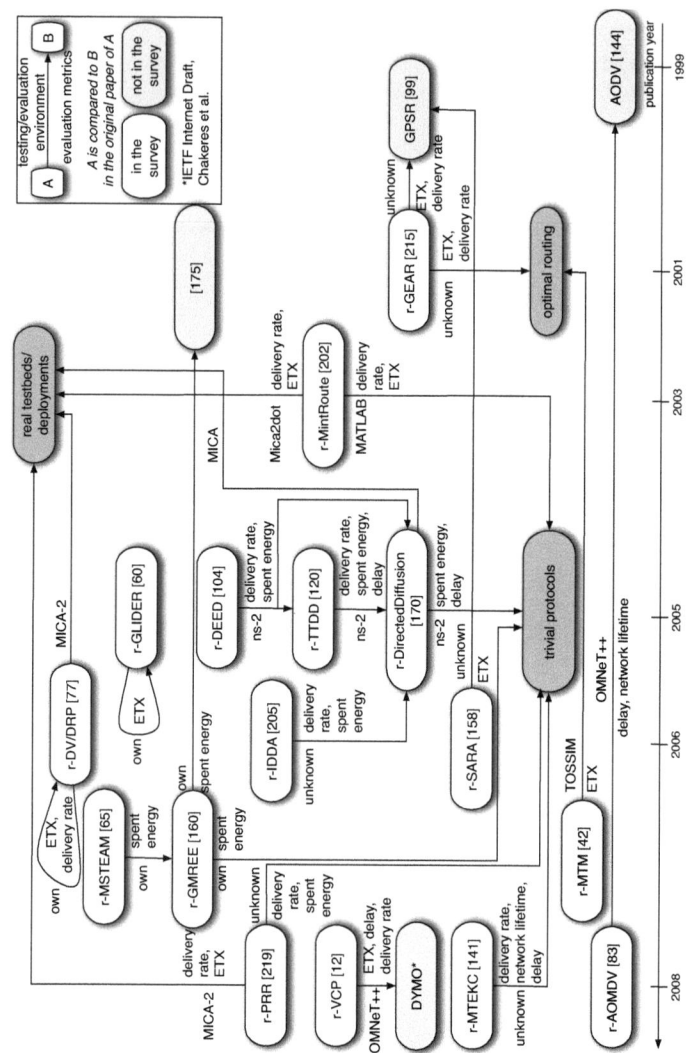

Figure 4.3. Comparison studies of state-of-the-art routing protocols. For each work, the arrows show to which other routing protocols the work was compared in the original paper, what was the testing environment (over or right of the arrow), and what were the evaluation metrics (below or left of the arrow).

4.2 Evaluating wireless sensor networks

tions. TOSSIM [136, 116] is especially designed to simulate TinyOS-based applications.

A comparison between many network simulators used for WSNs and their implemented models is presented in [57]. However, comparison is hard, since new models and extensions emerge continuously. r-TTDD, r-Directed Diffusion and r-DEED use ns-2, r-MTM and c-BP use TOSSIM, and r-MintRoute, c-EEPA, c-UUCP and c-FLOC use MATLAB. OMNeT++ with its extension Mobility Framework has emerged lately as a user-friendly simulator with a growing number of good network models. It has been used for example for simulating c-CLD, r-VCP and r-AOMDV. Thus, it seems like researchers use a low-level simulation environment for routing protocols and a more abstract one for clustering approaches.

However, looking at Figures 4.3 and 4.2, many researchers implement also their own simulators (c-LBR, r-DV/DRP, r-MSTEAM, r-GMREE, and r-GLIDER) and the overwhelming number of works do not state at all the used simulator or simulated network models (c-EDC, c-UCR, c-HEED, c-K-CONID, c-Max-Min, r-PRR, r-MTEKC, r-SARA, r-IDDA, and r-GEAR).

Recently there have been a lot of critiques about the credibility of simulated evaluations of wireless sensor networks lately [24, 57, 111, 142, 152, 225]. The main points of the critiques are about the network models used, mostly the radio propagation and energy models, the MAC layer models, the parameterization of the experiments (usually missing details or unmotivated parameters), and the comparative studies. In the next paragraphs we discuss in detail the network models, parameters and evaluation metrics used in the surveyed papers for simulation, and outline our own methodology.

Radio Propagation. Radio propagation in a simulated environment models how radio waves propagate through the wireless medium and how they interfere with obstacles and other radio waves. The main properties of radio propagation which need to be simulated are signal attenuation and fading, interfering signals, bit errors, and asymmetric links.

Many of the above surveyed works assume a perfect radio propagation model, often called the unit disk graph model. It assumes that each node can reach any of its neighbors, if the distance between them is less than some threshold value.

This is a highly abstracted network model which is inapplicable for the evaluation of MAC or routing protocols designed for real world sensor networks. In fact, it is not applicable even to application-level protocols like aggregation and clustering, since real world implementations of reliable MAC and routing layers are very expensive and these costs need at least to be considered and evaluated. The disadvantages of such perfect network models has been shown in many experimental studies, e.g. [57, 107, 200, 225].

From the above network simulators, ns-3 and OMNeT++ implement sophisticated probability or experimentally based radio propagation models. However, their use is not mandatory, like the OMNeT++ probabilistic radio propagation model [110] or a similar implementation for ns-2 [225]. Both models are designed and implemented according to latest research in the area and have been cross-validated with each other and with real hardware traces. These models allow not only for the most realistic network simulations, but also for many different network topologies and scenarios by using different parameters. This is also their main advantage against trace-based simulations, where data needs to be first gathered with great effort from real deployments, and is restricted to those topologies.

A simulator, which uses real traces to simulate radio links, is TOSSIM. The model does not implement any radio propagation. Instead, each link is assigned a bit error probability and bits of messages are flipped accordingly. On one side, this can be a very powerful model, as it allows for both ideal conditions during early evaluations, and for realistic network conditions taken, for example, from real deployments. The second choice is used for evaluating r-MTM to create simulated networks from real network deployment data. However, as stated above, this model does not allow for very many or different network topologies, since data needs to be gathered with great effort from real deployments. Additionally, it allows for "fake" networks, where bit error probabilities on links are invented instead of taken from real networks and signal interference and collisions are not captured.

MATLAB is usually used for simple, packet-level simulations, which is perfectly suitable for early feasibility studies or application-layer protocols like clus-

4.2 Evaluating wireless sensor networks

tering. There is also the Prowler simulator [172] for MATLAB, which has a slightly more realistic radio propagation model, which assumes signal strength decays with distance from the sender. However, this model is still circular. Similar models have been used also for c-HEED, c-EEPA, and r-DEED for self-implemented simulators. The simulation of r-MintRoute also used MATLAB and a similar radio propagation model, but their data is gathered from real deployments.

The simulator of r-DV/DRP is especially designed for supporting realistic radio propagation models as described in [225]. However, the simulator suffers from the common problems of self-implementations: there is no community to support it, models are very restricted and usually concentrated on the protocol level of the programmers. Only very rarely do these simulators develop into widely-used and community supported platforms. The other self-implemented simulators, used for studying r-MSTEAM, r-GMREE, r-GLIDER, and c-LBR, are neither published nor the motivation for developing them is stated.

However, as already mentioned above, an overwhelming number of the works do not discuss the used simulation environment. Some of them declare to use perfect radio propagation models (c-UCR, c-Max-Min, c-CMLDA, c-EDC, c-TRC, c-K-CONID, c-UUCP, c-LBR, r-SARA, r-GEAR, r-IDDA, r-GLIDER, r-GMREE, r-MSTEAM). The rest of the works do not give any details about the simulation environment or the radio propagation models. This makes comparison among different publications and research works very complicated.

Energy model. Many of the routing and clustering approaches have been evaluated in terms of network lifetime or energy expenditure. However, they use different energy expenditure models. Non-linear battery models, which accurately measure the energy expenditure of the radio and all other on-board components (CPU, sensors, LEDs, displays, etc.) are desirable, but hard to implement. Additionally, current research has already identified the radio (sending, receiving, idle listening and sleeping modes) as the main energy consumer [6, 112]. Thus, a well designed simple linear battery model is sufficient to evaluate routing and clustering approaches.

From the above surveyed works, many do not use any energy model: c-

radio	MSB430	Mica2	BTNode	FireFly	Imote
sleep	0.99 mW	36 mW	39.6 mW	24 mW	27 mW
listen	70.95 mW	66 mW	82.5 mW	30 mW	62.1 mW
RX	70.95 mW	117 mW	102.3 mW	83.1 mW	112.5 mW
TX	105.6 mW	117 mW	102.3 mW	76.1 mW	112.5 mW

Table 4.2. Power consumption for different WSN hardware platforms. Data compiled from the Sensor Network Museum [133] and hardware datasheets [87].

FLOC, c-GraphCluster, c-Max-Min, c-EDC, c-K-CONID, r-SARA, r-GLIDER, r-VCP, r-MTM, and r-MintRoute. They do they evaluate network lifetime or energy expenditure.

A widely used oversimplified model is to count the number of transmissions in the network, assuming that each node has a quota for sending packets. For example, c-TRC uses such a model. On one hand, this model is oversimplified and cannot be used for correctly estimating a node's or network's lifetime. On the other hand, a low number of transmissions implies less traffic in the network, less collisions, etc. Assuming that the right MAC and routing protocols are used, this evaluation is fully sufficient for clustering protocols. A similar model is also used for the evaluation of r-MSTEAM.

All of the other surveyed works use a more sophisticated battery model, which calculates the energy expenditure in terms of mAh or mW. Fixed energy expenditure per time step is assigned to each of the radio modes (receiving, sending, and sleeping) and the total energy expenditure is calculated. Usually energy expenditure values are taken from data sheets for a given sensor network platform. A summary of the most commonly used ones is presented in Table 4.2. Very often a higher energy is considered for sending messages than for receiving. However, this is not true according to the data in Table 4.2, and either the same amount of energy is dissipated, or even more (all platforms but Scatterweb's MSB430). Another often made mistake is assuming that "radio idle listening" (also called "low power listen") does not spend a lot of energy. While this might be true in lab environments from which the data for the hardware's data-sheet

4.2 Evaluating wireless sensor networks

is collected, in the real world there is no "silent" environment. The radio needs to sample regularly the medium for incoming packets.

An incomplete battery model is used for r-GEAR, where a sophisticated energy model is used for data packets, but routing of control packets is ignored all-together. Even if the control overhead is low, there is no reason for excluding it from the energy expenditure.

MAC layer model. Sensor nodes are extremely power-restricted and are usually expected to run unattended over months, or even years. Thus, it is very important to first identify the largest power consumers and then to minimize their consumption. As stated above, it is well known [6, 112] that the primary power consumer on any sensor node is the radio, and thus the MAC protocol becomes the crucial instrument to minimize energy expenditure in sensor networks. The MAC protocol sits on top of the physical layer and controls the radio. It schedules and manages its sleeping and idle phases, trying to minimize or avoid collisions, overhearing, and idle times. Many efforts have been invested recently to design the "ultimate" MAC protocol, which minimizes the energy spent for message transmission. A summary of state-of-the-art MAC protocols is given in [112].

Several well-known and extensively tested MAC protocols exist for WSNs. SMAC [210] is tuned to prevent the overhearing of unicast messages destined to other nodes, but does not perform that well in a broadcast environment. It has been used, for example, in the Great Duck Island habitat monitoring deployment [180]. In comparison, BMAC [145] assumes that higher layer protocols can extensively profit from overhearing messages and does not prevent it. Nevertheless it performs better in terms of network lifetime both in unicast and broadcast traffic than SMAC. BMAC has been used, for example, in the VigilNet surveillance application [151] and is the standard MAC protocol for the Mica2 sensor platform.

An alternative to BMAC is LMAC [192], which reserves a unique slot for each node in a 2-hop neighborhood. This enables a collision-free transmission of messages. Each node listens at the beginning of each slot to control messages for synchronization and destination addressing. LMAC has been implemented for the EYES sensor platform [223].

Many of the works do not state the used MAC protocol: c-GraphCluster, c-CMLDA, c-K-CONID, c-HEED, c-EEPA, r-GMREE, r-MTEKC, and r-DEED. Others use an ideal MAC protocol, which delivers all messages reliably and without retransmissions to their receivers: c-UCR, c-Max-Min, c-EDC, c-TRC, c-LBR, r-PRR, r-IDDA, r-SARA, r-GEAR, r-GLIDER, and r-MSTEAM . This is probably the only useful choice, if the unit disk graph is used as radio model. However, it does not represent a realistic network scenario.

From the rest of the works presented, r-AOMDV uses WiseMAC; r-VCP, r-Directed Diffusion and r-TTDD use IEEE 802.11; and r-DV/DRP, r-MTM, c-BP and r-MintRoute use BMAC. The CSMA-based MAC protocol from MATLAB's Prowler is used for c-FLOC. c-CLD and c-UUCP use a cluster-based scheme for medium access, where each of the nodes in each cluster is assigned its own transmission slot.

Parameterization of experiments. The last critical point we discuss here is the parameterization of experiments. Number of nodes, topologies, network sizes, densities, etc, need to be defined before conducting the experiments as they have a great influence on the final results. In general, a wide range of each parameter needs to be used to sufficiently explore the behavior of the communication protocol. Here we survey only one example: the range of network sizes and topologies for simulated experiments.

One of the main advantages of simulation is that any network size and topology can be easily created and evaluated, including very large networks, random networks, etc. Still, some researchers use only one fixed network topology for evaluation (c-FLOC, r-SARA, r-MintRoute and r-DEED) and evaluate the network with one source and one sink. However, the evaluation of r-GLIDER includes also only one network, but it is very large and many experiments with different source-sink pairs have been conducted. This makes the parameter space sufficiently large even with only one network.

A slightly improved evaluation is used for r-AOMDV, c-UCR, c-GraphCluster, c-Max-Min, c-UUCP, c-EEPA and c-CLD, where several controlled topologies are used. Indeed, some of these works carefully design the used networks to cover

4.2 Evaluating wireless sensor networks 83

most of the usual network topology challenges, e.g. void areas. However, an extensive evaluation of routing, and especially clustering algorithms, can be only performed with a wide range of network topologies and sizes. Best, several controlled topologies with designed challenges are first discussed (like void areas) and then extensive evaluation of randomly created networks is conducted. Such evaluations are presented for example for r-CVP, r-PRR, r-IDDA, c-CMLDA, r-GEAR, r-MTEKC, c-HEED, c-LBR, r-GMREE, r-MSTEAM, r-MTM, c-BP, r-Directed Diffusion, r-TTDD, and r-DV/DRP.

Comparative analyses. A widely used technique to show the new features or better performance of some new communication protocol is to compare it under certain network conditions with existing protocols. There are many possible comparison techniques: some researchers, for example, compare their protocol to an ideal protocol (r-MTM and r-MSTEAM). This a good way to show the ability of a routing protocol to find optimal (shortest) paths. However, it does not allow for protocol overhead evaluation, since ideal protocols usually do not have overhead at all. Additionally, excluding overhead from the evaluation falsifies the final results in terms of network lifetime or energy expenditure.

Other researchers implement a trivial or basic algorithm to compare against their protocols. This is often used when a new cost metric is introduced and needs to be evaluated, for example in the case of c-K-CONID. Another possible scenario is a novel protocol or technique, where no competing protocols exist, like for c-LBR. However, c-HEED, r-AOMDV, and r-MTEKC were compared against trivial or old protocols, already shown to perform poorly (LEACH) under certain network conditions. These comparisons were conducted even in the presence of better suited protocols. For better chronological order and comparison studies, see Figures 4.2 and 4.3.

However, there are also protocols, which have not been compared to existing works, like r-DV/DRP, r-GLIDER, c-GraphCluster, c-FLOC, and c-CLD. Even if theoretical analysis in terms of convergence or complexity has been conducted (see Section 4.2.3), the contribution of the work is not clear.

All of the other works present extensive comparative analysis against at least one up-to-date competing protocol: c-UUCP, c-TRC, c-EEPA, c-UCR, c-VCP, c-

Evaluation metric	Routing	Clustering
ETX (number of sent packets)	r-MintRoute, r-MTM, r-DV/DRP, r-GEAR, r-SARA, r-GLIDER, r-VCP	c-EDC, c-FLOC
delivery rate	r-MintRoute, r-DV/DRP, r-TTDD, r-MTEKC, r-GEAR, r-DEED, r-IDDA, r-PRR, r-VCP	c-BP, c-UUCP, c-CLD
total spent energy	r-MSTEAM, r-TTDD, r-Directed Diffusion, r-GMREE, r-DEED, r-IDDA, r-PRR	c-EEPA, c-UUCP, c-TRC
delay	r-TTDD, r-MTEKC, r-Directed Diffusion, r-VCP, r-AOMDV	c-UUCP, c-LBR
network lifetime	r-MTEKC, r-AOMDV	c-HEED, c-UUCP, c-CMLDA, c-LBR, c-UCR, c-CLD
number of cluster heads		c-BP, c-HEED, c-K-CONID, c-EDC, c-Max-Min, c-UCR, c-FLOC
clustering overhead		c-BP
nodes per cluster		c-HEED, c-EDC, c-Max-Min, c-LBR
remaining energy histogram/std dev.		c-TRC
time to stabilize		c-GraphCluster, c-FLOC

Table 4.3. Evaluation metrics under simulation for routing and clustering approaches.

Max-Min, c-CMLDA, c-BP, c-EEPA, r-GMREE, r-MintRoute, r-MSTEAM, r-TTDD, r-GEAR, r-Directed Diffusion, r-SARA, r-DEED, r-IDDA, and r-PRR. Thus, they can clearly show the network conditions in which their protocols perform better, and the reader gets a better understanding of the protocol's behavior.

Evaluation metrics for routing algorithms. It is interesting to observe which evaluation metrics researchers apply to their algorithms. Table 4.3 summarizes the evaluation metrics in the surveyed works, organized by routing and clustering approaches.

One of the most widely used and meaningful evaluation metrics for routing protocols is number of incurred transmissions. The assumption here is that less transmissions means shorter paths, thus less spent energy. It shows clearly the

4.2 Evaluating wireless sensor networks

ability of the evaluated routing protocol to find good routes. Delivery rate is used to show the actual success of delivery. In case the routing protocol does not rely on any neighborhood or link management beneath it, the delivery rate is a very useful metric. On the other hand, in case a neighborhood management protocol or a reliable MAC layer is used, this metric does not evaluate the routing protocol any more, but the used MAC and link protocols. The same is also true for measuring the delay.

Interestingly, many researchers measure the total spent energy, but only two of them evaluate the network lifetime. This can be problematic, especially in the case when routing is conducted between several nodes during long periods of time. Here, nodes on the shortest path will drain their batteries quickly, leaving others nearly unused. A histogram of the remaining energies on the nodes or a network lifetime evaluation would be helpful, but is rarely given. Such a histogram illustrates very well how energy was dissipated across the nodes in the network, and shows whether the routing protocol was able to balance the communication in the network so that no nodes die prematurely.

Evaluation metrics for clustering algorithms. Measuring energy expenditure or communication overhead is common, but not universal. This is unfortunate, because all clustering work is predicated on the fact that applying clustering reduces network energy expenditure. When energy expenditure is evaluated, sometimes it is considered after the clusters have been built while others include the overhead to build the clusters. Still others use network lifetime, usually defined as the time of first node death. Many of the protocols have been evaluated in terms of the number of clusters or cluster heads (CHs), interpreting a low number of clusters as *good* performance. The underlying assumption for this is that when the cluster size is bound to k-hop communication, a lower number of clusters means optimal clustering. While this may be true if the right k parameter is used, there is no investigation of how to find the right k. Furthermore, if the protocol does not restrict the size of the clusters, a low number of clusters may result in very high in-cluster communication overhead due to the increase in single cluster size.

One good evaluation criteria is the standard deviation of the number of nodes in a cluster. It is especially important for randomized algorithms, where the number of nodes in a cluster can vary dramatically. It shows clearly the balance of the cluster sizes, which ensures uniform data aggregation throughout the network. Unfortunately, however, this standard deviation is not provided by all researchers.

Clustering overhead and time to stabilize are interesting metrics which evaluate the clustering protocol in terms of how fast or how costly is the process of building clusters. However, they are already implicitly included in delay, network lifetime, and total energy spent metrics.

4.2.2 Evaluation on real hardware

Although almost all of the here surveyed works are in a late phase and most of them are described as final versions, only a few researchers actually implement their protocols on real hardware and test it in a real WSN environment. Of course, such an evaluation is very costly, both in terms of finance expenditures for hardware, and in terms of time and effort. However, shared remotely programmable sensor network testbeds exist, like MoteLab at Harvard University [186]. Furthermore, the most of the other university testbeds can be used by visiting researchers.

The already mentioned MoteLab [186] has been used to evaluate the existing ad hoc multicast routing protocol ADMR [37]. The testbed consisted of 30 MicaZ [184] motes at the time of the experiments. r-DV/DRP was implemented for proof-of-concept on Mica2 [184] motes. Mica2 motes were used also to evaluate r-PRR [219]. The first generation of Mica motes [184] was used to evaluate r-Directed Diffusion [170]. r-MintRoute [202] has been evaluated on Mica2dot motes [184].

While evaluation of routing protocols on real hardware is feasible, relatively easy to implement, and needs reasonable number of nodes, evaluation of clustering approaches meets the limits of real hardware testbeds. The only clustering approach which has been evaluated on hardware is c-FLOC, which included 25 sensor nodes arranged in a grid.

4.2 Evaluating wireless sensor networks

Evaluation metrics in real hardware environments. Similarly to simulation environments, routing protocols on real hardware have been evaluated for delivery rate (r-MintRoute, r-Directed Diffusion, and r-PRR) or number of transmissions per delivered packet (ETX) (r-MintRoute, r-PRR). Network lifetime or total spent energy are very hard to evaluate under real hardware, since they depend on many environmental properties, on exact battery levels, etc.

r-DV/DRP has been developed for real hardware only as proof of applicability; no evaluation or numerical results are reported. For clustering protocols, the number of built clusters is given for c-FLOC.

4.2.3 Theoretical analyses

Many researchers have also turned to theoretical analysis in terms of complexity, convergence, and correctness. Some works prove the theoretical optimality of their protocols (e.g. finding the shortest path), e.g. c-TRC, c-EDC, c-Max-Min, r-MTM, r-MSTEAM, r-SARA, r-IDDA, and r-PRR . Others discuss their complexity and memory and processing requirements (r-GMREE, c-BP, r-TTDD, c-UCR, c-FLOC, and r-DEED), and a few discuss both (c-HEED and c-GraphCluster). The rest do not give any theoretical results or discussions.

Theoretical analysis can be very helpful in several situations. First, at a very preliminary stage of evaluation, it can reveal weaknesses or strengths of the proposed algorithms. Second, it gives the reader a more complete understanding of the applied algorithm and its work. Third, it helps to explain better the results gathered in simulation or real hardware. Last but not least, theoretical analyses of WSN networks are invaluable for pointing out new directions in research and for identifying the "desired idea" solution, building the basis of new research.

However, the theoretical discussions and analyses of communication protocols, even the most thorough and complete ones, need to be used with care. While giving vital information about the design, goals, and properties of the protocols, these analyses most often need to assume ideal network and communication models. They do not show the real world behavior or cost of the protocols. For example, if a routing protocol assumes reliable broadcast, it becomes very costly in a real environment, where the nodes need to manage asymmetric links, link failures, radio quality fluctuations, etc. A simpler, non-reliable protocol would be better suited. Experimental evaluation through simulation or on real hardware is needed in any case to demonstrate a protocol's behavior and applicability.

4.2.4 Identified evaluation methodology

In the last paragraphs we have presented an extensive survey of current evaluation practices and methodologies. Given the insights gathered from this survey and our own application scenario and requirements as described in Chapter 2, we identify our own evaluation methodology. We use *theoretical analysis, evaluation through simulation and on real hardware* to show the most of the aspects and properties of the routing and clustering approaches developed in this thesis. We use a wide range of evaluation metrics across many different network scenarios and parameters. Of course, an exhaustive analysis under any possible environmental conditions is not possible for time and space reasons.

In the following paragraphs we identify the exact evaluation environments for our work as to be used in Chapters 5 and 6, where we present the routing and clustering protocols we have developed. Evaluation metrics and implementation details and parameters will be specified later in the appropriate evaluation sections.

Theoretical analysis. For both the routing and the clustering protocols presented in this thesis we provide short illustrative and intuitive theoretical analyses. We discuss the correctness, the complexity, and the convergence behavior of the protocols. Since both protocols are based on Q-Learning, which has a randomized behavior, the convergence of both protocols becomes critical. Additionally, we discuss the memory and processing requirements, which we will confirm then through real-hardware evaluations.

Simulation environment. Given the above discussion and survey of state-of-the-art evaluations under simulation, we decided to use the OMNeT++ network discrete event simulator, together with its extensions Mobility Framework and probabilistic radio propagation models[110]. This is the most complete and user

4.2 Evaluating wireless sensor networks

friendly environment from all presented simulators and it is easily extendable with our own models. Additionally, the community is very active, and the simulator is in constant development and improvement process. Unfortunately, there are no energy expenditure models, nor realistic MAC protocols for the Mobility Framework. Thus, we needed to implement the following additional simulation models:

- **Linear battery model.** As discussed above, a linear battery model which accounts for different energy expenditures for radio sleeping, receiving and sending, is sufficient for the evaluation of routing and clustering protocols, as designed and implemented in this thesis. For completeness, we use two different energy models taken from two different hardware platforms: Mica2 and MSB430, see Table 4.2.

- **MAC protocols.** In our experiments we use the already provided idle non-persistent CSMA MAC protocol. This MAC protocol comes as a part of the Mobility Framework and implements a simple carrier-sense multiple access protocol, where the radio is always idle and packets are not acknowledged nor resent. We use it together with the MSB430 energy expenditure model. Any of the other energy expenditure models from Table 4.2 assumes the same amount of dissipated energy for sending and receiving packets and thus an idle MAC protocol would result in constant network lifetime, independent from the traffic.

  In addition to the idle CSMA MAC protocol, we have implemented BMAC and LMAC as representatives of low power listening MAC protocols and TDMA based protocols. Both have been used for real WSN deployments and are widely accepted by the WSN community. Frame and slot durations were identified experimentally so that all evaluated data traffic models are accommodated without MAC buffer overflow. In LMAC we reserved 5 node IDs for mobile nodes to avoid continuous slot changing.

- **Comparative routing protocols.** For conducting a comparative analysis of the designed routing protocol, we have implemented three well known state-of-the-art routing protocols: the original unicast Directed Diffusion

MSB430	
Provider	ScatterWeb, Berlin, Germany
Processor	MSP430
Frequency	8MHz
Memory	5 KB RAM + 55 KB Flash
Radio	ChipCon 1020
OS	ScatterWeb2, TinyOS, Contiki, etc.
Other	SD-card slot

Figure 4.4. Characteristics of the MSB430 sensor nodes

(UDD) [170] as a representative of a simple, but powerful and widely tested WSN unicast routing protocol; our own variation of it multicast Directed Diffusion (MDD), which optimizes locally for sharing paths to multiple sinks; and MSTEAM [65], a very new geographic based multicast routing protocol. We decided to add the last protocol, MSTEAM, to our analysis since it represents a very well performing class of protocols for multicast applications. Indeed, most of the multicast protocols for WSNs are location-based and we desire to have a direct comparison with one of them. More details are given in the evaluation of our routing protocol in Section 5.5.

- **Comparative clustering protocols.** We also implemented a clustering protocol for WSNs, which is an improved version of the traditional randomized clustering algorithms and is based on the TRC clustering algorithm in [15]. Basically, it divided the network first in clusters of fixed size (builds a grid) and then runs the traditional randomized cluster head selection algorithm. Probability of becoming a cluster head is based on the number of nodes in the whole network and is parametrizable. More details are given in the evaluation section of our clustering algorithm in Section 6.3.

Evaluation on real hardware. We implement and test the developed routing protocol FROMS, as it will be presented next in Chapter 5, on a real hardware testbed, consisting of MSB430 nodes from ScatterWeb [87]. Their main characteristics are summarized in Figure 4.4. For implementation we use the OS-like ScatterWeb2 library, which provides simple interfaces for sending/receiving messages, setting timers, reading sensory data etc. We use the provided non-persistent idle CSMA MAC protocol without acknowledgments.

Unlike all here presented evaluations of routing protocols on real hardware, we decided to conduct also a comparative study between FROMS and our multicast extension of Directed Diffusion. We decided against the original Directed Diffusion, because it is a unicast routing protocol and against MSTEAM, because its implementation is very processing and memory intensive and did not fit on the used hardware.

4.3 Concluding remarks

In this chapter we presented some preliminary work vital for the development and evaluation of the targeted routing and clustering protocols. We identified Q-Learning as the general solution framework and inspiration for solving the main challenges of the application scenario and to achieve a highly flexible and robust behavior for the data dissemination protocols.

The second critical point is the evaluation of the designed protocol, which needs to be thoroughly planned in order to satisfactorily show the performance of the protocols under many different network scenarios and conditions. For this, we surveyed 30 state-of-the-art routing and clustering protocols for wireless sensor networks and identified the right evaluation environments, models, evaluation metrics and parameters.

Using the insights gained here, in the next two chapters we present our solutions to the main problems in our application scenario: Chapter 5 describes and evaluates our multicast routing protocol for mobile sinks called FROMS and Chapter 6 presents and evaluates our non-uniform clustering protocol CLIQUE.

Chapter 5

FROMS: Routing to Multiple Mobile Sinks in WSNs

In this chapter we present our solution to energy efficient routing to multiple mobile sinks. The resulting protocol is called **F**eedback **RO**uting to **M**ultiple **S**inks (FROMS). It successfully meets the challenges of our application scenario from Chapter 2. We follow the solution path and evaluation methodology as identified in Chapter 4 and show that it achieves better results than other state-of-the-art routing protocols in terms of various metrics, both in simulation and on real hardware.

First, we give a high level overview and intuition for FROMS in Section 5.1. Then we define the Q-Learning based solution of multicast routing in Section 5.2 and theoretically derive its optimality and convergence behavior in Section 5.3. Section 5.4 discusses the implementation details and challenges of FROMS. The evaluation is divided into a stand-alone evaluation of the parameters of FROMS in Section 5.5 and a comparative analysis in various network scenarios, including sink mobility and node failures, in Section 5.6. Finally, Section 5.7 summarizes the chapter and its findings.

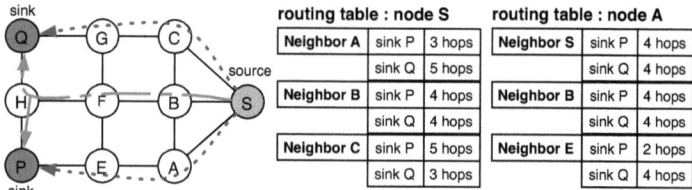

Figure 5.1. A sample topology with 2 sinks, the main routes to them from source S and the initial routing tables for nodes S and A.

5.1 Protocol intuition

The goal of our protocol is to find the optimal possible path for data to follow from its source to all interested sinks. Optimal can be defined as either minimum delay, minimum hop count, minimum geographic distance or maximum remaining energies. More complex cost metrics are also possible, such as combination of minimum hop and maximum remaining batteries. The cost function is a parameter of our protocol and will be discussed in detail later in the chapter. Here, we will use number of hops as an example.

Consider the sample network from Figure 5.1 with one source and two sinks. One possible path from the source to the sinks is formed by the union of the individual paths from the source to each sink (the dotted lines in the figure), however a shorter path often exists. This shorter path takes the form of a tree, as the one through nodes B, F and H. The challenge is to globally identify this tree without full topology information and using only local information exchange. The main task of our protocol is to update local information regarding "next-hops" to reach sinks from each node such that the resulting tree is as small as possible.

During an initial sink announcement phase, as proposed in Chapter 2, all nodes gather some initial routing information and register known sinks in the network. In our example from Figure 5.1 node S gathers hop information for each sink *individually* as shown in its routing table in the figure. When data

5.1 Protocol intuition

packets arrive at the node for routing, the node needs to select one or more next hops towards the sinks. However, instead of simply choosing the best looking one (in this example: node C for sink Q and node A for sink P), it also *explores* non-optimal routes in the assumption that some of them might have lower costs than in its own routing table. This is because its neighboring nodes may be able to share next hops too. For example, the source node S can conclude from its routing table that node A needs 7 hops to reach both sinks: it needs 5 hops to reach sink P, 3 hops to reach sink Q and the first hop is shared, thus the minus 1 or a total of 7 hops. However, node S does not know whether node A will be able also to share the next hop or will need to split the packet and send them through two different neighbors. In our example, node A is in fact able to share the next hop. It calculates that it can reach the sinks through node E (see the routing table of node A in the figure) in $(2+4)-1 = 5$ hops. Thus, node S will be able to reach both sinks in 1 hop to node A plus 5 hops from node A to all sinks or a total of 6 hops, which is 1 hop less than the initial information on the source node. Thus, node A needs to inform node S about its own estimation of the costs to both sinks. It can do so while sending the data packet further to the sink by making use of the broadcast environment and piggybacking its own cost estimation.

Similarly, node E piggybacks its cost estimation and informs node A and so on. There are four important observations to make: these piggybacked values, which we also call feedbacks, propagate exactly one step back until they reach the sinks, where the packet stops. Thus, the source needs to send several data packets to node A before its own cost estimation for node A represents the real hop cost of the route. In our example, the real costs through node A to reach both sinks is 5 hops. The source's cost estimation after the first data packet through node A is updated to 6 (see the last paragraph). At the same time (the same data packet), node A gets feedback from its next hop, etc. Thus, we need to send several data packets through node A until the feedbacks from the sinks propagate back to the source.

Second, the source needs to send data packets not only to node A, but to all neighboring nodes a sufficient number of times, before all of its cost estimations converge. The neighbors of the nodes need to also *explore* their neighbors and so on. Third, feedback can be used not only by the previous hop, but by all overhearing nodes of the transmitter and thus deliver additional information to the nodes. And fourth, keeping all of the routes at all nodes and always giving feedback to the neighbors with the current cost estimations, innately handles recovery and mobility. For example, in case node E fails, node A will switch to another route, for example through node B, will update its cost estimations and will inform the source S via feedback on the next data packet about its current costs. The information propagates together with the data packets, without incurring any additional communication overhead and update automatically the routes and their costs on all involved nodes.

The above made observations form a reinforcement learning based routing protocol. It first builds some initial cost estimations about routes through next hops. It immediately starts sending data to the sinks by taking possibly non-optimal routes, and simultaneously *learns* the real costs of the routes. After some time, the cost estimates on all nodes in the network *stabilize* and optimal routes are identified. The solution is elegant and efficient. However, we need to define some details. For example, how do the nodes know that all of the cost estimations have converged to the real costs and that optimal routes can be used from now on? How can we minimize communication overhead incurred by the non-optimal routes, while at the same time making sure that cost estimate converge and all route options are explored? In the next section we formalize the ideas presented here and present the details of the Q-Learning model, including the answers to the above questions.

5.2 Routing data to multiple sinks with Q-Learning

The main goal of this section is to model the multicast routing problem and solve it with reinforcement learning, as already discussed in Section 4.1. This will not only build the basis of our protocol, but also give us the possibility to make a theoretical analysis of the protocol in terms of complexity, correctness and convergence.

5.2.1 Problem definition

We consider the network of sensors as a graph $G = (V, E)$ where each sensor node is a vertex v_i and each edge e_{ij} is a bidirectional wireless communication channel between a pair of nodes v_i and v_j. Without a loss of generality, we consider a single source node $s \in V$ and a set of destination nodes $D \subseteq V$.

Optimal routing to multiple destinations is defined as the minimum cost path starting at the source vertex s, and reaching all destination vertices D. This path is actually a spanning tree $T = (V_T, E_T)$ whose vertexes include the source and the destinations. The cost of a tree T is defined as a function over its nodes and links $C(T)$. For example, it can be the number of one-hop broadcasts required to reach all destinations or in other words the number of non-leaf nodes in T. Further cost functions are presented in Section 5.4.8 and evaluated in Section 5.5.4.

5.2.2 Multicast Routing with Q-Learning

Finding the minimum cost tree T, also called the Steiner tree, is NP-hard, even when the full topology is known [147]. Our goal, therefore, is to approximate the optimal solution using localized techniques. As already proposed in the last Section 4.1, we turn to reinforcement learning and especially to Q-Learning [198].

In our multiple-sink scenario, each sensor node is an independent learning agent, and actions are routing options using different neighbor(s) for the next hop(s) toward a subset of the sinks, $D_p \subseteq D$, listed in the data packet. The main challenge in our application is to model the actions of the nodes, since they contain not a single next hop (route to some neighbor n), but a-priori unknown number of next hops. The following provides additional detail for the Q-Learning solution.

Agent states. For multiple sink routing, we define the state of an agent as a tuple $\{D_p, routes_{D_p}^N\}$, where $D_p \subseteq D$ are the sinks the packet must reach and $routes_{D_p}^N$ is the routing information about all neighboring nodes N with respect to the individual sinks. Depending on this state, different actions are possible.

Actions. In our model, an action is one possible routing decision for a data packet. However, the routing decision can include one or more different neighbors as next hops. Consequently, we need to change the original Q-Learning algorithm and define a possible action, a, as a set of sub-actions $\{a_1 \ldots a_k\}$. Each sub-action $a_i = (n_i, D_i)$ includes a single neighbor n_i and a set of destinations $D_i \subseteq D_p$ indicating that neighbor n_i is the intended next hop for routing to destinations D_i. A *complete* action is a set of sub-actions such that $\{D_1 \ldots D_k\}$ partitions D_p (that is, each sink $d \in D_p$ is covered by exactly one sub-action a_i).

Continuing with our example from Figure 5.1, consider a packet destined for $D_p = \{P, Q\}$. One possible complete action of the source S is the single sub-action $(B, \{P, Q\})$, indicating neighbor B as the next hop to all destinations. Alternately, node S may choose two sub-actions, $(A, \{P\})$ and $(C, \{Q\})$, indicating two different neighbors should take responsibility to forward the packet to different subsets of sinks.

The distinction between complete actions and sub-actions is important, as we assign rewards to sub-actions.

Q-Values. Q-Values represent the goodness of actions and the goal of the agent is to learn the *actual* goodness of the available actions. Here we differ from the original Q-Learning, which randomly initializes Q-Values, and where Q-Values serve only for quantitative comparison.

In our case, we bound the Q-Values to represent the real cost of the routes, for example, if the cost function is number of hops, the Q-Value of a route is also the number of hops of this route. To initialize these values, we use a more sophisticated approach than random assignment, which calculates an estimate of the cost based on the individual information about the involved neighbor and sinks. This non-random initialization significantly speeds up the learning process and avoids oscillations of the Q-Values.

For example, without loss of generality and continuing our example with a hop-based cost function, it estimates the route cost by using the hop counts available in a standard routing table, such as that in Figure 5.1. We first calculate the value of a sub-action, then of a complete action. Using the hop-based routing information, the initial Q-Value for a sub-action $a_i = (n_i, D_i)$ is:

5.2 Routing data to multiple sinks with Q-Learning

$$Q(a_i) = \left(\sum_{d \in D_i} hops_d^{n_i} \right) - 2(|D_i| - 1) \qquad (5.1)$$

where $hops_d^{n_i}$ are the number of hops to reach destination $d \in D_i$ using neighbor n_i and $|D_i|$ is the number of sinks in D_i. The first part of the formula calculates the total number of hops to individually reach the sinks, and the second part subtracts from this total based on the assumption that broadcast communication is used both (hence the 2) for transmission to n_i as well as by n_i to reach the next hop. Note that this estimation is an *upper bound* of the actual value, as it assumes that the packet will not share any links after the next hop. Therefore, during learning, Q-Values will always decrease and the best actions will be denoted with small Q-Values.

The Q-Value of a complete action a with sub-actions $\{a_1, \ldots, a_k\}$ is:

$$Q(a) = \left(\sum_{a_i \in a, i=1\ldots k} Q(a_i) \right) - (k-1) \qquad (5.2)$$

where k is the number of sub-actions. Intuitively this Q-Value is the broadcast hop count from the agent to all sinks.

The above is an example of calculating the Q-Values when using the specific hop-based cost. We will explore further cost metrics in Section 5.4.8.

Updating a Q-Value. To learn the real values of the actions, the agent must receive the reward values from the environment. In our case, each neighbor to which a data packet is forwarded sends the reward as feedback with its evaluation of the goodness of the sub-action. The new Q-Value of the sub-action is:

$$Q_{new}(a_i) = Q_{old}(a_i) + \gamma(R(a_i) - Q_{old}(a_i)) \qquad (5.3)$$

where $R(a_i)$ is the reward value and γ is the learning rate of the algorithm. We use $\gamma = 1$ to speed up learning. Usually a lower learning rate needs to be used with randomly initialized Q-Values, since otherwise they will oscillate heavily in the beginning of the learning process. However, since our values are guaranteed to decrease and not to oscillate, we can avoid the learning rate and the resulting delay in learning. Therefore, with $\gamma = 1$, the formula becomes

$$Q_{new}(a_i) = R(a_i) \qquad (5.4)$$

directly updating the Q-Value with the reward. The Q-Values of complete actions are updated automatically, since their calculation is based on sub-actions (Equation 5.2).

Reward function. Intuitively the reward function is the downstream node's opportunity to inform the upstream neighbors of its actual cost for the requested action. Thus, when calculating the reward, the node selects its *lowest (best) Q-Value* for the destination set and adds the cost of the action itself:

$$R(a_i) = c_{a_i} + \min_a Q(a) \qquad (5.5)$$

where c_{a_i} is the action's cost (always 1 in our hop count metric). This propagation of Q-Values upstream eventually allows all nodes to learn the actual costs.

In contrast to the original Q-Learning algorithm, low reward values are good and large values are bad. This is because we define the Q-Values to represent the real hop costs of some route and thus the lowest Q-Values are the best. Furthermore, rewards from the environment are generated and sent out without real knowledge of who receives them. Note that the reward values are completely localized and simply indicate the Q-Value of the best possible action. It depends only on the sub-set of destinations the node is asked for and thus implicitly on the previous hop of the data packet and its routing decision. We will come back to this when presenting our protocol implementation in Section 5.4.

Exploration strategy (action selection policy). One final, important learning parameter is the action selection policy. A trivial solution is to greedily select the action with the best (lowest) Q-Value. However, this policy ignores some actions which may, after learning, have lower Q-Values, resulting in a locally optimal solution. Therefore, a tradeoff is required between *exploitation* of good routes and *exploration* among available routes. This problem has been extensively studied in machine learning [179]. A simple, though efficient strategy is ϵ-greedy, which selects the best available action with probability $1 - \epsilon$ and a random one with probability ϵ. There are also variants of ϵ-greedy, where ϵ is decreased with time or where the range of random routes are restricted to the most promising ones. Section 5.4.9 gives more details about the exploration strategies we use for FROMS.

5.3 Theoretical analysis of FROMS

In this section we concentrate on the theoretical analysis of FROMS: on its convergence, complexity, memory, and processing requirements. First we explore an idealized model of the environment and later we introduce realistic properties like asymmetric links and link failures.

5.3.1 Worst-case complexity and convergence

We show first the worst-case complexity of FROMS (time to stabilize) and thus also implicitly its convergence. In our scenario, convergence means that first, the protocol is stable and the Q-Values do not change any more, and second and more importantly, that the optimal route has been identified. The original Q-Learning algorithm has been shown to converge after an *infinite* number of steps, see Section 4.1. Here we need to show that our Q-Learning based protocol converges after a *finite* number of steps. For this, we start by calculating the number of steps until convergence.

First, we assume a Q-Learning algorithm like the one we presented in the previous Section 5.2 with $\gamma = 1$, hop-based cost metric, and deterministic exploration strategy, which chooses the routes in a round-robin manner. We further assume a network N with the following properties: D is the number of destinations, M is the diameter of the network (the longest shortest path in the network between any two nodes in N) and Y is the density of the network (the maximum number of 1-hop neighbors at any node in N). The parameters are summarized in Table 5.1. We also assume static nodes and sinks and perfect

Parameter	Description
D	number of destinations
M	diameter of the network
Y	network density (maximum number of 1-hop neighbors)
|N|	number of nodes in the network
A	Maximum number of possible actions at each node
S	Maximum number of action steps (sent packets) at the source before convergence

Table 5.1. Summary of network scenario and complexity parameters, as used in the discussion of FROMS.

communication between the neighbors. Without loss of generality, we assume a single source, since the routes are constructed depending on the destinations, not on the sources. We will discuss multiple sources at the end of this section.

Further, the maximum number of possible actions A at any node is, according to the definition of actions in Section 5.2.2, the number of permutations of size D over all neighbors Y with repetitions (because we are allowed to use the same neighbor to reach multiple sinks) or:

$$A \leq Y^D \tag{5.6}$$

In the worst case the source of the data or the initiator of the learning process is at maximum distance M from all of the sinks. Our goal is to compute how many action selection steps have to be taken on all nodes in N, so that the Q-Values stabilize. With $\gamma = 1$ the feedback of any 1-hop neighbor is used for direct replacement of the old Q-Value. Thus, in order to learn the real costs of any route of length M we need exactly $M - 1$ steps. However, the source has to first wait for all other nodes to stabilize their Q-Values before it can be guaranteed that its Q-Values are stable too. In the worst case it has to explore the full network and

5.3 Theoretical analysis of FROMS

all possible routes in it. Let us count the number of action selection steps S we need for the whole system to converge.

Assuming the learning is always initiated by the source, we know that we need to select each of the routes available $M - 1$ times. Using Equation 5.6 we have:

$$S \leq (M - 1) \cdot Y^D$$

The 1-hop neighbors of the source need to do the same. Their distance to the sinks is also at most M. Note this is the worst case and it actually cannot exist in a real network: if all of the neighbors of some node are at the same distance from the sinks as the node itself, the network is disconnected. Thus, all of the nodes in the network have to select each of their routes at most M times. Thus, we have for the complexity:

$$S \leq (M - 1) \cdot |N| \cdot Y^D = O\left(M \cdot |N| \cdot Y^D\right) \tag{5.7}$$

This is the worst-case number of actions across all nodes (packet broadcasts) for the protocol to converge. After convergence, exploration can be stopped and the algorithm can proceed in a greedy mode, as the best route has been identified and has the best Q-Value among all available. If there are more than one best routes, they can be alternated to spread energy expenditure.

However, this is a very loose upper bound of the complexity - no real networks have the worst-case properties like "all neighbors are M hops away from the destinations". However, it gives us an idea about the scalability of the approach and its expected performance. In the next paragraphs we discuss in detail how the convergence behavior changes with various network parameters and what are the consequences for the protocol. We use experimental evaluations to show the real behavior of the protocol in Section 5.5.

Parameter analysis. The number of destinations D and the density Y are *not* directly dependent on the number of nodes $|N|$ in a network or on the diameter M. To understand better the expected performance, we explore these individual cases for each of the parameters:

The number of sinks D is completely independent from any of the other network properties, $|N|$, M, or Y, as it is a requirement of the application. The only limitation is that $D \leq |N|$. With a growing number of sinks the complexity grows exponentially, because D is in the power (see Equation 5.7).

With growing number of nodes $|N|$, usually either the *diameter M* or the *density Y* are growing, or both, but at a lower rate. In both cases, we expect the complexity to have a polynomial growth (from Equation 5.7).

In a network with constant number of nodes $|N|$, M and Y depend on each other. When the diameter is growing, the number of neighbors is decreasing; and vice versa. In the extreme case we have $M = |N| = c, Y = 2$, where we have a chain network with maximum number of neighbors 2. In this case we have:

$$S = O\left(|N|^2 \cdot 2^D\right) \qquad (5.8)$$

The other extreme case is when the density or Y grows towards $|N|$ and M decreases towards 2 - note that the case $M = 1$ does not make sense, because then any source will be exactly one hop from any sink and routing would be trivial. In the case of $M \to 2$ we have:

$$S = O\left(2|N|^{D+1}\right) \qquad (5.9)$$

However, these equations do not consider the behavior inbetween. It is more interesting to explore the complexity in a network with constant $|N|$ and different M and Y values. Figure 5.2 shows a case study for a network of 100 nodes, 3 sinks and different densities and diameters. The worst-case complexity is presented from two different points of view. Of course, as expected, with growing M and Y, the complexity grows. However, the thick line shows exactly the development when M is growing and Y decreasing - it shows that the function has a maximum between the two extreme cases. As a rule of thumb for practical networks it can be generalized, that having a lower density is always a good idea, since Y is in the power of D (see again Equation 5.7), unless M is very low,

5.3 Theoretical analysis of FROMS

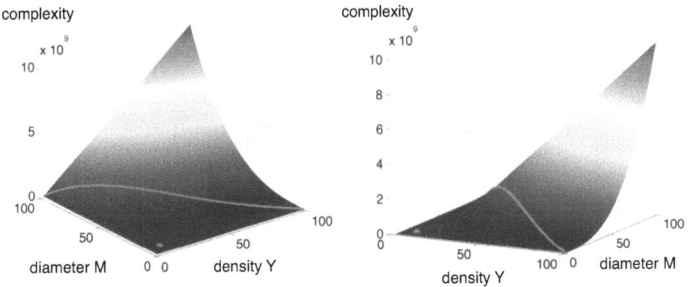

Figure 5.2. Worst-case complexity for some M and Y values from different views. The number of sinks is fixed to $D = 3, |N| = 100$. The thick line at the welding of the graph corresponds to maximum expected complexity and the single point near the origin to a real dense network with $M = 10$ and $Y = 10$.

as the complexity decreases again. Note also that the extreme case of Figure 5.2 where both M and Y are growing towards $|N|$ is impossible in practice [31]. Realistic values for a network with 100 nodes will be $M = 10$ and $Y = 10$, which corresponds to the single point in Figure 5.2.

Probabilistic exploration strategy. The above complexity is given for a deterministic round-robin exploration strategy. However, both the original Q-Learning algorithm, as well as our protocol, use probabilistic exploration strategies - for each route r there is a probability p_r to be chosen at any step s_t. If the probabilities of all routes are $p_r > 0$, convergence is guaranteed. However, complexity is hard to compute because of the non-deterministic nature of the algorithm. Instead, we will show experimental evaluations in the next sections.

Realistic communication environment. The above proof is built under the assumption of perfect communication. However, the real world of WSNs is seldom perfect. Packet losses are usual and have to be considered.

However, assuming some probability p_m for delivering a message between two nodes is enough to maintain the convergence criterium of the algorithm.

The convergence will take longer, but the correctness is not violated if the probability p_m is non-zero. In the special case of $p_m = 0$ for some link(s), the network model changes: these links are actually non-existing and under the new network model the algorithm will converge.

A scenario with asymmetric links is slightly more complex. Here, two neighboring nodes may have a one-way communication only. Thus, one of the nodes may hear from the other, but not vice versa. Consequently data packets may be forwarded through some node, but feedback will never be received by the sender. If the node with the asymmetric link happens to be on the optimal route, the sender of the packets will never learn its real costs and the protocol will not converge to the optimal route. However, in practice such links are often considered not-existing, because of their unreliable nature. If we assume this and come back to the above discussion of packet loss, convergence is guaranteed again. It is the responsibility of the protocol's implementation to recognize asymmetric links and to delete them and we will discuss how we do this in the next Section 5.4.

Multiple sources. In the above paragraphs we assumed a single data source learning the optimal routes to all sinks. However, what happens when more sources are present in the network? In fact, this speeds up the convergence process of all nodes in terms of data packets sent by one source. Imagine a network with 2 sources, sending data at the same rate to 3 identical sinks. In this case, nodes on the routes of both sources to the sinks receive double feedback from sending data packets from both sources. This is because our feedback is delivered to all neighboring nodes.

5.3.2 Correctness of FROMS

The correctness of FROMS is easily deducible from the definition of the used Q-Learning model in Section 5.2. The goal is to show that after convergence, the Q-Values of the full actions at any node will accurately reflect the hop-based costs. We use simple induction to sketch the proof in sufficient detail for our purposes. We begin by showing the correctness of FROMS for one sink, then

5.3 Theoretical analysis of FROMS

expand the proof to multiple sinks.

Assumptions. We assume perfect communication, static network, and the Q-Value calculation and update equations from Section 5.2.

Initial step. The induction starts with the sinks and we define the cost of the sinks of routing to themselves to be always 0, since no forwarding is needed any more. Thus, the reward of the sinks for routing to themselves is always $r = 0 + c_a$ with $c_a = 1$ from Equation 5.5. For $\gamma = 1$, the neighbors update the Q-Value for the corresponding sub-action to $Q = r = 1$, which we know is the correct cost of this sub-action, since the sink is exactly one hop away.

Induction step. Assume that a node N (sink or any other node) has a correct estimation of the costs to the sink Q_N. Its reward is always computed as $r = \min_a Q(a) + c_a$, where $\min_a Q(a)$ is necessarily the above Q_N and $c_a = 1$. When node N sends its reward to its direct neighbors, they will update their corresponding Q-Values for this node to $Q_N + 1$, which is the correct estimation of the cost through node N, since they are exactly one hop further away from the sink than node N. Thus, for any node N with correct estimations of the cost, its direct neighbors also have correct cost estimations.

We showed above that FROMS converges to the correct hop-based costs for one sink in the network. In fact we know that FROMS is correct for one sink also because of the sink announcement propagation. During this network-wide broadcast, every node easily learns about the best routes in terms of hops to a single sink. Thus, we have both a practical and a theoretical proof that FROMS converges to the correct costs for one sink. This is the beginning of the second induction proof, which shows that FROMS converges to the correct hop-based costs also for more than one sink.

Assume a network with 2 sinks that the Q-Values for each sink individually at all nodes have already converged (see the discussion above). For simplicity we call the sinks A and B. The costs of B to reach itself is 0 and to reach sink A is a constant $v = \min_a Q_B(a)$, which is the minimum Q-Value for A at node B. Thus, the cost of reaching *both* A and B at B is $0 + v$ and the reward of B is $r_B = (0 + v) + c_a = v + 1$. The direct neighbors of B will update their own Q-Values to this reward value, which is the right cost: they need one hop to reach sink *B* and further *v* costs to reach sink *A*. This trivially extends to the next hops, as shown already above. It also intuitively extends to more than 2 sinks.

Summarizing Sections 5.3.1 and 5.3.2, we have shown that FROMS *converges to the correct hop-based costs of the routes after finite number of steps.*

5.3.3 Memory and processing requirements

Before explaining the implementation details of FROMS and showing its experimental evaluation, we analyze the theoretical memory and processing requirements of the algorithm for each node in the network.

Each node has to store all locally available routes. According to Equation 5.6 the expected storage requirement is $O(Y^D)$. The processing requirements include selecting a route and updating a Q-Value. The first function requires in the worst case to loop through all available routes to compare them in terms of their costs and is thus bounded by $O(Y^D)$. The update of a Q-Value is itself an atomic action: given the old Q-Value and the reward, it calculates the new one. Assuming a data structure, organized by neighbor, we need as worst case for searching $O(Y + D)$.

5.4 Protocol implementation details and parameters

The multicast energy-aware routing protocol FROMS is built upon the formal Q-Learning model, presented in Section 5.2. A pseudo-code of the resulting protocol is given in Figure 5.3. Basically, the routing protocol consists of three main processes: sink announcement and initialization of routes (lines 3-4), selection of routes (lines 9-12) and learning and feedback (lines 8 and 14). Additionally, there are some parameters of FROMS like the exploration strategy (line 12), cost functions (line 2) and the sink mobility management module (line 7). We will step through all of these and give additional details in the following sections.

5.4 Protocol implementation details and parameters

```
1:  init:
2:    init_cost_function();

3:  on_receive(DATA_REQ req):
4:    add_nexthop(req.sinkID,req.neiID,req.hops,req.battery);

5:  on_receive(DATA d):
6:    // snoop on all incoming packets
7:    sinkControl.update(d.sinkStamps,d.neiID);
8:    add_feedback(d.feedback, d.neiID);
9:    // route packet to next hop(s)
10:   if (d.nexthops.includes(self))
11:     routes = get_possible_routes(d.my_sinks,cost_function);
12:     route = strategy.select_route(routes);
13:     d.routing = route;
14:     d.feedback = best_route_cost;
15:     broadcast(d);
16:   end if
```

Figure 5.3. The main FROMS algorithm

5.4.1 Sink announcement

Recall from our application scenario described in Chapter 2 that we assume each of the sinks announces itself via a network-wide broadcast of a DATA_REQ message, during which initial routing information like hops to the sink is gathered (line 3-4 in Figure 5.3). Additionally, position information, battery status of neighbors, etc, can be delivered to the nodes.

5.4.2 Feedback implementation

A substantial part of FROMS is the exchange of feedback. This is what enables FROMS to learn the global cost of the routes and to use the globally optimal paths. We piggyback the feedback, which is usually only a few bytes, on usual DATA packets (line 14 in Figure 5.3). There are several advantages of this implementation: feedback is sent only on-demand and only to local neighbors;

and overhead is kept minimal because no extra control packets need to be exchanged.

Note that feedback is accepted and route costs are updated even if the feedback is negative and the previously known costs were better. Thus, mobility and recovery are handled automatically. The feedback is usually received by all overhearing neighbors, which speeds up the learning process. However, feedback can also be delivered to the previous hop only, thus avoiding energy expenditure for overhearing of packets. This implementation requires a multicast MAC layer protocol, able to send the message only to a some subset of neighbors. Unfortunately there is no such a protocol designed for low-energy WSNs to the best of our knowledge and its implementation is not trivial, since it requires a well-designed scheduling together with variable-length preamble packets. We consider designing such a protocol and testing it with various routing techniques in the future.

5.4.3 Data management

One of the implementation challenges of FROMS is to design an efficient multi-destination routing data structure. This data structure is different from usual routing tables like the one in Figure 5.1 since it not only holds next hops for individual sinks and their costs, but also combines shared paths to multiple sinks. In other words, we need a data structure to hold the sub-actions as described in Section 5.2. For example, the possible sub-actions for node S from Figure 5.1 for each of the neighbors n_i are: $\{n_i,(P)\}$, $\{n_i,(Q)\}$ and $\{n_i,(P,Q)\}$.

Data structure API

As shown in the algorithm pseudocode from Figure 5.3, the multi-destination routing data structure used by FROMS has to implement efficiently and reliably the following API:

```
add_nexthop(sinkID, nexthop, hop_cost, battery)
```

This function is called when a DATA_REQ arrives, or when a feedback for an unknown sub-action arrives. The second case happens, when sink announcements were lost and some next hops are unknown at the node. However,

5.4 Protocol implementation details and parameters

the first time when the unknown neighbor broadcasts a data packet the node will repair its routing table.

```
add_feedback(feedback, previous_hop)
```

This is called every time the node hears a data packet. The data structure has to find the required sub-action and to update its cost. The cost is updated always and not only when it is better than before. The costs are expected to be higher than previously known when a node fails or when a sink moves away. All routes' full cost, using this sub-action, have to be updated. Additionally, if this sub-action cannot be found, it should be recovered (see add_nexthop).

```
get_possible_routes(sinks, cost_function)
```

This is called by the exploration strategy and should return all possible routes, which fulfill some requirements, like maximum hop cost, maximum total cost etc (for loop management, see below). The routing strategy will then select one of them for usage.

PSTable

Our FROMS implementation uses an instantiation of the above defined data structure called **PSTable**, or **P**ath **S**haring **T**able. Let us continue with our example of Figure 5.1. Figure 5.4 presents the resulting data structure for node S. For easy reference we have copied also the network topology. The PSTable consists of two simple tables, for the sub-actions and the routes (full actions), and three management variables. Note that this sample PSTable contains the initial Q-Values for all sub-actions and full actions and is based on hops for simplicity. Note that cost calculation for sub-actions occurs only once: at initialization. After that, feedbacks are used to update the Q-Values. Q-Values of full actions (Table allRoutes), which we also call Q-full, are computed according to Equation 5.2 from the Q-Values of the included sub-actions. Further details are given below:

- subActions: This table holds all available sub-actions for each of the neighbors. They are organized by neighbor ID for speeding up search in case of feedback. For each of the sub-actions, the table holds the Q-Value

5.4 Protocol implementation details and parameters

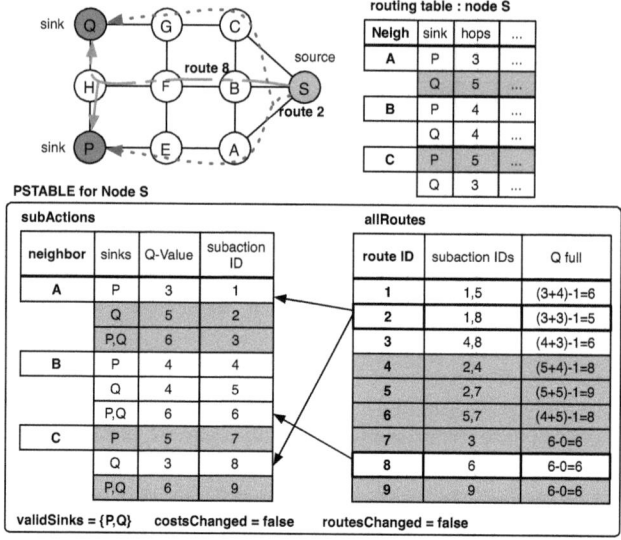

Figure 5.4. The PSTable for node S from Figure 5.1. Grey-shaded boxes are ignored sub-actions (not stored), which saves memory after applying route storage pruning heuristics $C = 1, Nr = 3$ (see Section 5.4.4).

of that action and assigns an ID, which is used as a pointer to that sub-action. The grey-shaded fields are pruned sub-actions to save memory and will be explained later in Section 5.4.4.

- allRoutes: This table holds basically all possible combinations of sub-actions, such that in each route all sinks are covered exactly once. The table holds the total Q-Value of the full action, computed from the Q-Value of the included sub-actions according to Equation 5.2. Two examples are emphasized in the figure, route 2 and 8. Route 2 (marked bold in the figure) consists of two sub-actions with IDs 1 and 8 and corresponds to the dashed route in the network topology in the same figure. Its full route

5.4 Protocol implementation details and parameters

costs (its full Q-Value) is 5, which is the cost in terms of hops for this route. In contrast, route 8 consists of only 1 sub-action with ID 6 and its full cost is also 6 hops.

Note that these two tables need to be separate: rewards are assigned and delivered by sub-actions, but full routes are needed when routing incoming data packets. Putting them together will increase significantly the search time for incoming rewards, because sub-actions will be presented several times in different routes and the full table would need to be traversed to find them.

- validSinks: The sinks, for which the full Q-Value is computed and stored. We apply lazy evaluation of routes to speed up the route selection. For example, if a route to only one of the sinks is desired (e.g. for sink Q), the Q-Values of the routes will be re-computed as to include only the desired sinks. If this computation is impossible, for example as it is for route 8, the Q-Value will be marked with -1. The computation is impossible, when needed and unneeded sinks are combined into the same sub-action: in our example, sub-action 6 of route 8 contains both sinks P and Q and thus separated computation of the cost to sink Q only is impossible.

- routesChanged: This variable indicates that the allRoutes table has to be rebuilt because new routes are available or old ones lost.

- costsChanged: This indicates that the costs of some routes have changed and have to be recalculated or that the costs are not valid any more (validSinks has changed). This happens usually when new feedback arrives, which in fact changes the routes Q-Values. Then all routes which use the updated Q-Value become invalid. For example, if sub-action 1 from our Figure 5.4 gets updated, routes 1 and 2 become invalid. However, instead of immediately searching for those routes and recalculating their costs, we mark the whole table as invalid and wait until a data packet arrives for routing. This saves processing effort when the node is overhearing a lot of feedback from its neighbors, but does not route data packets. When a new data packet arrives for routing, the table allRoutes is traversed and all routes' costs updated according to Equation 5.2.

In the simulation environment (described in Section 4.2.4) we use dynamic memory allocation for *subActions* and *allRoutes* and memory pointers to the subactions. In the real hardware environment (described in Section 4.2.4) we do not have dynamic memory allocation and use a static array of subActions items and a static array of allRoutes items. The size of both of them are large enough to accommodate all possible sink combinations and routes. Instead of memory pointers we use IDs, like in the example in Figure 5.4.

5.4.4 Route storage reducing heuristics

As pointed out in Section 5.3, the storage requirements for all routes grow exponentially with number of sinks and polynomially with number of neighbors. In practice this means that for large number of sinks and neighbors we are not able to store all routes. The consequence is that we cannot guarantee any more that the algorithm is optimal. However, its near-optimality can be easily preserved by wisely managing which routes to store and which not.

We have developed two route pruning heuristics: *C - cost over best maximum* and *Nr - maximum number of routes to sink*. The first one simply checks what is the currently best cost to the sink in question and if the newly arrived route has cost more than this best one plus the threshold C, it ignores the route. The second one is a limit over the number of routes per sink - when this number is exceeded, the newly arrived route is ignored. In Figure 5.4 ignored entries after applying $C = 1, Nr = 3$ are shown in grey.

Note that these heuristics not only limit the memory requirement at the nodes, but also the convergence time, since less routes need to be explored. In the following experimental setup we evaluate different pruning heuristics in terms of the optimality of routes found, see Section 5.5.2.

5.4 Protocol implementation details and parameters

5.4.5 Loop management

FROMS explores non-optimal routes for finding the globally best route. This means that it chooses a route with a non-limited length. Thus it can happen that a packet travels in a loop, even forever. In order to manage this, we have introduced the maximum allowed hop cost for a neighbor. Each node receives the data packet together with the subset of sinks which it has to care of, and a maximum hop cost for the selected route. We set this maximum allowed cost to the currently known cost for this sub-action. Thus, if the cost estimate is right and the node has no better routes, it will be forced to use the best one. The reason for requiring this is that if the cost estimate is right the probability that this estimate is also the real cost is very high.

5.4.6 Mobility management

The Q-Learning algorithm has the innate ability to manage changing network conditions. They will be delivered as feedback and the Q-Values will be updated accordingly in the usual learning process. However, practical challenges arise: growing costs of some route could either mean mobile sinks moving away or a disconnection from some sinks. The first case is normal and should be handled as usual. The second one, however, will cause looping packets, traveling forever and searching for non-existing routes.

An important special case for managing moving sinks is when a node is a direct neighbor of a sink. In this case we exclude this sink from learning and always send directly to it. However, this causes problems when the sink moves away and the sink needs to be included in normal learning again. Thus, we need a technique to recognize alive sinks moving out of range.

SinkControl is a simple data structure whose goal is to detect moving or disconnected sinks. It does not affect the Q-Learning algorithm, but manages the available routes, erasing invalid ones. It stores information about each known sink in the network. Figure 5.5 presents it for the sample topology of Figure 5.1. The feedback delivers a last timestamp for each included sink; this is the last time this neighbor has heard of the sink. If this timestamp is too old (a threshold

SinkControl : node E

sink	last timestamp	direct neighbor	direct timestamp
sink P	-2 sec	true	-2 sec
sink Q	-14 sec	false	-

Figure 5.5. SinkControl for node E (direct neighbor of sink P from Figures 5.1 and 5.4).

parameter), the sink is deleted. This is the case when either the sink itself has failed or disappeared from the network or the network is disconnected between the sink and the node. In both cases the application layer has to be notified to delete the data delivery task for those sinks and routing to them has to be stopped.

On the other hand, while the sink is "fresh" data delivery can continue even if the routes' costs to it are growing. In order to detect sinks in the direct neighborhood, we also store the last time the node has heard from a sink directly. if some threshold is exceeded, the flag for direct neighbor is deleted and FROMS is notified.

This simple module enables detection of sink mobility and learning of new routes with minimum communication overhead, the additional last timestamp feedback. Despite using timestamps, FROMS does not require a time synchronization protocol or any other means of global time. It is enough to use timestamps like in Figure 5.5: $(now - n \cdot sec)$. The goal is to detect sinks, which are not responsive for a long time.

Obviously, this sink mobility detection can be implemented for any routing protocol. However, it is not sufficient to handle sink mobility: it only checks whether a route can exist or not. Finding the optimal route is still performed by FROMS and its learning and feedback mechanism. Most importantly, delivery of data to the sinks continues while recovering the routes and learning the new costs.

5.4 Protocol implementation details and parameters

5.4.7 Node failures

Node failures are managed the same way as sink mobility. Each node stores the last time it heard from any 1-hop neighbor. Additionally, it stores the last time it routed something to that neighbor. In case the difference between both timestamps exceeds some threshold, the neighbor is deleted. Note that if this happens by mistake, the next time the node hears again from this neighbor, the route will be recovered.

Note that unlike many link management protocols, FROMS does not use any beacons or periodic full-network broadcasts. Only overhearing of data packets is used to check the status of neighbors.

5.4.8 Cost metrics

Here we present FROMS innate ability to incorporate different cost functions to reach different optimization goals. The cost function is used to calculate the initial Q-Values in FROMS. A simple hop-based metric was presented already in Section 5.2 with Equations 5.1 and 5.2. Its optimization goal is to find the shortest shared path for multiple sinks in terms of hops. The hop-based cost function can be easily exchanged with any other cost-per-link metric, like energy needed to reach the farthest neighbor, geographic distance or geographic progress to the sinks, etc. Various cost metrics and their properties are summarized in Table 5.2.

Another example for a cost-per-link function is a latency-based cost metric. Here we need to gather latency information during sink announcement to the sensor nodes. The latency needs to represent the radio propagation latency (where the differences will be negligible for usual sensor networks) and the latency caused by the packet queues on the nodes. However, note that such a cost metric is what we call here a *dynamic cost metric*: it is expected to change during network lifetime and to change fast. For FROMS this means that it will never globally converge, nor stay in a converged state. However, we show in the next paragraphs other dynamic cost functions and how to handle their behavior. In fact, we make use of this non-converging behavior and turn it into an advantage.

Beside these *simple cost functions*, which include only one metric, there exist

Cost metric	Calculation of initial values	Optimization goal	Convergence	Dynamic	Best Q-Values
simple metrics					
Hops	$\sum hops$	shortest shared path (Steiner tree)	guaranteed	no	lowest
Latency	$\sum latency$	least latency path	no	yes	lowest
Transmission energy	$\sum energies$	least energy path	guaranteed	no	lowest
Geographic distance	$\sum dist$	shortest shared path	guaranteed	no	lowest
Aggr. rate	$\sum rates$	maximum aggr. path	slow	no	highest
combined metrics					
Hops & rem. battery of nodes	$\sum hops \cdot hcm(bat_{hops})$	shortest shared path through nodes with high battery	no	yes	lowest

Table 5.2. Different possible cost metrics for FROMS and their main properties.

more complex, multiple objective *combined* cost metrics. Here we concentrate on one of them, a combination of remaining battery on the nodes and minimum hops. In this case we calculate the Q-Values as a combination of two metrics as follows:

$$Q_{comb}(route) = f(E_{hops}, E_{battery}) \qquad (5.10)$$

where E_{hops} is the estimated hop cost of the route exactly as we calculate it in equations 5.1 and 5.2, and $E_{battery}$ is the estimated battery cost of this route, which we define as the minimum remaining battery of all nodes along it:

$$E_{battery}(route) = \min_{n_i \in route} battery \qquad (5.11)$$

The function f that combines the two estimates into a single Q-Value is based on a simple and widely used function:

5.4 Protocol implementation details and parameters

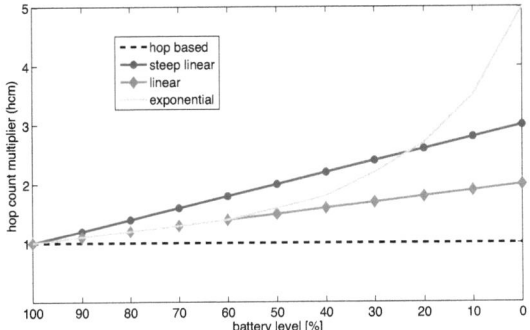

Figure 5.6. Hop count multiplier (*hcm*) functions for different optimization goals.

$$f(E_{hops}, E_{battery}) = hcm(E_{battery}) \cdot E_{hops} \qquad (5.12)$$

hcm is the hop-count-multiplier, a function that weights the hop count estimate based on the remaining battery. For simplicity we drop the "estimation" and denote the Q-Value components as *hops* and *battery*.

Figure 5.6 shows four different *hcm* functions. If the battery level is completely irrelevant, then *hcm(battery)* is a constant and $f(hops, battery)$ is reduced to a hop-based function only. Instead, if the desired behavior is to linearly increase f as the battery levels decrease, a linear *hcm* function should be considered. Figure 5.6 shows two linear functions. The first (labeled linear), has minimal effect on the routing behavior. For example, a greedy protocol which always uses the best (lowest) Q-Values available, when faced with two routes with $f(1, 10\%) = 1.9$ and $f(2, 100\%) = 2$, will select the shorter route even though the battery is nearly exhausted. Even when faced with longer routes of length 2 and 3 respectively, it will use the shorter route until its battery drops to 40%. Only when their values become $f(2, 40\%) = 3.2$ and $f(3, 100\%) = 3$, the protocol will switch to the longer route. Thus, this trade-off of weighing the hop count of routes (their length) versus the remaining batteries must be taken into account when defining hcm.

The main drawback of linear hcm functions is that they do not differentiate between battery levels in the low and high power domain. For example, a difference of 10% battery looks the same for $20-30\%$ and for $80-90\%$. Thus, to meet our goal of spreading the energy expenditure among the nodes, we require an exponential function that starts by slowly increasing the value of hcm with decreasing battery, initially giving preference to shorter routes. However, as batteries start to deplete, it should more quickly increase hcm in order to use other available routes, even if they are much longer, thus maximizing the lifetime of individual nodes. Of course, such a function gives preference to longer energy-rich routes, and will increase the per packet costs in the network.

The presented battery and hop based function is a dynamic function, which means that it is expected to change during the network lifetime. Obviously, the remaining batteries of the nodes will change and thus the Q-Values as well. The major consequence of this is that FROMS does not stabilize, because the Q-Values never stabilize. However, this is not necessarily a disadvantage: FROMS will just continue exploring routes throughout the network lifetime. Combining a dynamic cost function with a mostly greedy exploration strategy will ensure that FROMS is not spending too much energy on exploration of routes and is mostly using the best available routes. On the other side, we need to ensure that FROMS is still able to find the best routes. For this, we use the advantage of a dynamic cost function. The Q-Values change because of the dynamic nature of the cost metric and force FROMS to use different routes (because it mostly selects the best ones): thus, it implicitly forces FROMS to explore new routes.

This property of dynamic cost functions we call the *dynamic cost advantage of implicit exploration*, which is a very important property of FROMS. It allows FROMS to use a very simple greedy or ϵ-greedy exploration strategy with very low probability for exploration (see next section) and still ensures that the optimal routes are found. This simplifies significantly the implementation of FROMS both in terms of processing and memory requirements and make FROMS much more intuitive.

5.4 Protocol implementation details and parameters

Similarly, one can easily design and implement other cost metrics, both simple and combined. The used cost function depends on the application scenario and needs to be revisited for each deployment. However, the power of FROMS is its innate ability to accommodate nearly any cost function. The changes to the protocol are marginal and do not affect its basic functionality.

5.4.9 Exploration strategies

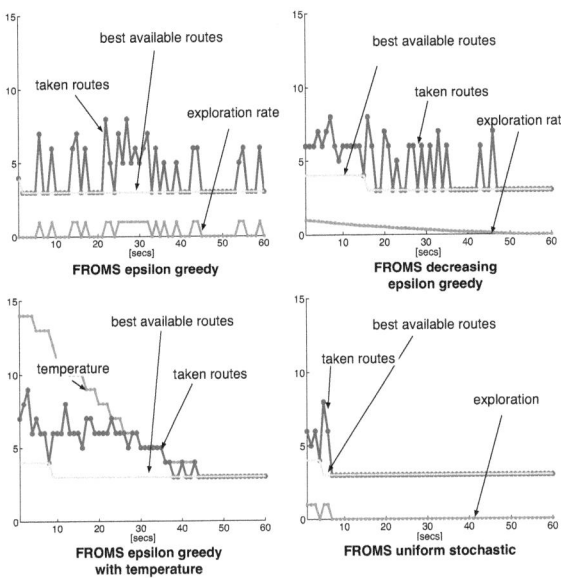

Figure 5.7. The route selection behavior at the source with different exploration strategies in a sample 50 node topology with 3 sinks and 1 source.

The exploration strategy controls how FROMS chooses between the available routes. It also controls the exploration/exploitation ratio, which is responsible for both finding the optimal route and minimizing routing costs. Early in this thesis, we have applied two different techniques for exploration: greedy and probabilistic. The *greedy* strategy simply ignores exploration and always chooses between the best available routes. *Stochastic* exploration strategies on the other hand assign a probability to each of the routes, depending or not on their current or initial Q-Values, and choose the routes accordingly. This type of exploration strategies show good results, but are very complicated to implement since they require updating the probabilities after each reward [63].

Here, we will turn to a new set of exploration strategies for two main reasons: to make them more intuitive and simple to implement and to complete the evaluation of FROMS with them. The behavior of the considered strategies are shown in Figure 5.7.

ϵ **- greedy.** This strategy is taken directly from the original Q-Learning algorithm and is very simple to apply and implement: with probability ϵ select any of the available routes; with probability $1 - \epsilon$, select one of the best routes. Note that when $\epsilon = 0$ we have the old greedy strategy from [63].

decreasing ϵ - greedy. This strategy is the same as before, but additionally decreases ϵ with time. The reason for this is that usually at the beginning of the algorithm the Q-Values change a lot, but with time these update become more rare and eventually stop. After convergence it is more appropriate for FROMS to be greedy, since no changes are expected and the routing costs should be as low as possible. ϵ increases again in case of failures or mobility.

ϵ **- greedy with temperature.** This strategy is again a variation of ϵ-greedy, but instead of decreasing ϵ itself, it limits the set of routes presented to the strategy. At the beginning, with high temperature T, all routes are presented to the strategy, independent from their current Q-Values. With decreasing T, however, only routes with better Q-Values are presented and with $T = 0$ only the best routes are presented. ϵ remains constant and the temperature is increased in case of failures or mobility.

uniform stochastic with stopping strategy. This strategy is taken from our previous work [63] (it performed the best out of all compared stochastic strategies there) and is used for comparison reasons. It assigns the same probability to each sub-action and updates it every time a reward arrives for it, decreasing it with neutral rewards, increasing it with negative rewards, and leaving it the same with positive rewards. It stops exploration completely after some number of continuous neutral rewards to the node and starts it again with negative/positive rewards.

5.4.10 Summary

In this section we presented all parameters and implementation details of FROMS. The main parameters which need to be specified before deploying FROMS are its cost function and exploration strategies. Additionally, node failure management is a necessary option in nearly any WSN. However, all other presented modules implement special features, like sink mobility support or route pruning heuristics for extremely memory-restricted hardware systems, and need to be deployed only when necessary. In the next paragraphs, we present an extensive evaluation of FROMS and all of its components and features both under simulation and on real hardware.

5.5 Stand-alone evaluation of FROMS

In this section we present results from testing and evaluating FROMS under two environments - in simulation and on real hardware. In particular we evaluate and analyze its stand-alone performance in terms of memory and processing requirements, and we offer a parameter analysis. We use the evaluation environments and our own network models and routing protocols implementation as identified and described in Section 4.2.4. First we give more details about the evaluated network scenarios and parameters.

Real hardware testbed. We compare the performance of FROMS with ϵ-greedy exploration strategy against the multicast version of Directed Diffusion [170]. We use two controlled network topologies as given in Figure 5.8. In these experiments, we allowed the nodes to process packets only from some predefined set of nodes and to drop immediately all others. We were forced to

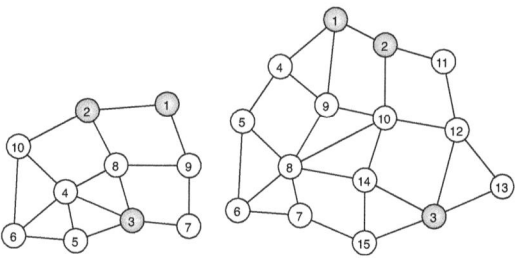

Figure 5.8. Topologies 1 (left) and 2 (right) for the real hardware testbed, sinks are shaded, source is node 6.

do this, because we were unable to create a natural multi-hop topology, which is essential for the evaluation of the routing protocol.

Simulation environment. We already discussed the needed simulated network models in Section 4.2.4. A summary of them, as used for the experiments of FROMS in this section, is presented in Table 5.3. We conducted experiments with randomly created connected topologies and each of the results presented is a mean of at least 5 different random runs on at least 50 different topologies. Consequently, we present means over at least 250 experiments and a standard deviation of the experimental results of 1-2%. We normalize all results on a topology-per-topology manner to abstract from differences coming from different network scenarios, like different network diameters.

We proceed first by evaluating FROMS' memory and processing requirements in Section 5.5.1, the implemented route storage heuristics in Section 5.5.2 and the various exploration strategies of FROMS in Section 5.5.3. In Section 5.5.4 we concentrate on the evaluation of different cost functions for FROMS. Then we compare FROMS performance with other routing protocols under simulation (Section 5.6) and on real hardware (Section 5.6.2). Section 5.6.3 deals with the ability of the compared routing protocols to recover after node failures and Section 5.6.4 shows their performance for mobile sinks.

5.5 Stand-alone evaluation of FROMS

Layer	Protocol / model	Parameters	Packet length
Application	regular data report	**data rate:** every 10 secs **data request rate:** every 100 secs	DATA: 17 B header, 20 B payload DATA_REQ: 31 B header
Routing	FROMS	cost functions, exploration strategies, route storage heuristics: see text	DATA: + (6 + 8*s) B DATA_REQ: + 4 B
	multicastDD	-	DATA: + (2 + 5*s) B DATA_REQ: + 4 B
	unicastDD	-	DATA: + 7 B DATA_REQ: + 4 B
	MSTEAM	cost per link: constant, variable (see text)	DATA: + (7 + 24*s) B DATA_REQ: + 10 B
MAC	BMAC	**frame length** 100 ms	preamble 120 B MAC header 6 B
	LMAC	**frame length** 2000 ms **# slots:** 32	preamble 12 B MAC header 6 B
Energy expenditure	linear battery	**SLEEP:** 36 mW **RX, TX:** 117 mW	n/a
Radio propagation	Nakagami	**shape factor m = 1**	n/a

Table 5.3. Summary of simulation environment models and their parameters for our experiments with FROMS.

5.5.1 Memory and processing requirements (hardware testbed)

Here we present and discuss the memory and processing requirements as obtained from the real hardware testbed. No simulated results are presented, since they depend strongly on the simulation environment used and are not comparable to real hardware requirements.

Memory usage. Figure 5.9 (left) presents the memory footprints at compile-time for MDD and FROMS together with the application layer. It shows the memory reserved for the flash ROM and the RAM. The footprint of the ScatterWeb2

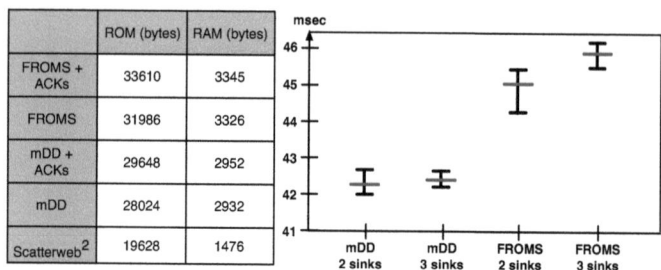

Figure 5.9. (left) Memory usage at compile time. The Scatterweb library alone is given for comparison. (right) Processing time to find a route in milliseconds for MDD and FROMS and max-min intervals.

library alone is given for comparison. The vanilla implementation of MDD on top of ScatterWeb e.g. consumes roughly 3KB of RAM at compile time, leaving 2KB for stack allocation and application-level protocols.

Both implementations of FROMS and MDD use static data structures, because there is no working dynamic memory management implementation for the microprocessor of the used hardware platform MSB430. No route storage heuristics are used for FROMS and thus all possible routes are kept at all times. Thus the data structures are already included also in the memory footprints in Figure 5.9. Although FROMS's data structures are more complex and larger than the routing table of MDD, its memory requirements are not significantly higher. MDD has a very tiny data structure, but despite this, its implementation size is not negligible. In fact, the majority of its memory is used for the functionality of the protocol, not for data structures.

Processing time. We measured the time needed to find a route for each packet in the network at every node in milliseconds. Basically, we discovered that it takes slightly longer to find a route to more sinks but the difference between the protocols is negligible. The results in Figure 5.9 (right) are summarized based on the number of sinks in the network. They are obtained from experiments with topology 2 only. The reason why FROMS needs more time to

5.5 Stand-alone evaluation of FROMS

	heuristic		number of sinks				
	Nr	C	2	3	4	5	6
PST size [bytes]	10	3	25	115	737	2469	17326
	5	1	29	77	369	1437	6590
	4	1	19	51	253	671	4682
	2	1	10	36	192	215	1731
Overhead [norm.]	10	3	1	1	1.03	1.03	1.06
	5	1	1	1.07	1.08	1.09	1.12
	4	1	1.05	1.06	1.04	1.06	1.12
	2	1	1	1	1.02	1.03	1.15

Table 5.4. PSTable pruning heuristics, evaluated in terms of PSTable size (in bytes) and achieved overhead per packet (normalized by optimal Steiner).

both to find a route for a data packet is its routing data structure. We need to search through all of the available routes to find the best available one. Consequently, with 3 sinks the processing time increases further.

These results are an important proof of the applicability of FROMS and in general of reinforcement learning based communication protocols on real hardware. They show that FROMS is easily implementable and that its memory and processing requirements are negligibly higher than those of a very simple routing protocol like MDD. The comparative evaluation of both protocols on the real testbed is discussed later in Section 5.6.2.

5.5.2 Route storage heuristics (simulation)

As discussed in Section 5.4.4, different heuristics can be applied to the PSTable, limiting its size and thus saving memory on the nodes and speeding up the learning process. We consider two PST route pruning heuristics: limiting the number of routes per sink to *Nr*, and limiting the maximum route cost to a sink to *bestCost* + *C*. Both types of information refer to the routing table (see Figure 5.4), *before* the sub-actions and actions are computed and initialized. As the PST size decreases, fewer actions are available for selection. Because the best route may be among those pruned, we expect the protocol performance to decrease as the size of the PST decreases. This trend is shown for FROMS ϵ - greedy in Table 5.4 for various values of Nr and C and for multiple numbers of sinks. In this experiment we compare the routing overhead of FROMS in terms of number of transmissions (ETX) against an optimal Steiner tree.

Interestingly the largest table (with ($Nr = 10, C = 3$) does not always discover the best routes. This is due mainly to packet loss, especially when the number of sinks in the network increases. This causes higher data traffic and thus more data loss.

In the remainder of our experiments, however, we do NOT use any route pruning heuristics in order to limit the number of used parameters and simplify evaluation and understanding of the results. Furthermore, as we already showed in the previous Section 5.5.1, we are able to implement FROMS with no route pruning heuristics on real hardware. In case the implementation needs to be restricted because of a very large number of sinks or very high density of the nodes, we suggest using a moderate size for the PSTable with ($Nr = 4, C = 1$) that yields route costs close enough to optimal.

5.5.3 Exploration strategies (simulation)

In the next paragraphs we explore the behavior and performance of FROMS with different exploration strategies. We consider the following four types of strategies: ϵ - *greedy*, ϵ - *greedy with temperature*, *decreasing ϵ - greedy* and *uniform-stochastic*. Please refer to Section 5.4.9 for a detailed explanation of all investigated strategies and for a theoretical discussion of their behavior.

The experimental results are shown in Figure 5.10. In the top graphs we fix the number of nodes to 50, the number of sources to 1 and vary the number of sinks from 1 to 5. All exploration strategies are normalized by FROMS *decreasing ϵ-greedy*. The deviation of the first node death time (left graph) is only insignificant and does not exceed 1%. On the other hand, the differences in the routing overhead (number of ETX per delivered packet in the network) reaches 10%. This deviation of the results is a result of the MAC layer. Even an unicast MAC protocol cannot avoid completely overhearing of packets and the used BMAC protocol in fact uses only broadcast. This diminishes small differences in the

5.5 Stand-alone evaluation of FROMS

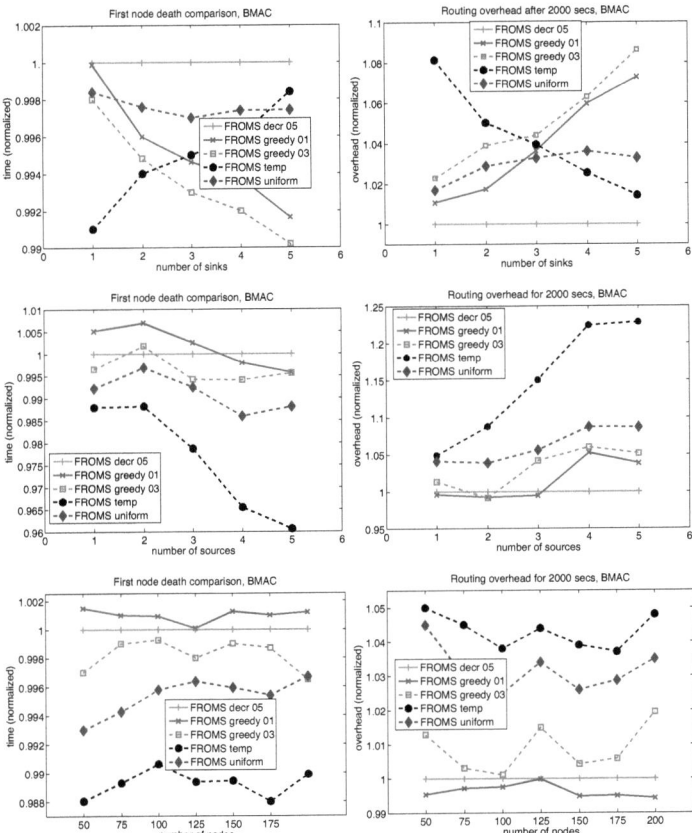

Figure 5.10. Evaluation of exploration strategies, mean over 50 different topologies, 5 runs each; the network consists of (top) 50 nodes, 1 source and 1-5 sinks; (middle) 50 nodes, 1-5 sources and 3 sinks; (bottom) 50-200 nodes, 1 source and 2 sinks. All experiments performed with BMAC.

number of sent packets (ETX) from the routing layer, and shows how important the MAC layer is for minimizing the energy spent and maximizing network lifetime. On the other hand, shorter routes usually result in higher source-to-sink delivery rates, since less hops are taken. Additionally, less traffic is always an advantage since it increases the delivery rate and thus the overall efficiency of the network.

The rest of the graphs in Figure 5.10 present experiments with varying number of sources and nodes respectively. They support the above made observations. Given the results obtained in this step, we will consider two exploration strategies in our comparative analysis experiments: decreasing ϵ-greedy with $\epsilon = 0.5$ and ϵ-greedy with $\epsilon = 0.1$.

5.5.4 Cost functions (simulation)

As we already showed in Section 5.4.8, FROMS can work with nearly any cost function: hops, location information, remaining energy on the nodes, delay, etc. An important property of the used cost function is its localized nature, as FROMS allows direct exchange of information only among one-hop neighbors. The cost function in FROMS is used in three places - initialization of route costs, computation of costs to reach some neighbor and comparison between routes. All these functions are independent from the rest of FROMS and can be easily exchanged.

In this section we concentrate on two main cost functions: a hop-based one and a combined hop and remaining energy based one, as already introduced in Section 5.4.8. Recall that the goal of the first one, *hop function* is to select globally shortest routes to reach all sinks. Instead, the second one, *hop-battery function*, favors shorter routes with higher remaining batteries of the involved nodes, thus spreading the energy expenditure throughout all nodes of the network. Everything else in the FROMS implementation remains the same: data structures, exploration strategies, feedback, etc.

Figure 5.11 presents different metrics for two exploration strategies of FROMS with both cost functions. The hop-battery cost functions extend slightly the network lifetime: however, only by at most 1% (top left graph). This is due to the

5.5 Stand-alone evaluation of FROMS

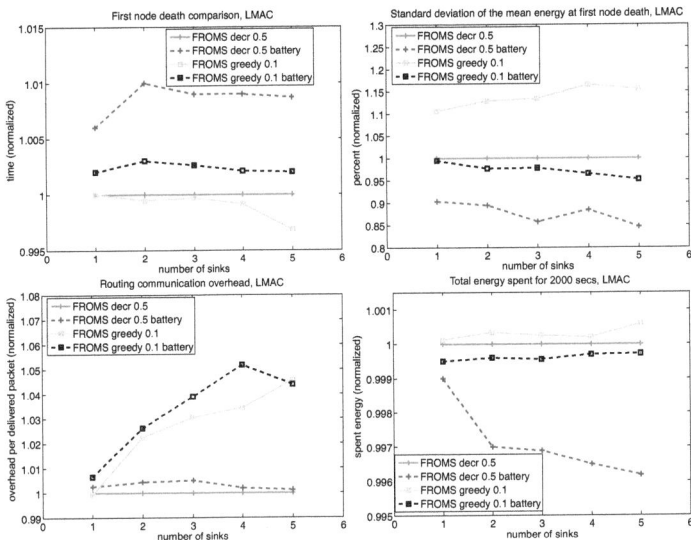

Figure 5.11. Comparison for two different exploration strategies of FROMS with *hop-based cost* and *hop-battery based cost*. All experiments performed with LMAC.

---

nature of the cost function: on one side, it uses nodes more uniformly and this can be observed in the standard deviations of remaining energies at the nodes from the top right graph. In fact, the hop-battery cost functions decreases the standard deviation of the remaining energies by 10-15%. However, at the same time FROMS is forced to use longer routes and the routing overhead increases (bottom left graph). These two effects combine into a slightly increased lifetime and slightly decreased spent energy, but the difference to the hop-based cost metric is only insignificant.

Our previous study in a less realistic simulation environment (MATLAB) in [64] showed different results. In that study we achieved a significantly longer network lifetime (by nearly 80%) because the nodes in the network were used more uniformly for routing. However, in a more realistic wireless simulation with a real implementation of a MAC protocol, overhearing of packets among neighbors cannot be avoided and spends a lot of energy. Even when switching to alternative routes with higher batteries, the hop-battery cost function selects routes near to the last used ones, thus further draining the batteries of the nodes. An extreme example are the direct neighbors of the source: whatever route is taken to the sinks, the neighbors of the source always overhear the packets and drain their batteries. In fact, we discovered that usually either the source itself, neighbors of the source, or direct neighbors of the sinks are the first to die.

However, battery-hop cost functions are a good solution when the data delivery task to the sinks is short. In such cases, the cost function is able to spread the usage of the nodes more uniformly, thus avoiding building low-battery bottlenecks in the network.

The result presented here could change if a multicast MAC protocol for WSNs is used. To the best of our knowledge, there is no such protocol for WSNs and it is also appears non-trivial to develop. The expected gain of such a protocol would be two-fold: compared to unicast MAC protocols, it would be able to send a single packet for many simultaneous receivers; and compared to broadcast MAC protocols it would save energy from overhearing of packets at non-receiving nodes. However, a real world implementation of a multicast MAC protocol could prove to be either impossible or not worth the gain, since some minimal overhearing is always necessary and synchronization/agreement among nodes is costly too.

In respect to the FROMS cost functions presented here, such a multicast MAC protocol might change the above presented results and prolong the lifetime of the network significantly, for example comparable with our MATLAB perfect communication simulations [64]. However, such a protocol would also force another change in the feedback mechanism of FROMS. In this thesis we assume a broadcast MAC protocol, which delivers all packets to all neighbors. Thus, delivering of feedback does not incur any communication overhead. Additionally, feedback can be delivered to all neighbors, not only to the previous hop. A multicast MAC protocol would force FROMS to identify clearly the receiver of the feedback, otherwise we will loose the advantage of using a multicast MAC protocol.

However, since such a MAC protocol does not exist currently for WSNs and, as discussed above, its implementation is rather questionable, we do not explore this question further.

5.6 Comparative evaluation of FROMS

As already proposed in Section 4.2.4, we compare the performance of FROMS against three other state-of-the-art routing protocols. We explore all of the routing protocols in terms of their routing overhead, network lifetime, standard deviation of the remaining energy on the nodes, and total spent energy in various network scenarios, including mobile sinks and node failures. We use the simulation and hardware environments as described in Section 4.2.4 and detailed in Section 5.5. The routing protocols used in our comparative study are:

1. MSTEAM [66] is a recent state-of-the-art geographic multicast routing protocol. The comparison between MSTEAM and FROMS is especially interesting and challenging, as they require different available information on the nodes to achieve the same goal. Thus, also a general performance comparison between hop-based and geographic based protocols is presented. We use the same application layer and sink announcement broadcasts for both FROMS and MSTEAM. They have several advantages against the typical pre-known set of sink coordinates, used by many geographic-based protocols. First, it replaces the use of beacons for discovering and maintaining neighbors and, second, it enables recovery and mobility, which are not covered by the original version of the protocol. Two versions of MSTEAM are evaluated: the original MSTEAM uses cost over progress to sinks metric to evaluate possible next hops, where the cost is a function of the geographic distance between the nodes. We also implemented a simplified version, called MSTEAM-CONST, where the cost is always 1 and thus only the progress to the sinks is considered.

2. UNICAST DIRECTED DIFFUSION (UDD) [170] is a well known, simple, and efficient routing paradigm, where each of the nodes builds gradients towards the sinks. We label this version of Directed Diffusion "unicast" (or UDD for short), since we consider the original one-phase pull version of the protocol, as opposed to MULTICAST DIRECTED DIFFUSION (or MDD), as explained next.

3. MULTICAST DIRECTED DIFFUSION (MDD) is a multicast-optimized variation of UDD of our own design [220]. It is searching locally on the nodes for shared paths for multiple sinks. It can be considered a simplified version of greedy-FROMS, which keeps only the best hops to individual sinks, does not explore, and the cost function is based on hops only. However, it does not incorporate the learning mechanism of FROMS, nor it is able to find the globally optimal path unless by chance.

5.6.1 Multi-source multi-sink routing (simulation)

In this section we make an extensive scalability analysis and comparison between FROMS, MSTEAM, MDD and UDD, as outlined in Section 4.2.4. Similar to the stand-alone evaluation of FROMS in the previous Section 5.5 we fix all network parameters except for one and give mean results over 50 different connected random topologies with 5 random runs each. Figure 5.12 presents the obtained results for different number of sinks (top), number of sources (middle) and number of nodes (bottom) while using BMAC as MAC layer protocol. The achieved results with LMAC were very similar and thus graphs are omitted. The first point of FROMS (e.g. one sink, one source or 50 nodes) is used as the point of normalization. Unlike the experiments for the stand-alone evaluation of FROMS in Section 5.5, here we are interested in the scalability analysis and comparison of all routing protocols. Thus, we need to use only a single point for normalizing the results and not a full line. Thus, we obtain scalability analysis and comparative analysis at the same time.

Coming back to Figure 5.12, with increasing number of sinks, all protocols have shorter network lifetimes (faster first node death). However, FROMS

5.6 Comparative evaluation of FROMS

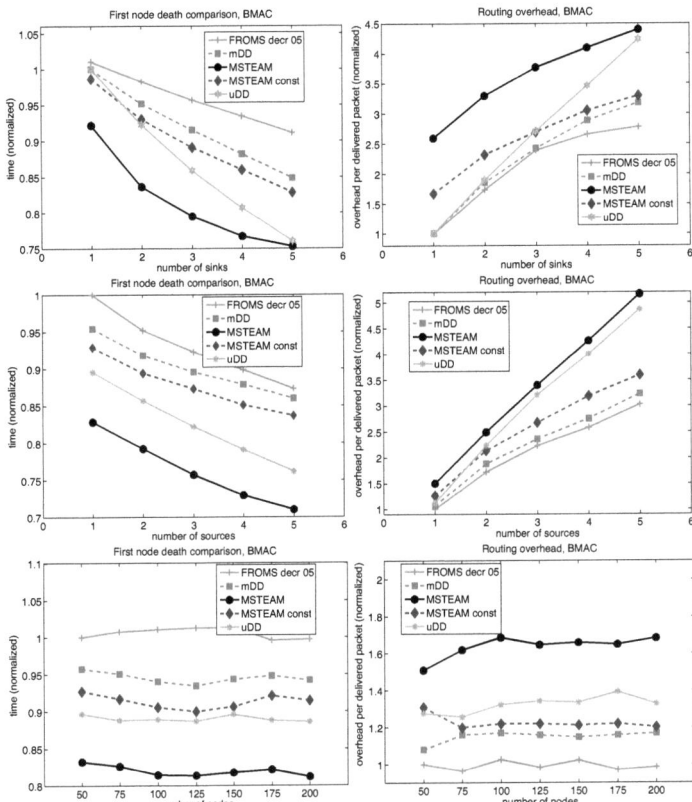

Figure 5.12. Evaluation of routing protocols in terms of first node death and routing overhead, 50 different topologies, 5 runs each; the network consists of (top) 50 nodes, 1 source and 1-5 sinks; (middle) 50 nodes, 1-5 sources and 3 sinks and (bottom) 50-200 nodes, 1 source and 3 sinks. All experiments performed with BMAC.

achieves the best network lifetimes compared to the other protocols. This is due to two reasons: its ability to find optimal multicast routes and the limited use of broadcast sink announcements. The longer lifetimes of FROMS compared to MDD are also due to these reasons. However, it is interesting to note that MSTEAM (both variations) achieve network lifetimes well below MDD and FROMS. In fact, MSTEAM-CONST (where the cost of sending a packet between two nodes is considered to be constant) performs much better than the original MSTEAM protocol. This is due to the fixed transmission power of the simulated nodes (which is often also the case in real hardware). The original MSTEAM protocol uses a special cost function, which increases the cost of sending a packet with increasing distance between the nodes. This cost function is based on geographic distance rather than taken from real experimental data and thus forces the protocol to take more, shorter hops instead of less long hops.

FROMS clearly outperforms any of the protocols in this comparative analysis in terms of network lifetime and achieved routing overhead per packet (see again Figure 5.12 top), but especially the geographic-based protocol MSTEAM. The reason for this is the so-called face routing in geographic protocols, which handles void areas (nodes with no progress against the sinks). In these cases, the packet is sent back and follows a predefined route over a "face" until reaching again a node with some positive progress towards the sinks. However, this face route is possibly very long. Second, and more importantly, the exact same route will be taken for each packet, including the sending back of the packet. This incurs excessive and unneeded routing overhead, where reinforcement learning will avoid the repetitive sending to void nodes and back.

The same observations can also be made for varying number of sources in Figure 5.12 (middle). There, all protocols have shorter network lifetimes and more routing overhead for increasing number of sources. The comparative analysis shows similar results as for varying number of sinks. In contrast, Figure 5.12 (bottom) shows the good scalability of all protocols when varying the number of nodes (the density of the network is constant). This is due to the localized nature of all protocols, which are independent of the size of the network. The comparative analysis, therefore, shows exactly the same trend as before.

5.6 Comparative evaluation of FROMS

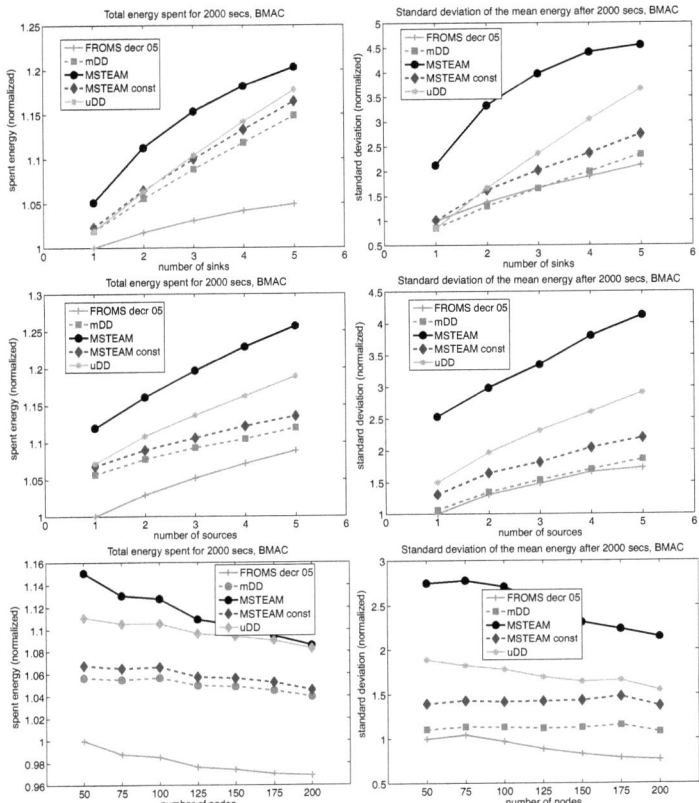

Figure 5.13. Evaluation of routing protocols in terms of total spent energy and standard deviation of remaining energy after the first 2000 seconds, 50 different topologies, 5 runs each; the network consists of (top) 50 nodes, 1 source and 1-5 sinks; (middle) 50 nodes, 1-5 sources and 3 sinks and (bottom) 50-200 nodes, 1 source and 3 sinks. All experiments performed with BMAC.

Besides network lifetimes and routing overhead, we have also measured the total energy spent for the first 2000 seconds of the network lifetime and the standard deviation of the remaining batteries at all nodes at this time. The results are presented in Figure 5.13. Less energy expenditure is an indicator of less routing overhead and little standard deviation of the remaining batteries at the nodes indicates that nodes are used more uniformly instead of taking always the same route and draining the batteries on the affected nodes faster. In this experiment we again vary the number of sinks (5.13 top), the number of sources (middle) and the number of nodes (bottom). The results for energy expenditure are analogous to the network lifetimes obtained in Figure 5.12. The standard deviations of the remaining batteries show similar comparative results: FROMS achieves the least deviation through its explorative nature and controlled switching between routes with the same costs, thus spreading the energy expenditure throughout the nodes. MDD achieves similar results, since it also makes use of the route switching in case of same route costs. In contrast, UDD uses always exactly one route. This is the reason why its standard deviation is higher than for FROMS and MDD. Additionally, it sends unicast packets to its neighbors, which further drains the batteries on the routes. MSTEAM-CONST, on the other hand, uses also exactly one route, but for shorter routes it drains the batteries more uniformly than the original MSTEAM.

In summary, FROMS achieves between 10 and 22% longer network lifetimes in terms of first node death, around 2 times less routing overhead, between 5 and 15 % less spent energy and 2 to 3 times less standard deviation of the remaining energies against the other compared routing protocols. The second best protocol in terms of these metrics is MDD, which is a hop-based multicast improvement of directed diffusion. Next comes the constant-cost variation MSTEAM-CONST, then UDD and then the original MSTEAM protocol.

Last, we present a comparison of all routing protocols over BMAC and LMAC, see Figure 5.14. This comparison is not intended as an evaluation of the MAC protocols in use. Its goal is rather to show the importance of cross-layer design between routing and MAC protocols. In fact, LMAC achieves longer network lifetime (by 20-25%) and lower energy expenditure (by 20-25%) against BMAC

5.6 Comparative evaluation of FROMS

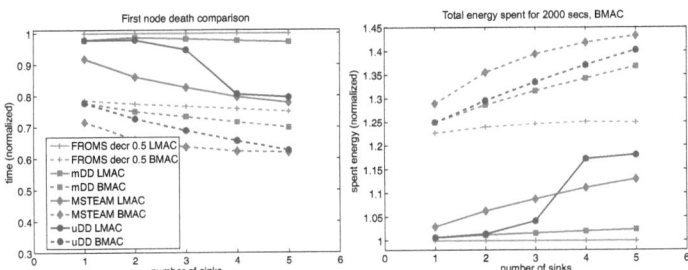

Figure 5.14. Joint comparison of routing protocols with LMAC and BMAC.

in the network scenarios which we explored. Thus, in our scenarios LMAC is the better choice. However, this evaluation will probably change with different data rates in the network and another choice of a MAC protocol might be necessary.

5.6.2 Multi-source multi-sink routing (hardware testbed)

Next, we compare the performance of FROMS and MDD on real hardware (see Section 4.2.4) in terms of delivery rate and routing costs. Figure 5.15 summarizes the results for several network configurations. As expected from our simulation experiments and theoretical analysis, FROMS achieves lower routing costs. This can be attributed to its learning algorithm which actively explores the network for optimal routes. We also compare the performance against the theoretically optimal cost of the Steiner tree.

In simulation we are unable to evaluate an accurate delivery rate since transmission failures cannot be reliably simulated. Here, instead, we confirm our theoretical expectation that FROMS is able to achieve higher delivery rates in any network scenario. Data is lost in MDD mainly due to the higher in-network communication caused by the periodic sink announcements (see Section 4.2.4) and the longer routes to the sinks. This increases the traffic and collision probability leading to packet losses. Figure 5.15 supports these observations, showing that the delivery rate of both protocols clearly drops in networks with larger numbers

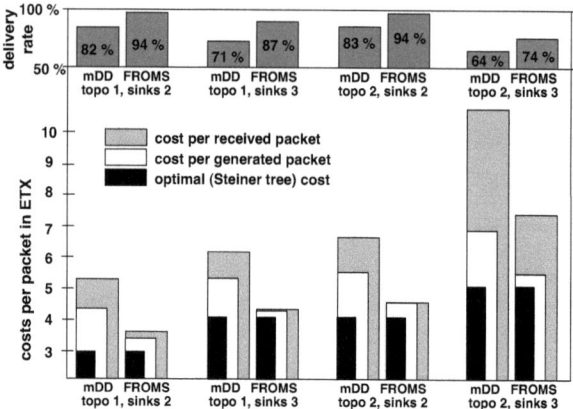

Figure 5.15. Routing costs and delivery rates for FROMS and MDD in various network scenarios.

of nodes and sinks.

Figure 5.16 presents the results when using transmission backoff, clearly showing that the technique is highly effective at improving delivery rates. We implemented a simple algorithm in which a parameter (in our case 0, 1 or 100 ms) is multiplied with the node's ID and this delay is applied before forwarding any packet. This backoff reduces packet collisions and thus increases successful delivery.

Another common mechanism to increase the delivery rate is to force packet acknowledgments. We use overhearing of DATA packets as implicit acknowledgments, avoiding additional costs. The incurred overhead stems from re-sending unacknowledged packets. Figure 5.17 shows how routing costs skyrocket, while the delivery rate also increase. Communication failures cause not only data loss, but also loss of acknowledgments. This results in resending packets which were actually received, but not acknowledged. Consequently, the communication traffic explodes, leading to even higher loss rates.

5.6 Comparative evaluation of FROMS

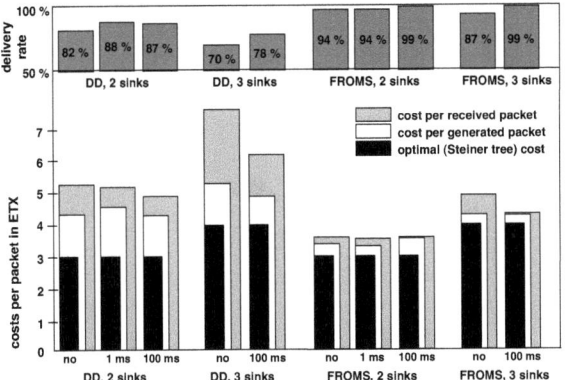

Figure 5.16. In-network performance when applying transmission backoff, results from topology 1.

5.6.3 Recovery after failure (simulation)

In this section we show the ability of the compared routing protocols (FROMS, MDD, UDD, and MSTEAM) to recover routes after node failures. We evaluate them under simulation. An important feature of FROMS is its ability to recover quickly after node failures. The protocol keeps track of which neighbors are responding and which are not, as explained in Section 5.6. In case some neighbor is not reachable any more, FROMS switches directly to the next best route. The new costs are propagated as feedback through the network and learned at all affected nodes.

We have designed a recovery experiment where all but a small set of nodes are given full battery levels. The small set of nodes is given only one third of the usual battery level and are thus expected to die quickly one after another. We consider this scenario more realistic compared to a controlled killing of nodes at some predefined time, since in real deployments nodes do not die simultaneously. The results of the experiment in terms of delivery rate achieved and total spent energy are given in Figure 5.18 for a set size of failed nodes between 2

5.6 Comparative evaluation of FROMS

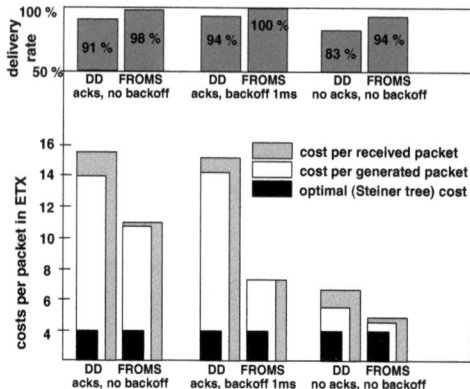

Figure 5.17. In-network performance when using acknowledgments, results from topology 2.

and 10 (approximately 4 – 20% of all nodes). Each point represents a mean over 50 different topologies, with 30 different random sets of failed nodes. Note that results are gathered only for connected topologies. In case failing of nodes actually disconnected the topology, the scenario was ignored. The achieved standard deviation of the experiments is around 2.3 – 3%.

FROMS achieves the highest delivery rate and the least energy spent. This is mainly due to the availability of alternative routes at each node and the feedback, which quickly propagates through the network, not only recovering routes but recovering the best ones. Similarly, MDD also monitors the neighborhood through the FROMS node failure detection module, and has alternative routes at the nodes. Its achieved delivery rate is 2-5% less than the one for FROMS, due to the learning behavior of FROMS. On the other side, MSTEAM (we tested here only the better performing constant cost variation of MSTEAM) uses much longer routes (see again Section 5.6), which incur more packet loss. Additionally, the neighborhood failure detection does not work as efficiently as for FROMS and MDD because MSTEAM uses exactly the same route over and over again. Thus,

5.6 Comparative evaluation of FROMS

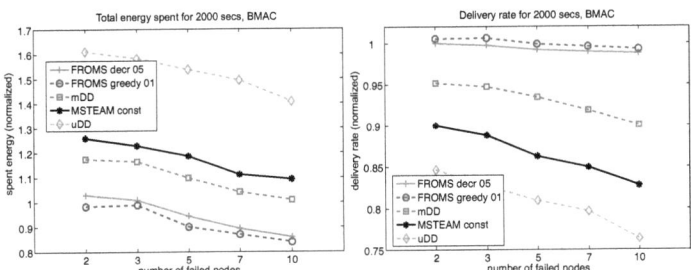

Figure 5.18. Comparison of delivery rate and spent energy for different routing protocols with varying number of failed nodes in the network.

in the case of failures of some nodes on a route, it will still be used until the failure detection module deletes the neighbor. Only then will an alternative be used, which might again have failed. In contrast, MDD and FROMS use same-cost alternative routes in a round-robin manner and thus spread the risk of taking a failed route. For UDD the scenario becomes even worse, since it relies on a single route which needs to be updated by sink announcements.

In terms of energy expenditure, FROMS ϵ-greedy performs the best, because of its continuous exploration. Instead of exploring only on demand, ϵ-greedy keeps track of all possible routes and updates their costs proactively. Thus, when a failure is detected, not only an alternative route is available, but its quality is up-to-date and the best possible route can be taken. Additional exploration and taking of non-optimal routes is avoided, delivery rate is increased because of shorter routes (Figure 5.18 right), and spent energy is minimized (Figure 5.18 left).

In summary, keeping alternative routes, using shortest possible routes, and keeping track of the real length of all available routes (not only of the shortest ones), is a good strategy to be able to recover quickly after failures.

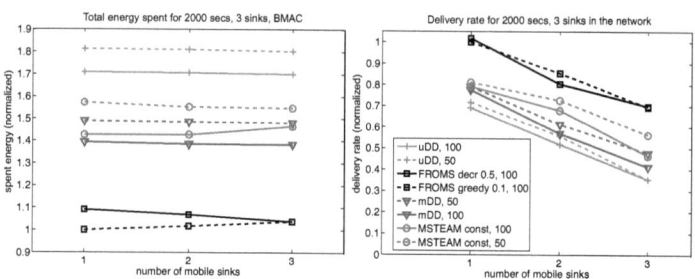

Figure 5.19. Evaluation of all routing protocols with various number of mobile sinks in the network.

5.6.4 Sink mobility (simulation)

For testing the performance of the routing protocols under scenarios with sink mobility, we designed two different experiments: one with different numbers of mobile sinks, and a second with different velocities of the mobile sinks. The experiments for both of them were conducted over 50 random topologies, with 10 random runs on each. We achieved a standard deviation of the results of $1.6 - 1.9\%$.

The results from the first experiment are presented in Figure 5.19. Here, we used a network size of 50 nodes, with 3 sinks and 1 source. We varied the number of mobile sinks from 1 to 3, leaving the rest of them static. The velocity of the mobile sinks is constant and is set to $1m/s$. We varied the sink announcement periods for MDD, UDD, and MSTEAM-CONST. The assumption is that refreshing the routes on the nodes more often would lead to better delivery rate and shorter routes in case of mobile sinks. This can be seen for all protocols in Figure 5.19 (right). In fact, the delivery rate compared to longer sink announcement periods increases slightly. However, this happens only at the cost of increasing data traffic and thus higher energy expenditure. Figure 5.19 (left) shows that energy expenditure increases non-proportionally to the achieved gain in delivery rate, and is thus not worth it.

In terms of energy expenditure (Figure 5.19 left), all protocols scale well with

5.6 Comparative evaluation of FROMS

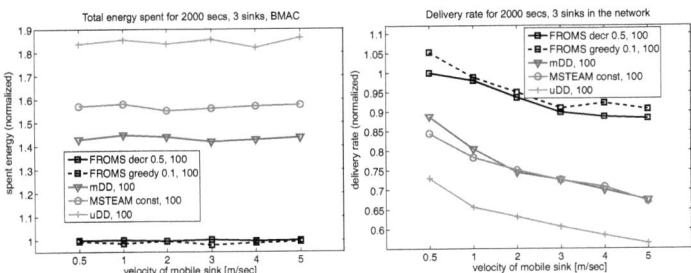

Figure 5.20. Evaluation of all routing protocols with various velocities of the mobile sinks in the network.

increasing number of mobile sinks. The reason for this is simple: the mobility of the sinks does not invoke any additional mechanisms, such as re-transmissions, which might influence the energy expenditure. However, it can be clearly seen that for all protocols the delivery rate drops with multiple mobile sinks (Figure 5.19 right). This is because the mobility affects the quality of the used links and some links disappear.

Comparing the routing protocols, FROMS has the least energy expenditure of all of them and still achieves the best delivery rates. This is again due to several factors: there are no regular retransmissions of sink announcements, data traffic is routed along shorter paths, and the learning mechanism keeps the routes up to date. As in our previous experiments, MDD and MSTEAM-CONST perform similarly well, while UDD spends the most energy and achieves the lowest delivery rate.

In our second experiment presented in Figure 5.20 we vary the velocity of the mobile sink. The network consists again of 50 random nodes, 1 source and 3 sinks. One sink is mobile and its velocity is $0.5m/s$ to $5m/s$, which corresponds to slow human walking ($2km/h$) through slow car driving ($20km/h$). We compare the routing protocols using normal sink announcement interval (every 100 secs) because the results of the previous experiment showed that the gain is negligible while the energy expenditure increases significantly with smaller intervals.

In terms of energy expenditure (Figure 5.20), the behavior of the routing protocols is the same as in the previous experiment. FROMS has a significantly lower energy expenditure than the others, followed by MDD, MSTEAM-CONST, and finally UDD. The reasons are the same as before.

The trend of the delivery rate in case of higher velocities is also as expected. It drops with higher velocities, less for FROMS and slightly more for the other protocols. The difference comes from the learning mechanism of FROMS, which not only substitutes the sink announcement re-broadcasts, but enables faster recovery of routes.

In summary, these experiments show clearly the innate ability of FROMS and its learning algorithm to quickly recover routes in case of mobile sinks, even for a moderate velocity of $20km/h$. Compared to the all other routing protocols, it spends significantly less energy, incurs less data traffic, and achieves considerably higher delivery rates.

5.7 Concluding remarks

In this chapter we presented our solution to the first of the identified problems, namely routing to multiple mobile sinks in a failure-prone wireless sensor network. We modeled and solved this complex routing problem with Q-Learning, and implemented a high performance reliable protocol called FROMS (**Feedback ROuting to Multiple Sinks**). We evaluated the protocol both analytically and experimentally, and showed an extensive discussion of its properties and parameters.

Most importantly, we showed that the protocol converges in finite number of steps, as opposed to the original Q-Learning algorithm which is guaranteed to converge after infinite number of steps. We also discovered that we can minimize exploration of non-optimal routes by applying a dynamic cost function, which itself *implicitly* explores the network.

The experimental evaluation of FROMS in simulation and on a real hardware testbed showed its superior performance over three state-of-the-art routing protocols in terms of delivery rate, network lifetime, energy expenditure, and in-

5.7 Concluding remarks

curred communication overhead. Most importantly, we clearly showed its applicability for real world scenarios and problems by implementing the protocol on a highly memory-restricted sensor platform.

Considering our goals identified in Chapter 2, we have fully met the requirements of our target application scenario. FROMS is able to handle failure-prone, multicast routing to possibly mobile sinks, scales very well with the number of sinks, sources, and growing size of the networks. The results achieved in this chapter are highly satisfying and fully support our intuition and initial study for using reinforcement learning for solving the challenges of our target application scenario. Thus, in the next chapter we proceed with the solution of the second problem, low overhead, non-uniform clustering for WSN.

Chapter 6

CLIQUE: Role-free Clustering for WSNs

The solution path to the target scenario as identified in Chapter 4 divides the problem into two main parts: first, organizing the nodes of the network into clusters and gathering the information of each cluster to its corresponding cluster head; and second routing the aggregated cluster data from the cluster heads to all sinks in the network. While Chapter 5 provides a solution to the routing problem, this chapter concentrates on the clustering problem: identifying the clusters, the cluster members and the cluster heads and gathering the data on the cluster heads.

While the general approach of clustering is seemingly simple and straightforward, efficiently achieving it involves solving five challenging problems. First, the clusters themselves must be identified. Second, the cluster heads must be identified. Third, routes from all nodes to their cluster head must be discovered. Fourth, the cluster heads must aggregate the received data. And finally, the cluster heads must efficiently route the aggregated data to the sink(s). This chapter focuses on the first three problems, using existing works to cover the last two.

The first problem, identifying the clusters, is specific to the application domain. Some solutions generate random clusters [149], others focus on semantically formed clusters, such as grouping all sensors in a geographic area [213] or those with similar data independent of sensor location [190]. We use the target scenario as described in Chapter 2 and define the clusters to be groups of nodes in geographic proximity to each other. The clusters are rectangular areas of variable size. An example of such a clustering scenario is a grid, overlaid on the network with clusters as grid cells as shown in Figure 6.1(a). However, any other shape of the clusters are also possible, for example hexagons. The clusters can also be pre-defined, like rooms or floors in a building. Additionally, we allow for non-uniform clustering as required by our target scenario, where the size of the grid's cells grow with increasing distance from some special points of interest (Figure 6.1 b).

Data aggregation, the fourth clustering challenge, is performed by the cluster heads to pre-process the data before forwarding it to the base stations. It is highly dependent on the type of the data and the application requirements. The aggregation methods are out of scope of this thesis. However, we assume that aggregation is possible and can be performed on any node of the network with minimal processing requirements and no communication overhead. Additionally, we allow for both tree-aggregation and cluster head central aggregation (see Section 3.2.8 and [41]).

Regarding the last problem, routing data from the cluster heads to the sinks, some approaches assume cluster heads communicate directly with the base station, e.g., by boosting transmission power. Such an approach places high energy demands on the cluster heads, and makes unrealistic assumptions about the network size or the position of the sink. Instead, we assume multi-hop communication between the cluster heads and the sinks. Any routing approach can be chosen and all nodes in the network are used for routing. Here, we employ our own multicast protocol FROMS, developed and evaluated in the previous chapter. This choice allows us to take advantage of cross-layer optimization between FROMS and the work presented here.

This chapter proceeds as follows: Section 6.1 describes the algorithm for organizing the nodes into clusters: both for uniform and non-uniform clustering. Section 6.2 presents the learning algorithm for finding the best cluster heads and the intra-cluster routes. Section 6.3 gives an extensive evaluation of CLIQUE in different uniform and non-uniform scenarios. Finally, Section 6.5 discusses the

6.1 Grid-based cluster membership computation

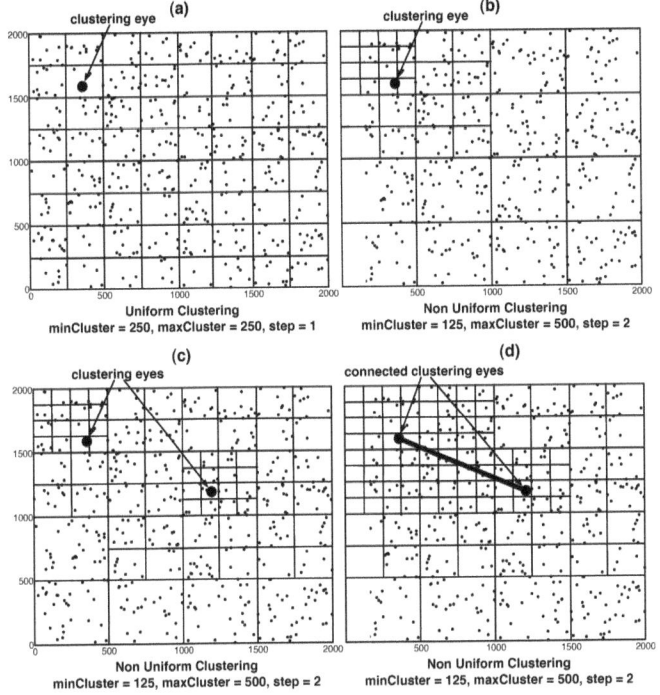

Figure 6.1. Uniform (a) and non-uniform (b-d) clustering scenarios.

achieved results and properties of CLIQUE and its application areas.

6.1 Grid-based cluster membership computation

One of the main goals of our clustering approach is to allow for non-uniform sizes of clusters. We assume that the size of the clusters is increasing with growing distance between the cluster and some special point of interest, which we call *eye*. Around the eye the clusters have some minimum required size and further away the size grows until reaching some maximum allowed size. The

6.1 Grid-based cluster membership computation

Parameter	Description
eyeCoord1	The coordinates of the 1st eye
eyeCoord2	The coordinates of the 2nd eye
maxCluster	The size of the largest cluster
minCluster	The size of the smallest cluster
stepCluster	The growing step of the clusters

Figure 6.2. Clustering parameters (left) and cluster IDs (right)

eyes can be any points in the network: they could be a rescue worker's current coordinates (sink's coordinates) in a disaster relief scenario, the worker's future target position etc. The combination of the given parameters (the eye's coordinates, the minimum and the maximum size of clusters, see Figure 6.2 left) allow for any non-uniform scenario based on distance. Examples of a non-uniformly clustered network are given in Figure 6.1(b-d). The network is divided into square-shaped clusters with *maxCluster* size of 500 meters and *minCluster* size of 125 meters directly around the eye(s). For comparison, Figure 6.1(a) shows a uniform scenario with a cluster size of 250 meters.

Identifying the cluster to which the node belongs simply means computing its cluster ID. The goal of this computation is to be able to identify which neighbors belong to the same cluster and which do not. The IDs of the clusters are defined as follows. First, the grid is divided into the maximum sized clusters. If the requirements of the sinks for the size of the maximum cluster are different, the smallest is taken. Each of these top-level clusters receives a unique global ID. For example, the clusters in Figure 6.1(b) can be numbered 1 : 16. Note that we take square networks as examples for simplicity, but the ID computation approach can handle any sizes or shapes for the network and the clusters.

For achieving non-uniformity, we need to divide some of the top-level clusters into smaller ones. We always divide a bigger cluster into 4 equally sized smaller clusters. However, any other equal-division is also possible: into 9, 16, etc. The smaller clusters are then assigned local IDs from 1 : 4 and the full ID of the

6.1 Grid-based cluster membership computation

cluster becomes for example {17 − 3} for top-level cluster 17 inner cluster 3. These scheme can be continued iteratively for any sub-division of clusters, for example {17 − 3 − 1}, {17 − 3 − 1 − 2}, etc. Figure 6.2 gives an example. Thus, there is a unique ID for each cluster in the network and the size of the cluster can be derived from the number of levels in the ID.

Clustering parameters include the coordinates of the eye(s), the minimum and maximum cluster sizes and the growing step. They are summarized in Figure 6.2 (left). Each sink defines its own clustering parameters and includes them into its data request packet (sink announcement). Thus, each node in the network receives the clustering parameters of each of the sinks. At each node, the parameters of all sinks need to be combined to achieve the same clustering in the whole network. We assume that sinks compute their parameters according to their minimum data requirements and thus the finest clustering (smallest clustering) is taken to meet all sinks' requirements. The cluster ID computation algorithm works as follows: first, the grid is divided into clusters with the maximum required size. Then, the cluster of the eye and the own cluster are identified and the distance between them is computed in number of clusters. If the distance is 0 (the node and the eye are in the same top-level cluster), the *minCluster* is applied. With each step further away from the eye, the *minCluster* is multiplied by *stepCluster* to identify the size of the cluster. For example, with *stepCluster* = 2, the resulting clustering is presented in Figure 6.1(b). With smaller steps, the cluster sizes will grow slower.

In case of two eyes (sinks) as in Figure 6.1(c), the cluster ID according to each of the eyes will be calculated separately and then the smaller sized-cluster will be taken. Many other scenarios are possible. For example, in Figure 6.1(d) we can require a second eye per sink to be connected with the first one and the minimum sized clusters to be applied to the region between the two eyes.

Note that the computation of the cluster ID is simple, takes only $O(1)$ steps to complete at each node and needs only to be recalculated with new data requests arriving at the node - e.g. in case the sink has new clustering requirements or has moved out of its top-level cluster (see Section 6.2.2 on mobility). The computation relies only on data available at the node directly (its own coordinates) and on data in the data request.

Other clustering scenarios. The main property of the presented cluster membership algorithm is its non-uniformity. However, it presents also a simple way of computing uniform clusters in a distributed manner by setting *minCluster* = *maxCluster* or *stepCluster* = 1. Next we present the cluster head learning algorithm which depends on *some* already available cluster membership information on the nodes: the presented non-uniform or uniform one or any other clustering which associates each node in the network with a cluster ID can be used. An example for such an alternative is a-priori floor or room information on the nodes.

6.2 Finding the cluster head with Q-Learning

Clustering and aggregation in WSNs is typically performed in two steps: first, clusters are identified, and second, cluster head roles are assigned to usually a single node in the cluster. Sometimes this scenario is reversed: the cluster head roles are first assigned, then nodes join the nearest cluster head, thus forming clusters. Nevertheless, in both scenarios the nodes need to agree on the cluster heads and to find routes to them.

In contrast, here we propose a cluster head assignment algorithm, where the nodes do not need to know the identities of the cluster heads. Given knowledge about their cluster identifier and basic information about their one-hop neighbors, each node tries to route its data directly to *all* sinks in the network while taking the simple decision of whether to act as a cluster head and aggregate data or whether to route the incoming data to a neighbor better suited for this role. The algorithm is fully distributed and localized.

While straightforward to explain, one major challenge remains: **how do nodes evaluate their neighbors to decide both the next hop and whether or not to act as a cluster head**? To address this, we observe that sinks flood the network with DATA_REQ packets, with the result that each node knows some routing information regarding each *individual* sink in terms of parameters such as hop count, geographic progress, or battery status. However, our challenge is

6.2 Finding the cluster head with Q-Learning

to route to multiple sinks, by first routing to the cluster heads most appropriate for each cluster. Therefore, each node must combine the single-sink routing information to identify the cost to route to multiple sinks *and* to decide whether or not to act as the cluster head. Unfortunately, the local information from the DATA_REQ packets provides only an approximate, upper-bound on the cost, and does not take into account the real multicast cost to the sinks. Therefore, a node can only approximate the total routing costs, and further can only make a best estimate about whether or not to serve as a cluster head.

To improve the localized cost estimates, we employ Q-Learning, incrementally learning the real globally valid costs to all sinks through the best cluster head. Additional information is gathered by exchanging feedback among neighbors while routing data packets. We calculate the routing cost using a combination of hop counts to reach the sinks (through the cluster heads) and battery status of the nodes on the routes to the sinks. Note that the data is always routed first to the cluster head where it is aggregated. Only after this point can it be duplicated to follow multiple paths to the sinks. Such splitting before aggregation would result in multiple cluster heads, aggregating data for each of the sinks and increasing significantly the communication overhead both for routing to the cluster heads and to the sinks.

Q-Learning was already introduced in Chapter 4.1. In our clusterhead routing scenario, each sensor node is an independent learning agent, and actions are routing options using different neighbors for the next hop toward the clusterhead. *The clusterhead is defined as the node in the cluster with the best (lowest) routing cost to all sinks.* The following provides additional detail for the Q-Learning solution.

Agent states. The state of an agent is a tuple $\{D, cost_D^{N+self}\}$, where D is the set of all sinks in the network and $cost_D^{N+self}$ is the routing cost to all sinks through all neighboring nodes N, plus the routing costs to the sinks at the node itself. Depending on this value, different actions are possible.

Actions. An action identifies the next hop to the cluster head. This could be a neighbor or the node itself if it is acting as cluster head and aggregating packets. Specifically, we define a possible action as $a_{n_i} = (n_i, D)$ with $i \in \{N, self\}$. In case the next hop is the node itself, the packet is buffered for some predefined time, all buffered packets are aggregated and sent to the sinks using the routing layer.

Q-Values. Q-Values represent the goodness of actions and the goal of the agent is to learn the *actual* goodness of the available actions. In our case, Q-Values represent an estimate of the cost of the neighbor, specifically the broadcast hop count to reach all sinks from the agent and the minimum battery level of the nodes on the route to the sinks through this neighbor. The first part of the cost function accounts for energy efficiency and minimizing communication overhead. The second, the minimum battery of the nodes, is necessary to avoid very low powered nodes. The two elements of the cost function are united with a *hop count multiplier (hcm)* value, which grows exponentially for decreasing battery levels, identical with the one designed for FROMS in Section 5.4.8. This means that when the batteries of the nodes are full, the routing cost of a neighbor is exactly the number of hops to reach the sinks; while with decreasing batteries this cost exponentially grows, giving preference to higher powered nodes on possibly longer routes.

To initialize these values, we could use random values, as is common in many learning approaches. However, we turn again to a more sophisticated approach that calculates an estimate of the hop count cost based on the individual hop counts available in a standard routing table, as described above, thus speeding up the learning process.

The initial Q-Value for an action $a_{n_i} = (n_i, D)$ is:

$$\begin{aligned} Q(a_{n_i}) &= Q_{hops}(a_{n_i}) \cdot Q_{battery}(a_{n_i}) \\ &= \sum_{d \in D} hops_d^{n_i} \cdot hcm(bat_{n_i}) \end{aligned} \quad (6.1)$$

where $hops_d^{n_i}$ is the number of hops neighbor n_i needs to reach sink d. The initial value of the battery element is initialized with the battery status of neighbor n_i. Note that the hop-count estimation is an *upper bound* of the real costs, because next hops are expected to be able to share routes to multiple sinks, decreasing the number of hops needed to reach the sinks. On the other hand, the

6.2 Finding the cluster head with Q-Learning

battery element is expected to decrease, because battery levels decrease. Thus, the Q-Values are expected first to drop, reflecting the learning of the real hop costs to reach the sinks, and then to slowly and constantly increase because of depleting energy on the nodes.

Updating a Q-Value. To learn the real values of the actions, the agent must receive the reward values from the environment. In our case, each neighbor to which a data packet is forwarded sends the reward piggybacked with the next data packet with its own best Q-Value. The new Q-Value of the action is:

$$Q_{new}(a_{n_i}) = Q_{old}(a_{n_i}) + \gamma(R(a_{n_i}) - Q_{old}(a_{n_i})) \tag{6.2}$$

where $R(a_{n_i})$ is the reward value and γ is the learning rate of the algorithm. We use $\gamma = 1$ to speed up learning and because we initialize the Q-Values with non-random values. Therefore, with $\gamma = 1$, the formula becomes

$$Q_{new}(a_{n_i}) = R(a_{n_i}) \tag{6.3}$$

directly updating the Q-Value with the reward.

Reward function. Intuitively the reward function is the downstream node's opportunity to inform the upstream neighbors of its actual cost for the requested action. Thus, when calculating the reward, the node selects its *lowest Q-Value* for the destination set and adds the cost of the action itself:

$$R(a_{n_i}) = c_{a_{n_i}} + \min_{n_i \in N} Q(a_{n_i}) \tag{6.4}$$

This propagation of Q-Values upstream is piggybacked on usual DATA packets and eventually allows all nodes to learn the actual costs.

Exploration strategy (action selection policy). One final, important learning parameter is the action selection policy. A trivial solution is to greedily select the action with the best (lowest) Q-Value. However, this policy ignores some actions which may, after learning, have lower Q-Values, resulting in a locally optimal solution. Therefore, a tradeoff is required between exploitation of good routes and exploration among available routes. Here we choose the standard

158 6.2 Finding the cluster head with Q-Learning

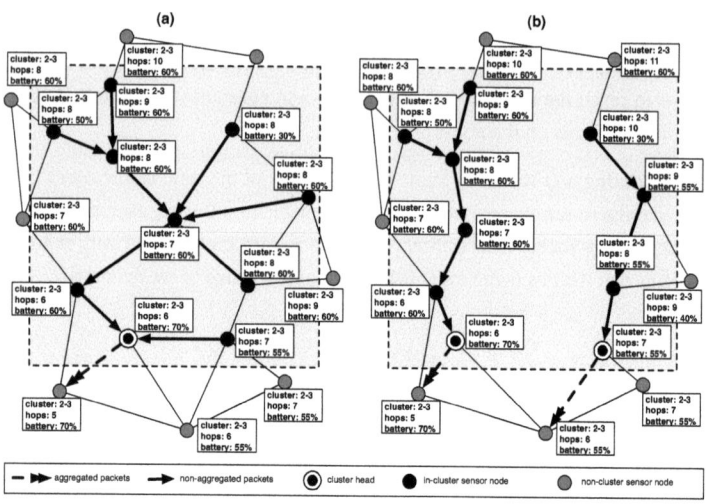

Figure 6.3. Learned cluster head in a connected scenario (a), and in a disconnected scenario (b). Data gathering and aggregation is shown only inside the cluster.

ϵ-*greedy strategy* (see Chapter 4.1), which selects a random route with probability ϵ and the best route otherwise. However, ϵ can be very low, as our study on dynamic cost functions for FROMS in Section 5.4.8 showed. This is because the changing costs of the routes force the protocol to switch to other, less costly routes, thus also learning their real costs and *implicitly* exploring routes.

6.2.1 Discussion of key properties and convergence of CLIQUE

The most important property of CLIQUE is its role-free nature. In contrast to most clustering algorithms, it does not try to find the optimal cluster head (in terms of cost) and to inform cluster members about it, but incrementally *learns* the best behavior without knowing where and who the real cluster heads are. As a result, especially at the beginning of the protocol, multiple nodes in the cluster may act

6.2 Finding the cluster head with Q-Learning

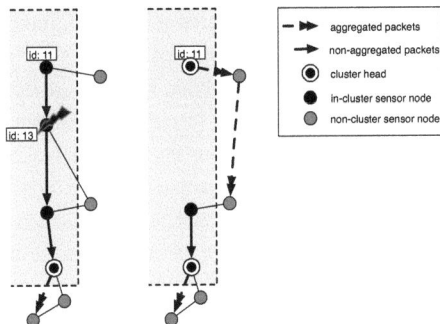

Figure 6.4. Recovery after node failure and new cluster heads.

as cluster heads. While this temporarily increases the overhead, this is a short-term tradeoff in comparison to the regular communication overhead required to agree on a single cluster head. Later in the protocol operation, after the real costs have been learned, multiple cluster heads can be seen only in disconnected clusters, where a single cluster head cannot serve all cluster members.

Even in case of a connected cluster in which two nodes have exactly the same routing costs and are *not* neighbors, there will exist a node in this cluster who needs to take the decision to which of the two possible cluster heads to route the data. If both options have exactly the same routing costs, which means that also the routes to them have the same costs, a simple ID-resolving process will decide on one of the options. If the routes to both possible cluster heads have different costs (e.g. there is a depleted node on the way to one of them), then the data will be routed automatically to the cluster head with lower cost route. This intuitively argues that CLIQUE *converges* to a single cluster head (if and only if the cluster is connected). However, convergence cannot be defined for CLIQUE in the usual way because of the used dynamic cost function. As we already showed for FROMS in Section 5.4.8, a dynamic cost function as the residual energy based one for CLIQUE, forces the protocol to switch to alternative routes while residual energy on the nodes decreases. Thus, there is no real "stable" phase of CLIQUE, where exactly the same optimal route is taken. Instead, routes are alternated to spread the communication load. In this sense, convergence to a single route or a single cluster head is not desired. What we are more interested in is the total incurred communication overhead in the network, both from clustering and routing. We will evaluate it experimentally in the next Section 6.3.

Figure 6.3 shows some cluster head learning scenarios. Scenario (a) presents a single cluster, where all nodes within the cluster are connected. The optimal cluster head lies in the lower left corner of the cluster because all sinks lie in this direction. A more problematic scenario is presented in Figure 6.3 (b), where the cluster is disconnected. Such a scenario is challenging for traditional clustering approaches: they need a complicated recovery mechanism which requires large control overhead. On the contrary, CLIQUE automatically identifies two cluster heads, as shown in the figure.

A recovery scenario is shown in Figure 6.4, in which node 13 fails. Node 11 is no longer able to send its data to the cluster head and needs to find a recovery solution. However, instead of searching for a new route to the cluster head it simply becomes a cluster head itself. Again, because of its learning properties and awareness of the network status, no control overhead is required for this.

It is also worth noting that CLIQUE is a reactive protocol: it only learns the optimal cluster heads when data traffic is flowing. In case some part of the network remains silent, it will not spend any energy on learning or clustering there. Note also that after aggregation, the packet is routed to the sink via the routing protocol, which is allowed to use any nodes in the network.

6.2.2 Sink mobility

Our CLIQUE clustering algorithm also handles sink mobility. In case the destinations move, they need to re-broadcast their data requests to all nodes in the network so that they can update their routing information. However, when we combine CLIQUE with FROMS, the full-network broadcasts can be avoided. They are compensated by the feedback (reward) mechanism, which updates the Q-Values at all nodes while forwarding sensory data to the destinations. Thus, the sinks need to broadcast their data request only one hop to their immediate

6.3 Comparative evaluation of CLIQUE

Layer	Protocol/ model	Parameters
Application	CLIQUE TRC	**data rate**: every 2 sec **sink announcement**: every 100 sec **wait before aggregate**: 200 msec **clusterhead round (TRC)**: 200 sec
Routing	FROMS	**expl. strategy**: ϵ - greedy, $\epsilon = 0.1$
Medium access	CSMA	not persistent, no ACKs
Energy expenditure	Linear battery (MICA-2)	**SLEEP**: 0.054 mW **RX**: 66 mW **TX**: 117 mW
Radio propagation	1-Nakagami	-

Table 6.1. Summary of simulation environment models and their parameters for our experiments with CLIQUE.

neighbors and update the routes there. The learning and reward mechanism will update the routes on all interested nodes.

This requirement changes in case of non-uniform clustering. Here, if the clustering eye moves away from its top-level cluster (refer back to Section 6.1) all nodes in the network need to be informed about the new clustering scenario. However, the spreading of the new data requests can be further limited by the nodes in the network: if the new data request in fact changes the cluster ID on the node, then re-broadcast it; if not, there is no need of re-broadcasting it. Thus, the data requests will be sent only to nodes which need to change their cluster membership, all others will be uninformed about the new eye's position.

In case of non-uniform clustering, it is important to stress the difference between eyes and sinks: when the eyes move and the sinks do not, only the clustering layer needs to be updated. On the contrary, if the sinks move and the eyes do not, the routing layer needs to be updated. In case both are moving, both layers need an update.

6.3 Comparative evaluation of CLIQUE

In this section we perform extensive simulation experiments with CLIQUE to validate our ideas and theoretical discussions from Section 6.2.1. We use a simulation evaluation environment as identified in Section 4.2.4 based on OMNeT++ and the Mobility Framework. All parameters and models, as used in this section are summarized in Table 6.1. The main difference of this experimental environment compared to the one used for FROMS in Chapter 5 is the MAC protocol: FROMS was evaluated using BMAC and LMAC and here we need to use a simpler protocol like a non-persistent idle CSMA. There are two reasons for this: the scalability of the simulation, and additional evaluation for FROMS with a third MAC protocol (see Sections 5.5 and 5.6). To evaluate extensively a clustering protocol we need bigger networks: here we use networks with 100 to 300 nodes. Additionally, all nodes in the network serve as data sources, exploding the data traffic in the network. While the routing protocol is independent form the amount of data traffic, the MAC protocol can handle only limited number of packets. LMAC has a very low throughput in dense big networks, since it needs to reserve a separate slot for each of the nodes in a 2-hop environment. In dense networks it needs many slots in a single frame, which increases the length of the frame. However, nodes are able to send only one data packet per frame. Furthermore, the battery lifetime is limited because of the battery model and the number of data packets, which nodes are able to send before the network dies, is too low. BMAC has a better throughput, but the large number of preambles before sending out the real data packets breaks the simulation environment in terms of memory. Thus, we decided to use a simpler MAC protocol, a non-persistent idle CSMA. Additionally to being able to run bigger simulations, these experiments also show that FROMS can run generally on top of any MAC protocol, including an error-prone and unreliable CSMA.

To obtain meaningful results with the CSMA protocol we needed to change slightly also the battery model and to take the energy expenditure of a MICA-2 sensor node, see Table 4.2 and Table 6.1. Recall that the previously used battery model assumed equal consumption for idle, listening and sending radio modes. Such a model will result in a constant network lifetime for any routing/clustering

6.3 Comparative evaluation of CLIQUE

protocol top of an idle CSMA MAC protocol.

In our experiments we measure performance for multiple network settings. Unless otherwise stated, our experiments run with 30 different random connected networks with 30 different random seeds (900 runs in total). The network scenario spans from 100 to 300 nodes in a network of 2000x2000 meters, from 1 to 5 sinks and with clustering sizes from 250m to 1000m. The achieved standard deviation of the experimental results is 1.3 − 2%.

Comparative study. We implemented the Traditional Random Clustering (TRC), based on the work in [15]. The original algorithm uses a head selection probability at each node in the network to decide whether or not to become a cluster head. In case it becomes a cluster head, the node broadcasts a notification. Non-cluster head nodes simply join the nearest cluster head. Our modification consists of first clustering the network exactly as in CLIQUE. Then, the probability-based cluster head assignment from [15] is applied, and nodes join the nearest in-cluster cluster head. In case no cluster head is announced after some waiting time, the algorithm is simply re-run and data packets are buffered on the nodes. The algorithm is performed periodically to spread the energy expenditure among the nodes. The probability of becoming a cluster head is derived from the expected number of nodes in one cluster and is different for various network deployments:

$$P_{clusterhead} = \frac{N_{clusters}}{N_{nodes}} \tag{6.5}$$

In both clustering protocols, the cluster heads wait for some predefined amount of time for packets to arrive (in our case 200 msec with a sensing period of 2 secs), aggregate them and send them to the sinks using the routing protocol.

For this study, we use FROMS from Chapter 5. We again emphasize on multi-hop routing protocols, since our application scenario is not able to send messages from cluster heads to the sinks directly in one hop. The routing protocol takes care of aggregated packets and forwards them to the sinks. It is allowed to use any nodes in the network. The combination of CLIQUE with FROMS is efficient since they both use the same cost metric and are designed for multiple mobile sinks. We also consider FROMS as a good choice to combine with TRC for the same reasons. However, any other multi-hop multicast routing protocol may be taken for either clustering approaches.

6.3.1 Uniform clustering evaluation

We begin with evaluating CLIQUE in a uniform grid scenario, where all clusters have the same size. Given that the main goal of our clustering approach is to minimize energy expenditure in the network, we measured the following cost metrics:

First node death is a good indicator for the expected lifetime of a given network. It shows how the clustering and routing approaches are able to avoid bottlenecks in the network and to spread the energy expenditure. The later the first node dies the better. We have evaluated the network lifetime and the scalability of CLIQUE in three dimensions: increasing number of sinks, increasing cluster sizes (and thus more nodes per cluster and higher hop radius of the cluster) and increasing density of nodes in the network.

Figure 6.5 (a) presents the results of the network lifetime study. The plots show that CLIQUE is able to prolong the network lifetime in terms of first node death by 20-25% and scales well in all load tests. Interestingly, while the gain is constant for different numbers of nodes or different cluster sizes, it increases with increasing number of sinks. This is because of the multicast nature of CLIQUE, which takes into consideration the routing costs to all sinks and is able to save communication overhead while routing from cluster heads to the sinks.

Standard deviation of the remaining energy on the nodes is closely related to the efficient balancing of energy consumption and shows how balanced or unbalanced the node usage was during the network lifetime (until first node death). Low standard deviation implies good balancing. Figure 6.5 (b) summarizes the results over the same three dimensions as before (number of sinks, node density and cluster sizes). It is worth noting that with an increasing number of sinks CLIQUE is not able to achieve much better energy spreading than TRC. This is because the overall communication load in the network increases so much that TRC also uses a lot of nodes, implicitly spreading the load among

6.3 Comparative evaluation of CLIQUE

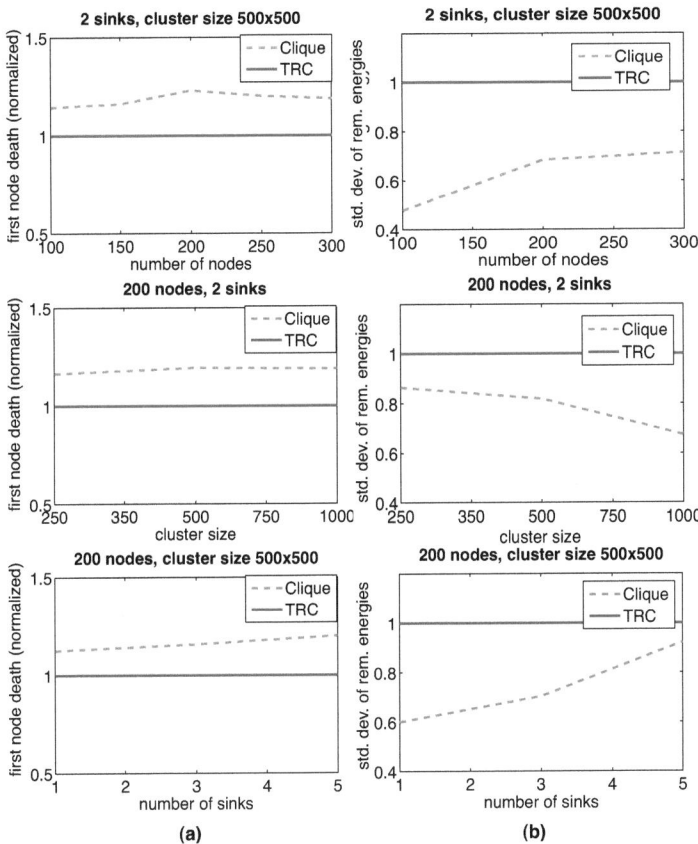

Figure 6.5. First node death (a) and standard deviation of remaining energies at first node death (b) for different number of sinks, cluster sizes and nodes in the network

6.3 Comparative evaluation of CLIQUE

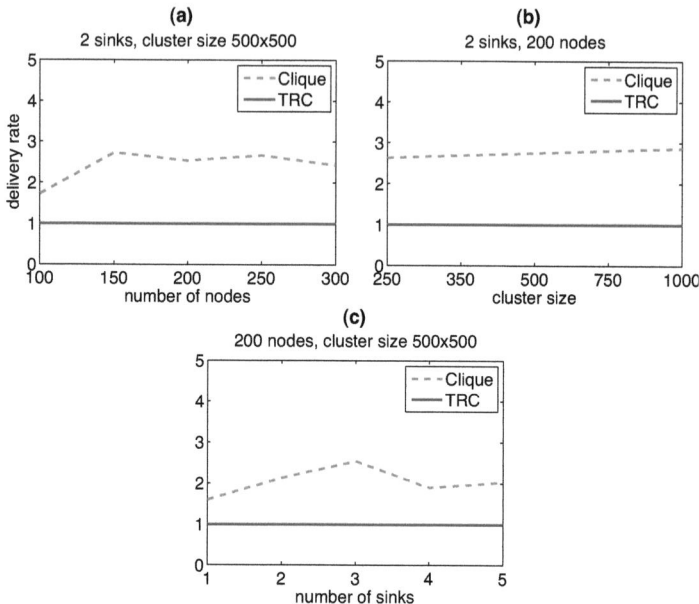

Figure 6.6. Delivery rate at the sinks for different number of sinks, cluster sizes and node densities

them. However, note again that in the same scenario CLIQUE prolongs the network lifetime by almost 25% (Figure 6.5 (a) bottom).

The ability of CLIQUE to spread the energy expenditure is especially clear in Figure 6.5 (a) center. Here, with increasing node density, CLIQUE makes extensive use of the many different options available for routing, thus spreading the load among the nodes.

Delivery rate is closely related to the communication overhead in the network: with more packets being transmitted the probability of collisions or overflowing MAC layer buffers increases. However, it should be noted that delivery

6.3 Comparative evaluation of CLIQUE

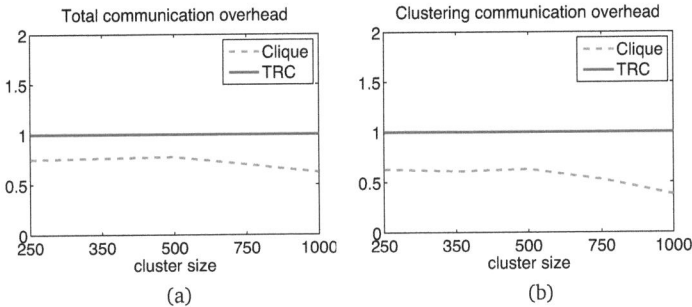

Figure 6.7. Communication overhead for clustering and in total in number of generated packets of all types

rate is not an absolute metric in a simulation environment and instead simply provides an intuition of the real expected behavior. Figure 6.6 summarizes the results. The behavior of CLIQUE can be characterized as stable, as it shows always a delivery rate increase of between 20%-30%. These results are mostly interesting to observe together with those in Figure 6.7, where the total number of generated packets is presented (see below).

Generated packets. Here we counted the number of packets created in the whole network of all types - data requests, aggregated and non-aggregated data packets and cluster head selection packets. Figure 6.7 (a) shows that the overall communication overhead was reduced with CLIQUE by 25%-30%, due mostly to the reduced in-cluster communication, see Figure 6.7 (b). We have shown these results for increasing cluster sizes (increasing number of nodes in one cluster with constant node density) since it shows clearly how CLIQUE saves even more communication overhead with growing clusters.

Total energy spent measures the ability of the clustering approach to minimize communication in the network as a whole. While longer network lifetimes can be due either to better balancing of resources or to less communication overhead, the total spent energy clearly shows the incurred communication

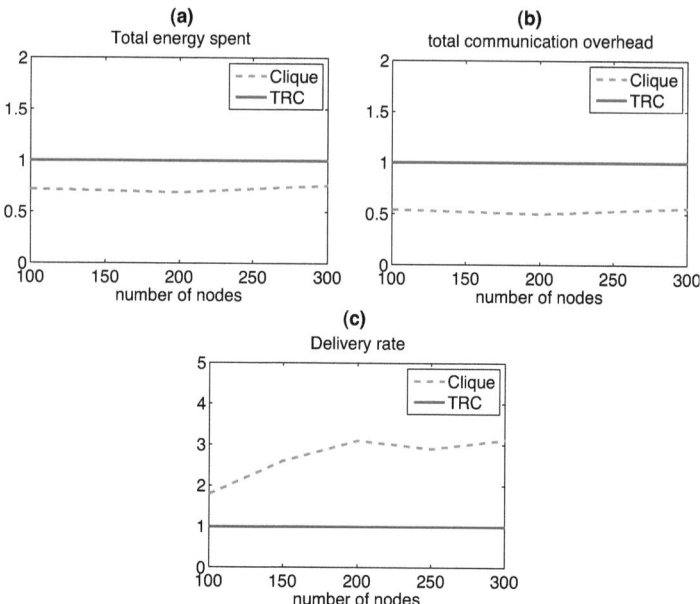

Figure 6.8. Energy expenditure, total communication overhead and delivery rate for networks with unlimited energy for 1000 seconds.

overhead. Low energy spent implies less overhead.

The results are presented in Figure 6.8. Not only does CLIQUE reduce the spent energy by 25% (a), it also increases the delivery rate by more than 2 times (bottom plot). This is because the overall communication overhead is reduced significantly, thus also reducing collisions. The total communication overhead (top right plot) is nearly halved: however, this does not result in halving the total spent energy because of packet overhearing.

6.3 Comparative evaluation of CLIQUE

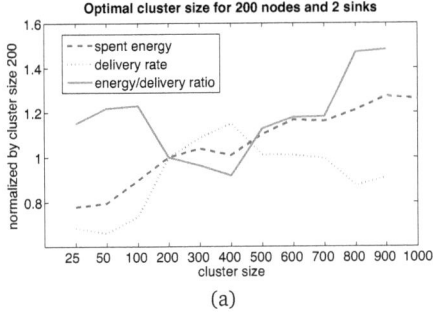

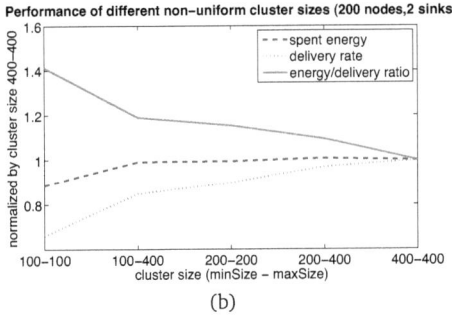

Figure 6.9. Optimal cluster size and non-uniform clustering performance. Experiments with CLIQUE and FROMS.

6.3.2 Non-uniform clustering evaluation

The non-uniformity feature of CLIQUE needs to be used carefully and its evaluation is not trivial. It is a well-known fact that growing the size of clusters infinitely does not minimize the communication overhead. When clusters grow in size, the inner-cluster communication (non-aggregated packets) is increasing too. At the same time, the intra-cluster communication (aggregated packets) is decreasing non-proportionally. Thus, there is a balance somewhere between size of the clusters, data quality and communication overhead, which has to be found for each network, depending on the node density, link qualities and application requirements. Figure 6.9 (a) shows this balance for 30 different networks of 200 nodes with 2 sinks over a field of 2000x2000 meters. The spent energy in the network is growing constantly with increasing the cluster sizes and it looks like the minimum cluster sizes perform best. However, looking at the delivery rate of packets it becomes clear that the low energy expenditure comes at the price of loosing too many packets because of packet collisions. Thus, the ratio between them gives us the optimal cluster size - in this case it is around 400 meters or one-hop radius of the cluster (in our simulations the maximum communication radius lies at around 400-450 meter).

Given the optimal cluster size for a network it becomes clear when and how non-uniformity can achieve lower energy expenditure. For example, if the application scenario requires very small cluster sizes for some regions of interest, CLIQUE can use the optimal cluster sizes in all other regions. Thus, it is not necessary to divide the whole network into small-sized clusters and CLIQUE will reduce the energy expenditure to the minimum possible. Figure 6.9(b) demonstrates this by comparing again the delivery rate, the energy expenditure and their ratio for different uniform and non-uniform scenarios. For example, clustering the network non-uniformly with $\{minSize = 100, maxSize = 400\}$ performs around 20% worse in terms of the energy/delivery rate ratio than the uniform clustering with optimal $size = 400$, but at the same time 20% better than the uniform clustering with $size = 100$.

6.4 Optimal cluster sizes

In the previous section we introduced a novel Q-Learning based clustering protocol CLIQUE, able to avoid all-together the communication overhead for selecting cluster heads. It is able to handle multi-hop clusters as well as one-hops clusters and does not depend on node density, number of sinks, etc. However, this freedom of selecting any cluster sizes poses a new question: which cluster size is optimal? We define the *optimal* cluster as the one sized such that routing data from the cluster members to cluster heads and subsequently to base stations in-

6.4 Optimal cluster sizes

curs the minimal communication overhead. In this section, we step back from our clustering protocol and we concentrate on this question. We explore the parameter space of a wide variety of clustering scenarios to give a general answer independent of the used clustering protocol.

There have been previous efforts on answering this question and we already described them in Chapter 3.2.9. In [194], the author addresses the question: given a network with N uniformly spread sensors, how big is the optimal cluster measured in the number of sensors? In this work the network model assumes that the network can be divided into cells with each cell containing a single sensor with a very high probability. Additionally, sensors can communicate to all their adjacent sensors. The cluster heads are always in the center of the cluster and have more powerful radios to be able to communicate to all adjacent cluster heads. In this model, the question of the optimal size of a cluster is reduced to the calculation of the number of transmissions required to reach the cluster head and the single base station. The author's answer to the above question is:

Proposition 1. *[194] In a network with $A \times A$ cells, where each cluster is $x \times x$ cells big, the optimal x is as close to $\sqrt[3]{2N}$ as possible and divides A.*

For example, for a very big network, e.g. 1156 nodes (34x34 cells) the optimal cluster size is 12 (or 6 hop cluster radius). For a small network, e.g. with 256 nodes (16x16 cells) the optimal cluster size is 4 (or 2 hop radius).

In contrast, the study in [206] comes to the conclusion:

Proposition 2. *[206] For any network with 300 to 2000 nodes, the optimal cluster has a radius of 2 hops or any node in the cluster can reach the cluster heads in maximum 2 hops.*

However, a slightly different network model is used. The authors use multi-hop routing through normal sensors to reach the base station instead of cluster heads only.

These results are not only contradictory. The parameter space is rather limited, since it permits a very limited variety of network scenarios, for example different network densities. On the other hand, the communication model (unit disk graph symmetric and reliable communication) is appropriate, since the goal

PARAMETER	DESCRIPTION
N	number of nodes
A	size of network (meters)
r_c	communication radius of nodes (meters)
C	size of cluster (meters)
P_{CH}	position of cluster head [center, random, station]
I_N	in-network processing [tree, center]
M	number of base stations

Figure 6.10. Network and clustering parameters as used in this study.

of the study is to answer a general high level question about which clustering scenario is *in theory* the best possible one.

In the next paragraphs, we define first optimal clusters in a formal way and the used network parameters. Then, in Section 6.4.2 we step through the network parameters and study their effect on the clustering scenario and communication overhead.

6.4.1 Defining the optimal cluster

Next we extend the network models used by [194, 206] to incorporate multiple network and cluster parameters and to make an extensive analysis of the optimal cluster sizes. We define the WSN to be a flat network with N nodes, uniformly and randomly spread over a square area with size A. We assume that clusters are also squares with some size C. Nodes can communicate to all their neighbors, defined as those nodes whose distance is less than some communication radius r_c (unit disk graph communication model). Energy is spent when a node sends or receives a packet. We do not use a specific energy model to calculate the exact energy expenditure, but instead always show the number of sent/received messages (ETX+ERX). As we assume a broadcast environment neighbors receive messages even if they are not destined to them.

6.4 Optimal cluster sizes

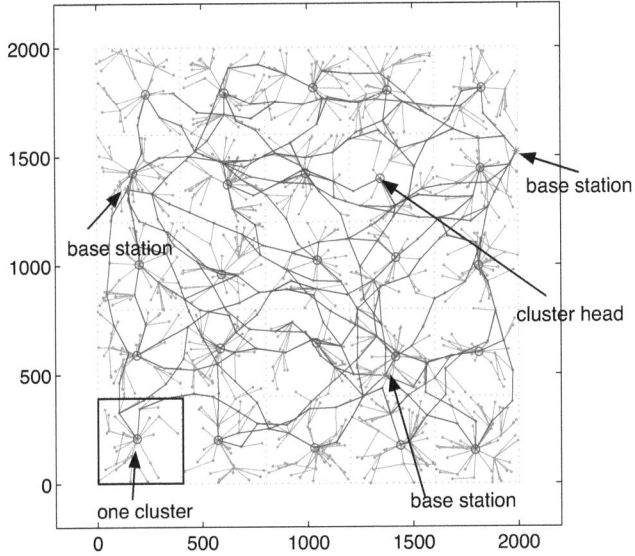

Figure 6.11. A sample network from our MATLAB evaluation scenario with 2000 nodes, 3 base stations, clusters and cluster heads.

In every cluster there is a single cluster head, reachable in k hops by all cluster members. The position of the cluster head inside the cluster is an input parameter, P_{CH}, that can be set to: next to the center of the cluster, next to the base stations (in case of multiple base stations the minimum distance sum to all of them is used as metric), or random. Each node gathers sensory data and sends it first to the cluster head, then the cluster head aggregates the received packets and sends a single packet to all base stations. Multi-hop routing through all sensor nodes (cluster heads and cluster members) are used for both aggregated and non-aggregated packets. There are M base stations in the network, randomly selected among all nodes, therefore they have no special properties such as increased battery or communication range. In-network processing is either tree-based or centralized at the cluster head [41] (parameter $I_N = \{tree, CH\}$). The network parameters we use are summarized in Figure 6.10. A sample network for our study is shown in Figure 6.11.

We evaluate the performance of a clustering scheme with its parameters $N, A, r_c, C, P_{CH}, M, I_N$ in terms of the number of received/sent packets for routing the sensory data from the sensors through the cluster heads to the base stations. We define:

Definition 1. *The optimal clustering scenario is the 3-tuple $\{C, P_{CH}, I_N\}$ which incurs the minimum communication overhead for the network $\{A, N, r_c, M\}$.*

Definition 2. *The communication overhead of a network $\{A, N, r_c, M\}$ with clustering scenario $\{C, P_{CH}, I_N\}$ is the sum of sent packets and received packets for all nodes in the network for one round of data reporting. In one round of data reporting each node sends exactly one packet to its cluster head and the cluster heads send exactly one packet to all base stations M. Multi-hop routing is used for all transmissions.*

Note that the network model and clustering scenarios we define here are more general and sophisticated than those previously proposed [194, 206]. We allow more parameters (node density, communication radius, multiple base stations) and different aggregation schemes (tree-based, centralized). Some of the parameters are novel, like the position of the cluster head and have not been evaluated before. We are particularly interested in this one, since our own clustering protocol CLIQUE selects cluster heads next to the base stations, based on the intuition that intra-cluster communication will be minimized.

The questions we address in the next section are:

1. Are there some general rules for optimal clusters? For example, do 2-hop clusters perform the best for all network sizes, independent of the number of nodes, network area or node density? (see Propositions 1 and 2)

2. If there are no rules for all parameters, what are the rules of thumb for selecting the cluster parameters C, P_{CH}, M for some given network N, A, r_c, M?

6.4 Optimal cluster sizes

3. Are the above results different when a different in-network aggregation scheme is used, e.g., tree-based vs. centralized?

4. How does the position of the cluster head inside the cluster P_{CH} influence the optimal clustering, inter and intra-cluster communication overhead?

6.4.2 Finding the optimal cluster

Unlike previous efforts [194, 206], we take an experimental approach for two reasons. First, it is hard if not impossible to derive generally valid formulas for the network communication overhead that consider all parameters, especially random topologies. Such a theoretical approach has been previously done [194, 206], however several required, simplifying assumptions make the results difficult to apply in practice. Further, we extend the network models of these works to accommodate different densities and fully random topologies, which makes the parameter space even larger. Our second motivation is to make our results immediately applicable: a WSN practitioner can select the most relevant scenarios from our experiments and directly derive the optimal clustering parameters.

We performed our simulations in MATLAB. Figure 6.11 shows a sample network. Nodes are spread randomly through the network field. The network area is divided into equal-size clusters, and all results are presented for a variety of cluster sizes that allow the area to be precisely divided into such equal-size clusters. Shortest distance (in terms of ETX - expected number of transmissions) is computed between each node and its corresponding cluster head and between all cluster heads and the base stations. The energy expenditure is calculated as the sum of ETX and ERX (expected number of receivers) for one round of data gathering. Cluster formation overhead is ignored. Each of the reported experiments is the mean of 100 independent random connected topologies.

Our analysis addresses the energy expenditure of different clustering schemes by exploring the parameters A, C, M, P_{CH}, I_N, N. Our goal is always to identify the optimal cluster size for scenarios, first studying the optimal cluster size for a scenario with no intra-cluster aggregation ($I_N = center$), the cluster head near the center of the cluster (P_{CH} = center), and constant node density (N/A^2 = $CONST \approx 500 nodes/km^2$). We then vary the number of base stations, the position of the cluster head, the use of in-network processing, and finally the node density.

Cluster size C. We first consider a single setting whose key parameters are described in Figure 6.12. To understand the components of the communication cost, Figure 6.12 (top) separates the cost into intra and inter cluster communication. Intuitively, as cluster size grows communication inside the clusters also grows, since data needs to be forwarded multi-hops to the cluster head. At the same time communication from cluster heads to the base station drops significantly, since fewer cluster heads are present. The intersection of these lines shows the optimal cluster to be approximately 250, or 1-hop clusters because in our scenario $r_c = 150m$.

Figure 6.12 (bottom) confirms the optimality of 1-hop clustering for a wide range of network sizes with 30–3000 nodes, but always constant density.

This result stands in contrast to those previously reported in the literature and summarized as Propositions 1 and 2. Differences from Proposition 1 follow from different network models. Notably, [194] does not take into account routing from cluster heads to base stations and assumes a very regular topology with a single node able to communicate to exactly four neighbors. Instead, our random topologies allow different node densities in different parts of the network plus we include routing overhead to reach the base stations. On the other hand, we believe the difference from Proposition 1 [206] is due to the fundamental difference between an analytical analysis and experimentation. They provide general formulas with parameters for the network and cluster sizes. In their analysis, they rely heavily on the same virtual grid topology as [194] and make many assumptions and generalizations about the energy expenditure.

Number of base stations M. Another key parameter to evaluate is the clustering behavior with different number of base stations collecting the results. We keep the same parameters as in the previous section and Figure 6.12 (bottom), but extend the number of base stations to $M = 2$ in Figure 6.13 (top) and $M = 3$

6.4 Optimal cluster sizes

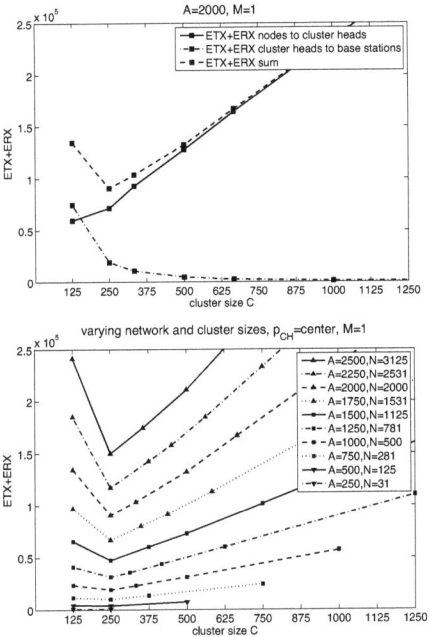

Figure 6.12. (top) Energy expenditure for $A = 2000m, M = 1, r_c = 150m, P_{CH} = center, I_N = center, N = const$ separated into intra and inter-cluster communication overhead. (bottom) Total communication overhead for varying network sizes.

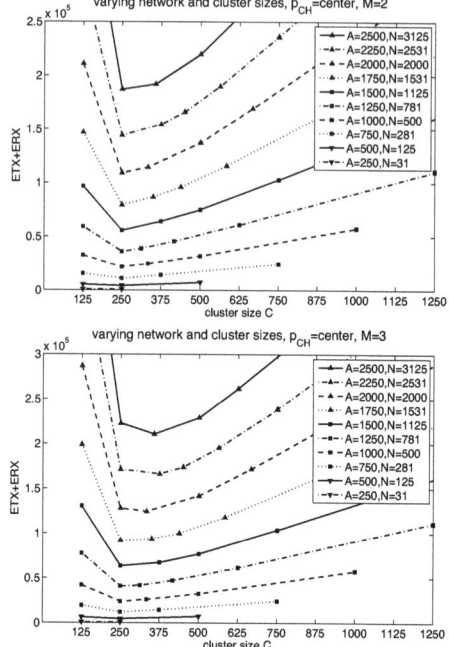

Figure 6.13. Varying numbers of base stations M. Energy expenditure for $r_c = 150m, P_{CH} = center, I_N = center, N = const$ and (top) M = 2; (bottom) M = 3.

in Figure 6.13 (bottom). As the number of base stations increases, inter cluster communication grows too. In terms of the independent overheads represented in Figure 6.12 (top), the intersection moves to the right, implying larger optimal clusters. This trend is visible in Figure 6.13 (top), where for large networks (e.g., the top line) the energy expenditure is nearly the same for 1 and 2 hop clusters. However, with three base stations and large networks the optimal cluster size is 2 hops (cluster size $\approx 375m$ with $r_c = 150m$). We expect this trend to continue for very large networks of tens of thousands of nodes and plan to verify this in the future.

6.4 Optimal cluster sizes

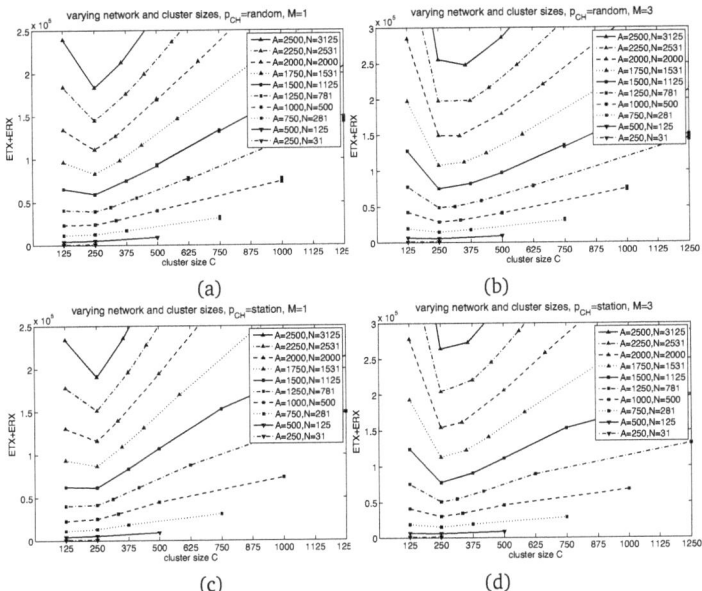

Figure 6.14. Varying position of cluster head P_{CH}. Energy expenditure for $r_c = 150m, I_N = center, N = const$ and (a) $P_{CH} = random, M = 1$; (b) $P_{CH} = random, M = 3$; (c) $P_{CH} = station, M = 1$; (d) $P_{CH} = station, M = 3$.

Position of the cluster head P_{CH}. Next, we explore the effect of the cluster head position inside the cluster. While the previous experiments shown in Figures 6.12 and 6.13 placed the cluster head close to the center of the cluster, here we allow it to be random (Figure 6.14(a-b)) or to be closest to the base stations (Figure 6.14(c-d)). The position of the cluster head is important for two reasons. First, it affects the load balance, and therefore energy consumption, inside the cluster for routing and data aggregation. Second, the routing overhead inside the cluster changes with the head placement. Based on our analysis, we make two key observations: first, the optimal cluster size is not af-

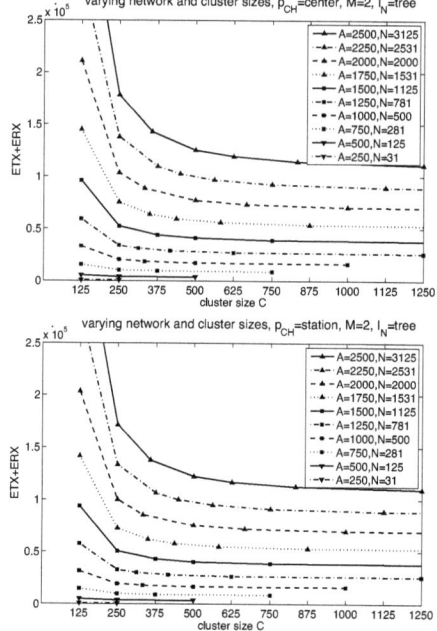

Figure 6.15. Studying in-network processing I_N. Energy expenditure for $r_c = 150m, I_N = tree, N = const, M = 2$ and (top) $P_{CH} = center$; (bottom) $P_{CH} = station$.

fected by P_{CH}. Second, the cluster head position does, however, affect the total energy spent in the network. Specifically, when the cluster head is at the cluster center (Figure 6.12), it requires 15% less energy than a random placement due to intra cluster routing costs. Notably, with head placement closest to the base stations, the clustering scenario does not perform better than the other options (Figure 6.14(c-d)). Even though the routing overhead between the cluster heads and the base stations is minimized, this is outweighed by the increased routing inside the clusters.

On the other hand, this result cannot be taken literally: placing the cluster

6.4 Optimal cluster sizes

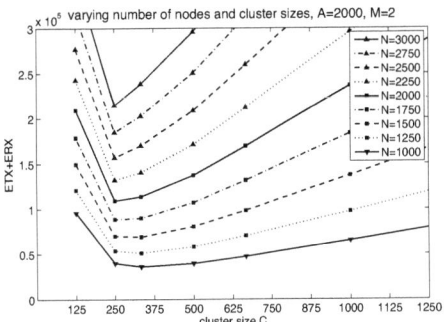

Figure 6.16. Varying node density N/A^2. Energy expenditure for $A = 2000, r_c = 150m, P_{CH} = center, I_N = center, M = 2$

head in the center of the cluster might minimize the communication of one round of data gathering. However, over time nodes around the cluster head and the cluster head itself will drain their batteries too fast. Thus, some spreading of the load is needed like randomly positioning the cluster head. In fact, in this case also our CLIQUE protocol is a very good option despite the placement of the cluster head next to the base stations. We already showed that it is performing much better in terms of energy spreading, spent energy and network lifetime compared to random clustering. Additionally, CLIQUE is able to accommodate in-tree aggregation inside the clusters and thus further minimizing spent energy, which we evaluate next.

In-network processing I_N. Next we consider the possibility to process the data inside a cluster, as it is being forwarded to the cluster head. While this ability typically depends on the application and cannot be changed simply to reduce overhead, in applications where either option is feasible our analysis in Figure 6.15 shows that tree-based aggregation is preferable. Intuitively, the total energy expenditure decreases with increasing cluster sizes because the data aggregation rate grows and data traffic decreases. However, for very large clusters the gainings are rather insignificant. Consequently, preference should be given to 3-4 hop clusters since they have simultaneously low energy expenditure and lower data aggregation rates.

Interestingly, the tree-based aggregation diminishes the importance of the cluster head position, as seen by comparing Figures 6.15(a) and (b). The energy expenditure is the same because the effect of in-cluster routing was also eliminated.

Node density N/A^2. In our final last experiment we vary the node density with a fixed network size. Figure 6.16 shows a clear trend that lower densities ($\approx$250-375 $nodes/km^2$) result in larger optimal clusters. For higher densities ($\approx$400-500 $nodes/km^2$) the optimal cluster size is again 1 hop. This is because low node densities lower the total intra cluster communication overhead, giving the inter cluster communication more weight.

6.4.3 Optimal clustering summary and rules

Here we return to the questions raised in Section 6.4.1 and summarize the results of the last paragraphs.

We are able to identify several rules: First, *1-hop clustering performs best for a large spectrum of different network sizes, node densities and number of base stations.* For very large networks (more than 1000 nodes), multiple base stations (more than three) or very low densities (less than 400 $nodes/km^2$) 2-hop clustering performs better, although not significantly. Additionally, *the optimal cluster head position is the center of the cluster.* In comparison to random locations or those closest to the base station, it spends approximately 15% less energy. However, keeping the cluster head always in the center of the cluster would drain the batteries of some nodes around it too fast. Thus, the other options (random, next to the base stations) are also feasible assuming that energy spreading is taken explicitly into account.

For tree-based aggregation, 3- to 4-hop clustering performs best in terms of energy expenditure and data aggregation rate. Here the position of the cluster head inside the cluster is not important. Tree-based aggregation minimized significantly the communication overhead inside the clusters and is thus always a good decision. However, this also depends on the application scenario.

In some sense our results are in between the results achieved by other researchers. They support partially Proposition 1 in the sense that optimal cluster sizes grow with increasing size of the network. However, the optimal cluster sizes grow at a much slower rate. This could be a consequence of our additional network density parameter, which changes significantly the communication overhead in the network.

Our results overlap in part also with Proposition 2, where the authors claim that optimal clusters have a radius of 2 hops for all practical networks with 300 to 2000 nodes. We are able to confirm this conclusion only for very large networks with more 1000 nodes.

The most important contribution of our analysis of optimal cluster sizes is the insight that small clusters with a radius of only 1 hop are usually more energy efficient than larger ones. Thus, research on clustering algorithms needs to concentrate on lowering the clustering overhead and balancing the communication overhead in small 1-hop clusters.

6.5 Concluding remarks

In this chapter we introduced a novel clustering algorithm for wireless sensor networks based on Q-Learning and able to avoid all-together the cluster head agreement communication overhead. CLIQUE exhibits some very important properties, which might prove path-breaking in the area of WSN clustering. First and most importantly it is able to decide on cluster head roles without explicitly assigning this role to any node in the network: instead, each node can evaluate itself and its neighbors in terms of who *seems* to be *currently* better suited for this job. In case some neighbor is the better choice, the node forwards the packet without any knowledge or interest of what will happen to this packet further. The emphasis of this technique is on properties like *current* or *seemingly better* and very importantly on *local neighbors and local knowledge*.

Additionally to these novel properties, CLIQUE proved to perform very well under realistic simulation scenarios too, e.g. by increasing the lifetime of the network by approximately 25% compared to a traditional simple random clustering protocol. Its implementation is rather simple and straight forward and is thus realistic also for highly restricted hardware platforms.

Clearly, the same Q-Learning based technique can be applied also to various other clustering applications. As we have seen on Section 6.4, the optimal clustering scenario for a network is identified by rather small clusters with centralized data aggregation or bigger clusters with in-tree aggregation. CLIQUE is able to handle both of them and can be easily extended to optimize the network performance for other metrics, such as maximum aggregation.

Last but not least, CLIQUE together with FROMS build a complete unified data dissemination architecture able to handle a wide variety of network scenarios and applications. Both are based on Q-Learning and can be used separately or together, paving the way towards autonomic, self-organizing scalable communications with minimum protocol overhead and naturally dealing with mobility and failures.

Chapter 7

Conclusions

The main contribution of this thesis is the design, implementation and evaluation of an energy-efficient, robust and flexible data dissemination framework, able to cope with various network scenarios and applications. Some of the considered application requirements are novel, such as the non-uniform data requirement or fast route recovery without data loss. Others are well-known and have been addressed often in the research literature, like energy efficient routes or multiple mobile sinks.

We conducted an extensive survey of the current state-of-the-art routing and clustering approaches, their properties, assumptions and evaluation methodologies. Further, we have studied the requirements and network scenarios of various existing and planned WSN deployments in order to better understand their needs and in order to identify the important network parameters to be considered. We supported our initial intuition of using machine learning to solve this hard problem efficiently and elegantly by studying various machine learning and computational intelligence techniques and their applications to WSNs. During this study, we identified Q-Learning as the most suitable technique and used it to solve both the routing and clustering problems. The result is a holistic cross-layer optimized data dissemination framework consisting of a routing protocol called FROMS and a clustering protocol called CLIQUE. Both exhibit vital properties such as robustness against mobility, node and link failures, fast recovery after failures, very low control overhead and a wide variety of supported network scenarios and applications.

In fact, FROMS achieves 5–25% longer network lifetime and 10–50% shorter routes compared to other state-of-the-art routing protocols. In scenarios with failing nodes or mobile sinks, FROMS is able to deliver approximately 30 – 40% more data packets to the sinks. On real hardware, FROMS achieves 30 – 40% shorter routes and approximately 15% higher delivery rate than an implementation of Directed Diffusion.

At the same time, CLIQUE is able to lower the spent energy in the network by approximately 25% compared to a traditional clustering approach. Additionally, it gives a distributed solution to the requirement of non-uniform data dissemination.

We evaluated the protocols analytically, in a realistic simulation environment and on real hardware. Thus, we show not only that machine learning is applicable to real-world wireless sensor networks, but that it also achieves significantly better performance in terms of energy savings, network lifetime, load spreading and delivery rate under various network conditions compared to other state-of-the-art routing and clustering approaches.

Given the highly satisfying results achieved in this thesis, we believe machine learning proves to be a practical and efficient approach to solve many other problems in WSNs. This thesis paves the way to further applications, protocols and optimizations, which will inherently improve the performance of wireless sensor networks, lower their design and deployment complexity, and expand their application areas.

Acronyms

ACO	Ant Colony Optimization
ANN, NN	Artificial Neural Networks, Neural Networks
BMAC	Berkeley Medium ACcess protocol [145]
CH	Cluster Head
CI	Computational Intelligence
CSMA	Carrier Sense Multiple Access
DD, uDD	Directed Diffusion, as described in [170]
ETX	Expected number of transmissions
FROMS	Feedback Routing to Multiple Sinks
GA	Genetic Algorithms
LEACH	Low Energy Adaptive Clustering Hierarchy [149]
LMAC	Lightweight Medium ACess protocol [192]
MAC	Medium ACcess
MANET	Mobile Ad Hoc Networks
mDD	Multicast version of Directed Diffusion, as described in [220]

ML	Machine Learning
MSTEAM	Minimum spanning tree based energy aware multicast protocol [66]
PSO	Particle Swarm Optimization
RL	Reinforcement Learning
RSSI	Received Signal Strength Indication
SVM	Support Vector Machines
TDMA	Time Division Multiple Access
TRC	Traditional Random Clustering, based on [15]
uDD	unicast Directed Diffusion, the original Directed Diffusion, as described in [170]
WSN	Wireless Sensor Network

Bibliography

[1] V. Abhishek. Localization in ad-hoc sensor network: A machine learning based approach. Technical Report CS229 project report, Stanford University, 2005.

[2] I. F. Akyildiz, Ö.B. Akan Akan, C. Chen, J. Fang, and W. Su. Interplanetary internet: state-of-the-art and research challenges. *Computer Networks*, 43(2):75–112, 2003.

[3] I. F. Akyildiz, W. Su, Y. Sankarasubramaniam, and E. Cayirci. Wireless sensor networks: a survey. *Computer Networks*, 38(4):393–422, 2002.

[4] J. N. Al-Karaki and A. E. Kamal. Routing techniques in wireless sensor networks: A survey. *IEEE Wireless Communications*, 11(6):6–28, 2004.

[5] J. N. Al-Karaki, R. Ul-Mustafa, and A. E. Kamal. Data aggregation in wireless sensor networks - exact and approximate algorithms. In *Proceedings of the Workshop on High Performance Switching and Routing (HPSR)*, pages 241–245, Phoenix, AZ, 2004.

[6] M. Ali, U. Saif, A. Dunkels, T. Voigt, K. Römer, K. Langendoen, J. Polastre, and Z.A. Uzmi. Medium access control issues in sensor networks. *SIGCOMM Computation and Communication Review*, 36(2):33–36, 2006.

[7] A.D. Amis, R. Prakash, T.H.P. Vuong, and D.T. Huynh. Max-min d-cluster formation in wireless ad hoc networks. In *Proceedings of the 19th Annual Joint Conference of the IEEE Computer and Communications Societies (INFOCOM)*, volume 1, pages 32–41, Tel-Aviv, Israel, 2000.

[8] T. Anker, D. Bickson, D. Dolev, and B. Hod. Efficient clustering for improving network performance in wireless sensor networks. In *Proceedings of the 5th European Conference on Wireless Sensor Networks (EWSN)*, pages 221–236, Bologna, Italy, 2008.

[9] P. Arabshahi, A. Gray, I. Kassabalidis, El M. A. Sharkawi, R. J. Marks, A. Das, and S. Narayanan. Adaptive routing in wireless communication networks using swarm intelligence. In *Proceedings of the 19th AIAA International Communications Satellite Systems Conference (AIAA-ICSSC)*, page 9pp., Toulouse, France, 2001.

[10] R. Arroyo-Valles, R. Alaiz-Rodrigues, A. Guerrero-Curieses, and J. Cid-Suiero. Q-probabilistic routing in wireless sensor networks. In *Proceedings of the 3rd International Conference on Intelligent Sensors, Sensor Networks and Information Processing (ISSNIP)*, pages 1–6, Melbourne, Australia, 2007.

[11] N. Aslam, W. Phillips, and W. Robertson. A unified clustering and communication protocol for wireless sensor networks. *IAENG International Journal of Computer Science*, 35(3), 2008.

[12] A. Awad, C. Sommer, R. German, and F. Dressler. Virtual cord protocol (vcp): A flexible dht-like routing service for sensor networks. In *Proceedings of the 5th IEEE International Conference on Mobile Ad Hoc and Sensor Systems (MASS)*, pages 133–142, Atlanta, GA, USA, 2008.

[13] A. Bachir and D. Barthel. Localized max-min remaining energy routing for wsn using delay control. In *Proceedings of IEEE International Conference on Communications (ICC)*, volume 5, pages 3302–3306, Seoul, Korea, 2005.

[14] P.F. Baldi and K. Hornik. Learning in linear neural networks: A survey. *IEEE Transactions on Neural Networks*, 6(4):837–858, 1995.

[15] S. Bandyopadhyay and E.J. Coyle. An energy efficient hierarchical clustering algorithm for wireless sensor networks. In *Proceedings of the An-*

nual *Joint Conference of the IEEE Computer and Communications Societies (INFOCOM)*, volume 3, pages 1713 – 1723, San Francisco, CA, USA, 2003.

[16] S. Banerjee and S. Khuller. A clustering scheme for hierarchical control in multi-hop wireless networks. In *Proceedings of the 20th Annual Joint Conference of the IEEE Computer and Communications Societies (INFOCOM)*, volume 2, pages 1028–1037, Anchorage, USA, 2001.

[17] T. Banka, G. Tandon, and A.P. Jayasumana. Zonal rumor routing for wireless sensor networks. In *Proceedings of the International Conference on Information Technology: Coding and Computing (ITCC)*, pages 562–567, Washington, DC, USA, 2005.

[18] J. Barbancho, C. León, J. Molina, and A. Barbancho. Giving neurons to sensors: QoS management in wireless sensors networks. In C. Leon, editor, *Proceedings of the IEEE Conference on Emerging Technologies and Factory Automation (ETFA)*, pages 594–597, Prague, Czech Republic, 2006.

[19] G. Barrenetxea, F. Ingelrest, G. Schaefer, and M. Vetterli. The hitchhiker's guide to successful wireless sensor network deployments. In *Proceedings of the 6th ACM conference on Embedded network sensor systems (SenSys)*, pages 43–56, New York, NY, USA, 2008.

[20] G. Barrenetxea, F. Ingelrest, G. Schaefer, and M. Vetterli. Wireless sensor networks for environmental monitoring: The sensorscope experience. *2008 IEEE International Zurich Seminar on Communications (IZS)*, pages 98–101, March 2008.

[21] E. A. Basha, S. Ravela, and D. Rus. Model-based monitoring for early warning flood detection. In *Proceedings of the 6th ACM conference on Embedded network sensor systems (SenSys)*, pages 295–308, New York, NY, USA, 2008.

[22] S. Bashyal and G.K. Venayagamoorthy. Collaborative routing algorithm for wireless sensor network longevity. In *Proceedings of the 3rd Interna-*

tional Conference on Intelligent Sensors, Sensor Networks and Information Processing (ISSNIP), pages 515–520, Melbourne, Australia, 2007.

[23] P. Beyens, M. Peeters, K. Steenhaut, and A. Nowe. Routing with compression in wireless sensor networks: A Q-learning approach. In *Proceedings of the 5th European Workshop on Adaptive Agents and Multi-Agent Systems (AAMAS)*, page 12pp., Paris, France, 2005.

[24] S. Biaz, Y. Ji, B. Qi, and S. Wu. Realistic radio range irregularity model and its impact on localization for wireless sensor networks. In *Proceedings of the International Conference on Wireless Communications, Networking and Mobile Computing (IWCMC)*, volume 2, pages 669–673, Hawaii, USA, 2005.

[25] T. Bokareva, N. Bulusu, and S. Jha. A competitive learning algorithm for checking sensor data integrity in unknown environments. Technical Report UNSW-CSE-0516, University of New South Wales, Sydney, NSW, Australia, 2005.

[26] T. Bokareva, N. Bulusu, and S. Jha. Learning sensor data characteristics in unknown environments. In *Procedings of the 1st International Workshop on Advances in Sensor Networks (IWASN)*, page 8pp., San Jose, California, USA, 2006.

[27] E. Bonabeau, F. Henaux, S. Guérin, D. Snyers, P. Kuntz, and G. Theraulaz. Routing in telecommunications networks with "smart" ant-like agents. In *Proceedings of the 2nd International Workshop on Intelligent Agents for Telecommunications Applications (IATA)*, pages 60–71, Paris, France, 1998.

[28] A. Boukerche, H.A.B.F. Oliveira, E.F. Nakamura, and A.A.F. Loureiro. Localization systems for wireless sensor networks. *IEEE Magazine of Wireless Communications*, 14(6):6–12, 2007.

[29] J. A. Boyan and M. L. Littman. Packet routing in dynamically changing

networks: A reinforcement learning approach. *Advances in Neural Information Processing Systems*, 6:671–678, 1994.

[30] D. Braginsky and D. Estrin. Rumor routing algorithm for sensor networks. In *Proceedings of the 1st Workshop on Sensor Networks and Applications (WSNA)*, pages 1–12, Atlanta, GA, USA, 2002.

[31] U. Brandes and T. Erlebach. *Network Analysis - Methodological Foundations*. Springer-Verlag, Berlin, Germany, 2005.

[32] C. Buratti, A. Giorgetti, and R. Verdone. Cross-layer design of an energy-efficient cluster formation algorithm with carrier-sensing multiple access for wireless sensor networks. *EURASIP Journal on Wireless Communications and Networking*, 5(5):672–685, 2005.

[33] D. Camara and A. A. F. Loureiro. A novel routing algorithm for ad hoc networks. In *Proceedings of the 33rd Hawaii International Conference on System Sciences (HICSS)*, page 8pp., Hawaii, USA, 2000.

[34] J. A. Carballido, I. Ponzoni, and N. B. Brignole. CGD-GA: A graph-based genetic algorithm for sensor network design. *Information Sciences*, 177(22):5091–5102, 2007.

[35] A. Carzaniga and A. L. Wolf. Content-based networking: A new communication infrastructure. In *NSF Workshop on an Infrastructure for Mobile and Wireless Systems (NSF-IMWS)*, number 2538 in Lecture Notes in Computer Science, pages 59–68, Scottsdale, AZ, USA, 2001.

[36] E. Cayirci and T. Coplu. SENDROM: sensor networks for disaster relief operations management. *Wireless Networks*, 13(3):409–423, 2007.

[37] B.-R. Chen, K.-K. Muniswamy-Reddy, and M. Welsh. Ad-hoc multicast routing on resource-limited sensor nodes. In *Proceedings of the 2nd International Workshop on Multi-hop ad hoc networks: from theory to reality (REALMAN)*, pages 87–94, Florence, Italy, 2006.

[38] G. Chen, C. Li, M. Ye, and J. Wu. An unequal cluster-based routing protocol in wireless sensor networks. *Wireless Networks*, 15:193–207, 2009.

[39] Q. Chen, J. Ma, Y. Zhu, D. Zhang, and L.M. Ni. An energy-efficient k-hop clustering framework for wireless sensor networks. In *Proceedings of the 4th European Conference on Wireless Sensor Networks (EWSN)*, pages 17–33, Delft, The Netherlands, 2007.

[40] Y.S Chen, S.Y. Ann, and Y.W. Lin. Ve-mobicast: A variant-egg-based mobicast routing protocol for sensornets. In *Proceedings of the IEEE International Conference on Communications (ICC)*, volume 5, pages 3020–3024, Seoul, Korea, 2005.

[41] L. Chitnis, A. Dobra, and S. Ranka. Aggregation methods for large-scale sensor networks. *ACM Transactions on Sensor Networks*, 4(2), 2008.

[42] P. Ciciriello, L. Mottola, and G.P. Picco. Efficient routing from multiple sources to multiple sinks in wireless sensor networks. In *Proceedings of the 4th European Conference on Wireless Sensor Networks (EWSN)*, pages 34–50, Delft, The Netherlands, 2007.

[43] M. S. Corson and S. G. Batsell. A reservation-based multicast (RBM) routing protocol for mobile networks: overview of initial route construction. In *Proceedings of the 14th Annual Joint Conference of the IEEE Computer and Communications Societies (INFOCOM)*, volume 3, pages 1063–1074, Boston, MA, USA, 1995.

[44] N. Cristianini and J. Shawe-Taylor. *An Introduction to Support Vector Machines and Other Kernel-based Learning Methods*. Cambridge University Press, 2000.

[45] A. Das and D. Dutta. Data acquisition in multiple-sink sensor networks. *SIGMOBILE Mobile Computation and Communication Revue*, 9(3):82–85, 2005.

Bibliography

[46] K. Dasgupta, K. Kalpakis, and P. Namjoshi. An efficient clustering-based heuristic for data gathering and aggregation in sensor networks. In *Proceedings of the IEEE Wireless Communications and Networking (WCNC)*, volume 3, pages 1948–1953, New Orleans, USA, 2003.

[47] M.T. Dela Cruz, M. Whyte, Z. Yu, and T. Hanselmann. Q learning routing protocol. Display demonstration of real hardware implementation at the International Conference on Intelligent Sensors, Sensor Networks and Information Processing (ISSNIP), Melbourne, Australia, 2007.

[48] M. Demirbas, A. Arora, V. Mittal, and V. Kulathumani. Design and analysis of a fast local clustering service for wireless sensor networks. In *Proceedings of the 1st International Conference on Broadband Wireless Networking (BroadNets)*, pages 700–709, San Jose, CA, USA, 2004.

[49] M. Di and E.M. Joo. A survey of machine learning in wireless sensor networks. In *Proceedings of the 6th International Conference on Information, Communications and Signal Processing (ICICS)*, pages 1–5, Singapore, 2007.

[50] G. Di Caro and M. Dorigo. AntNet: Distributed stigmergetic control for communications networks. *Journal of Artificial Intelligence Research*, 9:317–365, 1998.

[51] G. Di Caro, F. Ducatelle, and L.M. Gambardella. AntHocNet: an adaptive nature-inspired algorithm for routing in mobile ad hoc networks. *European Transactions on Telecommunications*, 16:443–455, 2005.

[52] OMNeT++ discrete event simulator. http://www.omnetpp.org.

[53] M. Dorigo. *Optimization, Learning and Natural Algorithms*. PhD thesis, Politecnico di Milano, Italy, 1992.

[54] M. Dorigo, G. Di Caro, and L.M. Gambardella. Ant algorithms for discrete optimization. *Artificial Life*, 5(2):137–172, 1999.

[55] M. Dorigo and T. Stuetzle. *Ant Colony Optimization*. MIT Press, 2004.

[56] J. Dowling, E. Curran, R. Cunningham, and V. Cahill. Using feedback in collaborative reinforcement learning to adaptively optimize MANET routing. *IEEE Transactions on Systems, Man and Cybernetics*, 35(3):360–372, 2005.

[57] E. Egea-Lopez, J. Vales-Alonso, A. Martinez-Sala, P. Pavon-Mario, and J. Garcia-Haro. Simulation scalability issues in wireless sensor networks. *IEEE Communications Magazine*, 44(7):64–73, July 2006.

[58] A. Egorova-Förster and A. L. Murphy. Exploring non uniform quality of service for extending WSN lifetime. In *Proceedings of the 3rd International Workshop on Sensor Networks and Systems for Pervasive Computing (PerSens)*, pages 285–289, White Plains, NY, USA, 2007.

[59] A.P. Engelbrecht. *Computational Intelligence: An Introduction*. John Wiley & Sons, New York, USA, 2 edition, 2007.

[60] Q. Fang, J. Gao, L.J. Guibas, V. de Silva, and L. Zhang. GLIDER: gradient landmark-based distributed routing for sensor networks. In *Proceedings of the 24th Annual Joint Conference of the IEEE Computer and Communications Societies (INFOCOM)*, volume 1, pages 339–350, Miami, FL, USA, 2005.

[61] K. P. Ferentinos, L. D. Albright, and B. Selman. Neural network-based detection of mechanical, sensor and biological faults in deep-trough hydroponics. *Computers and Electronics in Agriculture*, 40(1-3):65–85, 2003.

[62] A. Förster. Machine learning techniques applied to wireless ad-hoc networks: Guide and survey. In *Proceedings of the 3rd International Conference on Intelligent Sensors, Sensor Networks and Information Processing (ISSNIP)*, pages 365–370, Melbourne, Australia, 2007.

[63] A. Förster and A. L. Murphy. FROMS: Feedback routing for optimizing multiple sinks in WSN with reinforcement learning. In *Proceedings 3rd International Conference on Intelligent Sensors, Sensor Networks and Information Processing (ISSNIP)*, pages 371–376, Melbourne, Australia, 2007.

[64] A. Förster and A. L. Murphy. Balancing Energy Expenditure in WSNs through Reinforcement Learning: A Study. In *Proceedings of the 1st International Workshop on Energy in Wireless Sensor Networks (WEWSN)*, page 7pp., Santorini Island, Greece, 2008.

[65] H. Frey, F. Ingelrest, and D. Simplot-Ryl. Localized minimum spanning tree based multicast routing with energy-efficient guaranteed delivery in ad hoc and sensor networks. Technical Report 0337, Institut national de recherche en informatique et en automatique, 2007.

[66] H. Frey, F. Ingelrest, and D. Simplot-Ryl. Localized minimum spanning tree based multicast routing with energy-efficient guaranteed delivery in ad hoc and sensor networks. In *Proceedings of the 9th IEEE International Symposium on a World of Wireless, Mobile and Multimedia Networks (WOWMOM)*, pages 1–8, Newport Beach, CA, USA, 2008.

[67] D. Ganesan, B. Greenstein, D. Estrin, J. Heidemann, and R. Govindan. Multiresolution storage and search in sensor networks. *ACM Transactions on Storage*, 1(3):277–315, 2005.

[68] J. J. Garcia-Luna-Aceves and E. L. Madruga. The core-assisted mesh protocol. *IEEE Journal on Selected Areas in Communications*, 17(8):1380–1394, 1999.

[69] M. Gerla, T.J. Kwon, and G. Pei. On demand routing in large ad hoc wireless networks with passive clustering. In *Proceedings of IEEE Wireless Communications and Networking Conference (WCNC)*, pages 100–105, Chicago, USA, 2000.

[70] B. Gong, L. Li, S. Wang, and X. Zhou. Multihop routing protocol with unequal clustering for wireless sensor networks. In *Proceedings of the ISECS International Colloquium on Computing, Communication, Control, and Management (CCCM)*, pages 552–556, Changzhou City, China, 2008.

[71] S. Gonzalez-Valenzuela, S. T. Vuong, and V. C. M Leung. A reinforcement-learning approach to service directory placement in wireless ad-hoc net-

works. In *Proceedings of the IEEE 5th International Workshop on Aplications and Services on Wireless Networks (ASWN)*, page 8pp., Paris, France, 2005.

[72] A. Gopakumar and L. Jacob. Localization in wireless sensor networks using particle swarm optimization. In *Proceedings of the IET International Conference on Wireless, Mobile and Multimedia Networks*, pages 227–230, 2008.

[73] P. Gross and G. Kaiser. Automated component interconnection for scaling scale-resistent services. In *Proceedings of the 21st IEEE/ACM International Conference on Automated Software Engineering (ASE)*, pages 15–24, Tokyo, Japan, 2006.

[74] C. Gui and P. Mohapatra. Overlay multicast for MANETs using dynamic virtual mesh. *Wireless Networks*, 13(1):77–91, 2007.

[75] I. Gupta, D. Riordan, and S. Sampalli. Cluster-head election using fuzzy logic for wireless sensor networks. In *Proceedings of the 3rd Annual Communication Networks and Services Research Conference (CNSR)*, pages 255–260, Halifax, Nova Scotia, Canada, 2005.

[76] S.M. Guru, S.K. Halgamuge, and S. Fernando. Particle swarm optimisers for cluster formation in wireless sensor networks. In *Proceedings of the 2nd International Conference on Intelligent Sensors, Sensor Networks and Information Processing (ISSNIP)*, pages 319–324, Melbourne, Australia, 2005.

[77] C. P. Hall, A. Carzaniga, and A. L. Wolf. DV/DRP: A content-based networking protocol for sensor networks. Technical Report 2006/04, Faculty of Informatics, University of Lugano, 2006.

[78] E. B. Hamida and G. Chelius. Analytical evaluation of virtual infrastructures for data dissemination in wireless sensor networks with mobile sink. In *Proceedings of the First ACM workshop on Sensor and actor networks (SANET)*, pages 3–10, Montreal, Canada, 2007.

[79] S. Hao and T. Wang. Sensor networks routing via bayesian exploration. In *Proceedings of the 31st IEEE Conference on Local Computer Networks (LCN)*, pages 954–955, Tampa, FL, USA, 2006.

[80] P. Hebden and A.R. Pearce. Distributed asynchronous clustering for self-organisation of wireless sensor networks. In *Proceedings of the 4th Conference on Intelligent Sensing and Information Processing (ICISIP)*, pages 37–42, Bangalore, India, 2006.

[81] J. Hu, J. Song, X. Kang, and M. Zhang. A study of particle swarm optimization in urban traffic surveillance system. In *Proceedings of the IMACS Multiconference on Computational Engineering in Systems Applications (CESA)*, volume 2, pages 2056–2061, Bejing, China, 2006.

[82] Q. Huang, S. Bhattacharya, C. Lu, and G.-C. Roman. Far: Face-aware routing for mobicast in large-scale sensor networks. *ACM Transactions on Sensor Networks*, 1(2):240–271, 2005.

[83] P. Hurni and T. Braun. Energy-efficient multi-path routing in wireless sensor networks. In *Proceedings of the 7th international conference on Ad-hoc, Mobile and Wireless Networks (ADHOC-NOW)*, pages 72–85, Sophia Antipolis, France, 2008.

[84] S. Hussain and A. W. Matin. Hierarchical cluster-based routing in wireless sensor networks. In *Proceedings of the 5th International Conference on Information Processing in Sensor Networks (IPSN)*, page 2pp., Nashville, TN, USA, 2006.

[85] S. Hussain, A. W. Matin, and O. Islam. Genetic algorithm for energy efficient clusters in wireless sensor networks. In *Proceedings of the 4th International Conference on Information Technology (ITNG)*, pages 147–154, Las Vegas, Nevada, USA, 2007.

[86] K. Hwang, J. In, and D. S. Eom. Distributed dynamic shared tree for minimum energy data aggregation of multiple mobile sinks in wireless

sensor networks. In *Proceedings of the 3rd European Worskhop on Wireless Sensor Networks (EWSN)*, pages 132–147, Zurich, Switzerland, 2006.

[87] Scatterweb Inc. http://www.scatterweb.de/.

[88] C. Intanagonwiwat, R. Govindan, D. Estrin, J. Heidemann, and F. Silva. Directed diffusion for wireless sensor networking. *Transactions on Networking*, 11:2–16, 2003.

[89] M. Iqbal, I. Gindal, and L. Dooley. An energy-aware dynamic clustering algorithm for load balancing in wireless sensor networks. *Journal of Communications*, 1(3):10–20, 2006.

[90] O. Islam and S. Hussain. An intelligent multi-hop routing for wireless sensor networks. In *Proceedings of the IEEE/WIC/ACM international conference on Web Intelligence and Intelligent Agent Technology (WI-IAT)*, pages 239–242, Hong Kong, 2006.

[91] S. S. Iyengar, H.-C. Wu, N. Balakrishnan, and S. Y. Chang. Biologically inspired cooperative routing for wireless mobile sensor networks. *IEEE Systems Journal*, 1(1):29–37, 2007.

[92] Ki Y. Jang, Kyung T. Kim, and Hee Y. Youn. An energy efficient routing scheme for wireless sensor networks. In *Proceedings of the International Conference on Computational Science and its Applications (ICCSA)*, pages 399–404, Kuala Lumpur, Malaysia, 2007.

[93] J. G. Jetcheva and D. B. Johnson. Adaptive demand-driven multicast routing in multi-hop wireless ad hoc networks. In *Proceedings of the 2nd ACM International Symposium on Mobile Ad Hoc Networking & Computing (MobHoc)*, pages 33–44, Long Beach, CA, USA, 2001.

[94] L. Ji and M. S. Corson. A lightweight adaptive multicast algorithm. In *Proceedings of the IEEE Global Telecommunications Conference (GLOBECOM)*, volume 2, pages 1036–1042, Sydney, Australia, 1998.

Bibliography

[95] M.H. Jin, W.Z. Liu, D.F. Hsu, and C.Y. Kao. Compact genetic algorithm for perfor mance improvement in hierarchical sensor networks management. In *Proceedings of the 8th International Symposium on Parallel Architectures, Algorithms and Networks (ISPAN)*, page 6pp., Las Vegas, Nevada, USA, 2005.

[96] L.P. Kaelbling, M.L. Littman, and A.P. Moore. Reinforcement learning: A survey. *Journal of Artificial Intelligence Research*, 4:237–285, 1996.

[97] J. M. Kahn, R. H. Katz, and K. S. J. Pister. Next century challenges: mobile networking for "Smart Dust". In *Proceedings of the 5th annual ACM/IEEE international conference on Mobile computing and networking (MobiCom)*, pages 271–278, Seattle, WA, USA, 1999.

[98] S. Kaplantzis, A. Shilton, N. Mani, and Y.A. Sekercioglu. Detecting selective forwarding attacks in wireless sensor networks using support vector machines. In *Proceedings of the 3rd International Conference on Intelligent Sensors, Sensor Networks and Information (ISSNIP)*, pages 335–340, Melbourne, Australia, 2007.

[99] B. Karp and H. T. Kung. GPSR: greedy perimeter stateless routing for wireless networks. In *Proceedings of the 6th annual international conference on Mobile computing and networking (MobiCom)*, pages 243–254, Boston, MA, USA, 2000.

[100] I. Kassabalidis, M. A. ElSharkawi, R. J. Marks, P. Arabshahi, and A. A. Gray. Swarm intelligence for routing in communication networks. In *Proceedings of the IEEE Global Telecommunications Conference (GLOBECOM)*, pages 3613–3617, San Antonio, TX, USA, 2001.

[101] J. Kennedy and R.C. Eberhart. *Swarm Intelligence*. Morgan Kaufmann, 2001.

[102] H. Kim, Y. Seok, N. Choi, Y. Choi, and T. Kwon. Optimal multi-sink positioning and energy-efficient routing in wireless sensor networks. *Information Networking*, 3391:264–274, 2005.

[103] H.S. Kim, T.F. Abdelzaher, and W.H. Kwon. Minimum-energy asynchronous dissemination to mobile sinks in wireless sensor networks. In *Proceedings of the 1st International Conference on Embedded Networked Sensor Systems (SenSys)*, pages 193–204, Los Angeles, CA, USA, 2003.

[104] H.S. Kim, T.F. Abdelzaher, and W.H. Kwon. Dynamic delay-constrained minimum-energy dissemination in wireless sensor networks. *Transactions on Embedded Computing Systems*, 4(3):679–706, 2005.

[105] S. Koenig. Agent-centered search. *AI Magazine*, 22(4):109–131, 2001.

[106] R. E. Korf. Real-time heuristic search. *Artificial Intelligence*, 42(2-3):189–211, 1990.

[107] D. Kotz, C. Newport, R. S. Gray, J. Liu, Y. Yuan, and C. Elliott. Experimental evaluation of wireless simulation assumptions. In *Proceedings of the 7th ACM international symposium on Modeling, analysis and simulation of wireless and mobile systems (MSWiM)*, pages 78–82, Venice, Italy, 2004.

[108] S.B. Kulkarni, A. Förster, and G.K. Venayagamoorthy. A survey on applications of computational intelligence for wireless sensor networks. *under review*, 2009.

[109] S. Kumar and R. Miikkulainen. Dual reinforcement Q-routing: An on-line adaptive routing algorithm. In *Proceedings of the Conference on Artificial Neural Networks in Engineering (ANNIE)*, pages 231–238, St. Loius, MI, USA, 1997.

[110] A. Kuntz, F. Schmidt-Eisenlohr, O. Graute, H. Hartenstein, and M. Zitterbart. Introducing Probabilistic Radio Propagation Models in OMNeT++ Mobility Framework and Cross Validation Check with NS-2. In *Proceedings of the 1st International Workshop on OMNeT++*, page 7pp., Marseille, France, 2008.

[111] S. Kurkowski, T. Camp, and M. Colagrosso. Manet simulation studies: the incredibles. *SIGMOBILE Mobile Computation and Communication Revue*, 9(4):50–61, 2005.

[112] K. Langendoen. Medium access control in wireless sensor networks. In H. Wu and Y. Pan, editors, *Medium Access Control in Wireless Networks, Volume II: Practice and Standards*, page 22pp. Nova Science Publishers, Inc., 2007.

[113] K. Langendoen, A. Baggio, and O. Visser. Murphy loves potatoes: experiences from a pilot sensor network deployment in precision agriculture. In *Proceedings of the 20th International Symposium on Parallel and Distributed Processing Symposium (IPDPS)*, page 8pp., Rhodes Island, Greece, 2006.

[114] B. Lazzerini, F. Marcelloni, M. Vecchio, S. Croce, and E. Monaldi. A fuzzy approach to data aggregation to reduce power consumption in wireless sensor networks. In *Proceedings of the Annual meeting of the North American Fuzzy Information Processing Society (NAFIPS)*, pages 436–441, Montreal, Canada, 2006.

[115] S. J. Lee, W. Su, and M. Gerla. On-demand multicast routing protocol in multihop wireless mobile networks. *Mobile Networks and Applications*, 7(6):441–453, 2002.

[116] P. Levis, N. Lee, M. Welsh, and D. Culler. Tossim: accurate and scalable simulation of entire tinyos applications. In *Proceedings of the 1st international conference on Embedded networked sensor systems (SenSys)*, pages 126–137, Los Angeles, CA, USA, 2003.

[117] Z. Li and H. Shi. Design of gradient and node remaining energy constrained directed diffusion routing for wsn. In *Proceedings of the International Conference on Wireless Communications, Networking and Mobile Computing (IWCMC)*, pages 2600–2603, Honolulu, Hawaii, USA, 2007.

[118] Z. Liu and I. Elahanany. RL-MAC: A reinforcement learning based MAC protocol for wireless sensor networks. *International Journal on Sensor Networks*, 1(3/4):117–124, 2006.

[119] L.Kleinrock and K.Stevens. Fisheye: A lenslike computer display transformation. Technical report, University of California, Los Angeles, 2004.

[120] H. Luo, F. Ye, J. Cheng, S. Lu, and L. Zhang. TTDD: Two-tier data dissemination in large-scale wireless sensor networks. *Wireless Networks*, 11(1-2):161–175, 2005.

[121] S. R. Madden, M. J. Franklin, J. M. Hellerstein, and W. Hong. TinyDB: an acquisitional query processing system for sensor networks. *ACM Transactions on Database Systems*, 30(1):122–173, 2005.

[122] B. Malakooti, H. Kim, and K. Bhasin. Human & robotics technology space exploration communication scenarios: Characteristics, challenges & scenarios for developing intelligent internet protocols. In *Proceedings of the 2nd IEEE International Conference on Space Mission Challenges for Information Technology (SMC-IT)*, pages 322–329, Pasadena, CA, USA, 2006.

[123] A. Manjeshwar and D. P. Agrawal. TEEN: A routing protocol for enhanced efficiency in wireless sensor networks. In *Proceedings of the 15th International Parallel and Distributed Processing Symposium (IPDPS)*, pages 2009–2015, San Francisco, CA, USA, 2001.

[124] A. Manjeshwar and D. P. Agrawal. APTEEN: A hybrid protocol for efficient routing and comprehensive information retrieval in wireless sensor networks. In *Proceedings of the 16th International Parallel and Distributed Processing Symposium (IPDPS)*, pages 195–202, Fort Lauderdale, FL, USA, 2002.

[125] M. Marks and E. Niewiadomska-Szynkiewicz. Two-phase stochastic optimization to sensor network localization. In *Proceedings of the International Conference on Sensor Technologies and Applications (SensorComm)*, pages 134–139, Valencia, Spain, 2007.

[126] K. Martinez, P. Padhy, A. Riddoch, R. Ong, and J. Hart. Glacial Environment Monitoring using Sensor Networks. In *Proceedings of the 1st*

Workshop on Real-World Wireless Sensor Networks (REALWSN), page 5pp., Stockholm, Sweden, 2005.

[127] A. W. Matin and S. Hussain. Intelligent hierarchical cluster-based routing. In *Proceedings of the International Workshop on Mobility and Scalability in Wireless Sensor Networks (MSWSN)*, page 9pp., San Francisco, CA, USA, 2006.

[128] MATLAB. http://www.mathworks.com.

[129] John McCulloch, Paul McCarthy, Siddeswara Mayura Guru, Wei Peng, Daniel Hugo, and Andrew Terhorst. Wireless sensor network deployment for water use efficiency in irrigation. In *Proceedings of the Workshop on Real-world Wireless Sensor Networks (REALWSN)*, pages 46–50, Glasgow, Scotland, 2008.

[130] C. Mendis, S.M. Guru, S. Halgamuge, and S. Fernando. Optimized sink node path using particle swarm optimization. In *Proceedings of the 20th International Conference on Advanced Information Networking and Applications (AINA)*, volume 2, page 5 pp., Vienna, Austria, 2006.

[131] T.M. Mitchell. *Machine Learning*. McGraw-Hill, 1997.

[132] R. Muraleedharan and L. A. Osadciw. A predictive sensor network using ant system. In *Proceedings of the SPIE Conference on Digital Wireless Communications*, volume 5440, pages 181–192, Orlando, FL, USA, 2004.

[133] Sensor Network Museum. http://www.btnode.ethz.ch/projects/ sensornetworkmuseum.

[134] Guo-Fang Nan, Min-Qiang Li, and Jie Li. Estimation of node localization with a real-coded genetic algorithm in WSNs. In *Proceedings of the International Conference on Machine Learning and Cybernetics (ICMLC)*, volume 2, pages 873–878, Hong Kong, 2007.

[135] T. Naumowicz, R. Freeman, A. Heil, M. Calsyn, E. Hellmich, A. Braendle, T. Guilford, and J. Schiller. Autonomous monitoring of vulnerable

habitats using a wireless sensor network. In *Proceedings of the 3rd Workshop on Real-World Wireless Sensor Networks (REALWSN)*, pages 51–55, Glasgow, Scottland, 2008.

[136] TOSSIM: Simulating TinyOS Networks. http://www.cs.berkeley.edu/~pal/research/tossim.html.

[137] P.N. Ngatchou, W.L.J. Fox, and M.A. El-Sharkawi. Distributed sensor placement with sequential particle swarm optimization. In *Proceedings of the IEEE Swarm Intelligence Symposium (SIS)*, pages 385–388, 2005.

[138] F.G. Nocetti, J.S. Gonzalez, and I. Stojmenovic. Connectivity based k-hop clustering in wireless networks. *Telecommunications Systems*, 22(1-4):205–220, 2003.

[139] E. I. Oyman and C. Ersoy. Multiple sink network design problem in large scale wireless sensor networks. In *Proceedings of the IEEE International Conference on Communications (ICC)*, volume 6, pages 3663–3667, Paris, France, 2004.

[140] C. Pandana and K. J. R. Liu. Near-optimal reinforcement learning framework for energy-aware sensor communications. *IEEE Journal on Selected Areas in Communications*, 23(4):788–797, 2005.

[141] C. Pandana and K.J.R. Liu. Robust connectivity-aware energy-efficient routing for wireless sensor networks. *IEEE Transactions on wireless communications*, 7(10):3904–3916, 2008.

[142] K. Pawlikowski, H.-D. J. Jeong, and J.-S. R. Lee. On credibility of simulation studies of telecommunication networks. *IEEE Communications Magazine*, 40(1):132–139, 2001.

[143] G. Pei, M. Gerla, and T. W. Chen. Fisheye state routing in mobile ad hoc networks. In *Proceedings of the ICDCS Workshop on Wireless Networks and Mobile Computing*, page 8pp., Taipei, Taiwan, 2000.

[144] Charles E. Perkins and Elizabeth M. Royer. Ad-hoc on-demand distance vector routing. In *Proceedings of the 2nd IEEE Workshop on Mobile Computer Systems and Applications (WMCSA)*, pages 90–100, New Orleans, USA, 1999.

[145] J. Polastre, J. Hill, and D. Culler. Versatile low power media access for wireless sensor networks. In *Proceedings of the the 2nd ACM Conference on Embedded Networked Sensor Systems (SenSys)*, pages 95–107, Baltimore, MD, USA, 2004.

[146] J.B. Predd, S.B. Kulkarni, and H.V. Poor. Distributed learning in wireless sensor networks. *IEEE Signal Processing Magazine*, 23(4):56–69, 2006.

[147] H. J. Prömel and A. Steger. *The Steiner Tree Problem*. Vieweg, 2002.

[148] QualNet. http://www.scalable-networks.com/.

[149] W. Rabiner-Heinzelman, A. Chandrakasan, and H. Balakrishnan. Energy-efficient communication protocol for wireless microsensor networks. In *Proceedings of the 33rd Hawaii International Conference on System Sciences (HICSS)*, page 10pp., Hawaii, USA, 2000.

[150] P. Radivojac, U. Korad, K. M. Sivalingam, and Z. Obradovic. Learning from class-imbalanced data in wireless sensor networks. In *Proceedings of the 58th IEEE Vehicular Technology Conference (VTC)*, volume 5, pages 3030–3034, Orlando, Florida, USA, 2003.

[151] V. Raghunathan, S. Ganeriwal, and M. Srivastava. Emerging techniques for long lived wireless sensor networks. *IEEE Communications Magazine*, 44(4):108–114, 2006.

[152] B. Raman and K. Chebrolu. Censor networks: A critique of "sensor networks" from a systems perspective. *ACM SIGCOMM Computer Communication Review*, 38(3):75 – 78, 2008.

[153] V. Ramos and A. Abraham. Swarms on continuous data. In *Proceedings of the Congress on Evolutionary Computation (CEC)*, volume 2, pages 1370–1375, Canberra, Australia, 2003.

[154] Q. Ren and Q. Liang. Fuzzy logic-optimized secure media access control (FSMAC) protocol wireless sensor networks. In *Proceedings of the IEEE International Conference on Computational Intelligence for Homeland Security and Personal Safety (CIHSPS)*, pages 37–43, Orlando, FL, USA, 2005.

[155] R. Rojas. *Neural Networks - A Systematic Introduction*. Springer-Verlag, 1996.

[156] K. Römer and F. Mattern. The design space of wireless sensor networks. *IEEE Transactions on wireless communications*, 11(6):54–61, 2004.

[157] M.T. Rosenstein and A.G. Barto. *Learning and Approximate Dynamic Programming: Scaling Up to the Real World*, chapter Supervised actor-critic reinforcement learning, pages 359–380. John Wiley & Sons, 2004.

[158] M. Rossi, M. Zorzi, and R. R. Rao. Statistically assisted routing algorithms (SARA) for hop count based forwarding in wireless sensor networks. *Wireless Networks*, 14(1):55–70, 2008.

[159] S.J. Russell and P. Norvig. *Artificial Intelligence: A Modern Approach*. Prentice Hall International, 2003.

[160] J. A. Sanchez, P. M. Ruiz, and I. Stojmenovic. Energy-efficient geographic multicast routing for sensor and actuator networks. *Computer Communications*, 30(13):2519–2531, 2007.

[161] R. Schoonderwoerd, O.E. Holland, J.L. Bruten, and L.J.M. Rothkrantz. Ant-based load balancing in telecommunications networks. *Adaptive Behavior*, 2:169–207, 1996.

[162] C. Schurgers and M. B. Srivastava. Energy efficient routing in wireless sensor networks. In *Proceedings of the IEEE Military Communications Conference (MILCOM)*, volume 1, pages 357–361, Washington, DC, USA, 2001.

[163] M.W.M. Seah, C.K. Tham, K. Srinivasan, and A. Xin. Achieving coverage through distributed reinforcement learning in wireless sensor networks. In *Proceedings of the 3rd International Conference on Intelligent Sensors, Sensor Networks and Information Processing (ISSNIP)*, 2007.

[164] S. Shakkottai, X. Liu, and R. Srikant. The multicast capacity of large multihop wireless networks. In *Proceedings of the 8th ACM international symposium on Mobile ad hoc networking and computing (MobiHoc)*, pages 247–255, Montreal, Canada, 2007.

[165] Y. Shang, M. P. J. Fromherz, Y. Zhang, and L. S. Crawford. Constraint-based routing for ad-hoc networks. In *Proceedings of the International Conference on Information Technology: Research and Education (ITRE)*, pages 306–310, Newark, New Jersey, USA, 2003.

[166] D. Shaoqiang, P. Agrawal, and K. Sivalingam. Reinforcement learning based geographic routing protocol for UWB wireless sensor network. In *Proceedings of the IEEE Global Telecommunications Conference 2007 (GLOBECOM)*, pages 652–656, Washington, DC, USA, 2007.

[167] C.-C. Shen and C. Jaikaeo. Ad hoc multicast routing algorithm with swarm intelligence. *Mobile Networks and Applications*, 10(1-2):47–59, 2005.

[168] Y. J. Shen and M. S. Wang. Broadcast scheduling in wireless sensor networks using fuzzy hopfield neural network. *Expert Systems with Applications*, 34(2):900–907, 2008.

[169] Zhang Shi, Zhang Zhe, Lu Qian-nan, and Chen Jian. Dynamic alliance based on genetic algorithms in wireless sensor networks. In *Proceedings of the International Conference on Wireless Communications, Networking and Mobile Computing (WiCOM)*, pages 1–4, Wuhan, China, 2006.

[170] F. Silva, J. Heidemann, R. Govindan, and D. Estrin. *Frontiers in Distributed Sensor Networks*, chapter Directed Diffusion, page 25pp. CRC Press, Inc., 2003.

[171] K. M. Sim and W. H. Sun. Ant colony optimization for routing and load-balancing: Survey and new directions. *IEEE Transactions on Systems, Man and Cybernetics*, 33(5):560–572, 2003.

[172] G. Simon, P. Volgyesi, M. Maroti, and A. Ledeczi. Simulation-based optimization of communication protocols for large-scale wireless sensor networks. In *Proceedings of IEEE Aerospace Conference*, volume 3, pages 1339–1346, Big Sky, MT, USA, 2003.

[173] NS-3: The Network Simulator. http://www.nsnam.org/.

[174] S. Soro and W.B. Heinzelman. Prolonging the lifetime of wireless sensor networks via unequal clustering. In *Proceedings of the 19th International Parallel and Distributed Processing Symposium (IPDPS)*, page 8pp., Denver, CO, USA, 2005.

[175] I. Stojmenovic and X. Lin. Power-aware localized routing in wireless networks. *IEEE Transactions on Parallel and Distributed Systems*, 12(11):1122–1133, 2001.

[176] P. Stone. TPOT- RL applied to network routing. In *Proceedings of the 17th International Conference on Machine Learning (ICML)*, pages 935–942, San Francisco, CA, 2000.

[177] P. Stone and M. Veloso. Team-partitioned, opaque-transition reinforcement learning. In *Proceedings of the 3rd annual Conference on Autonomous Agents (AGENTS)*, pages 206–212, Seattle, WA, USA, 1999.

[178] D. Subramanian, P. Druschel, and J. Chen. Ants and reinforcement learning: A case study in routing in dynamic networks. In *Proceedings of the 15th Joint Conference on Artificial Intelligence (IJCAI)*, pages 832–838, Nagoya, Japan, 1997.

[179] R. S. Sutton and A. G. Barto. *Reinforcement Learning: An Introduction*. The MIT Press, March 1998.

Bibliography

[180] R. Szewczyk, E. Osterweil, J. Polastre, M. Hamilton, A. Mainwaring, and D. Estrin. Habitat monitoring with sensor networks. *Communications of the ACM*, 47(6):34–40, 2004.

[181] R. Szewczyk, J. Polastre, A. Mainwaring, and D. Culler. Lessons From a Sensor Network Expedition. In *Proceedings of the 1st European Workshop on Sensor Networks (EWSN)*, pages 307–322, Berlin, Germany, 2004.

[182] I. Talzi, A. Hasler, S. Gruber, and C. Tschudin. Permasense: investigating permafrost with a wsn in the swiss alps. In *Proceedings of the 4th Workshop on Embedded Networked Sensors (EmNets)*, pages 8–12, Cork, Ireland, 2007.

[183] Q. Tang, N. Tummala, S.K.S. Gupta, and L. Schwiebert. Communication scheduling to minimize thermal effects of implanted biosensor networks in homogeneous tissue. *IEEE Transactions on Biomedical Engineering*, 52(7):1285–1294, 2005.

[184] Crossbow Technologies. http://www.xbow.com/.

[185] K. Teknomo. Online tutorial on q-learning. http://people.revoledu.com/kardi/tutorial/ReinforcementLearning/index.html.

[186] MoteLab: A Sensor Network Testbed. http://motelab.eecs.harvard.edu/.

[187] C. Tham, S. Marwaha, and D. Srinivasan. Mobile agents based routing protocol for mobile ad hoc networks. In *Proceedings of the IEEE Global Telecommunications Conference (GLOBECOM)*, volume 1, pages 163–167, Taipei, Taiwan, 2002.

[188] S. Tilak, A. Murphy, and W. Heinzelman. Non-uniform information dissemination for sensor networks. In *Proceedings of the 11th International Conference on Network Protocols (ICNP)*, pages 295–304, Atlanta, GA, USA, 2003.

[189] D.A. Tran and T. Nguyen. Localization in wireless sensor networks based on support vector machines. *IEEE Transactions on Parallel and Distributed Systems*, 19(7):981–994, 2008.

[190] D. Tulone and S. Madden. Paq: Time series forecasting for approximate query answering in sensor networks. In *Proceedings of the 3rd European Conference for Wireless Sensor Networks (EWSN)*, pages 21–37, Zurich, Switzerland, 2006.

[191] R. Vaishampayan and J. J. Garcia-Luna-Aceves. Efficient and robust multicast routing in mobile ad hoc networks. In *Proceedings of the IEEE International Conference on Mobile Ad-hoc and Sensor Systems (MASS)*, pages 304–313, Fort Lauderdale, FL, USA, 2004.

[192] L. van Hoesel and P. Havinga. A lightweight medium access protocol (LMAC) for wireless sensor networks. In *Proceedings of the 1st International Conference on Networked Sensing Systems (INSS)*, pages 946–953, Tokyo, Japan, 2004.

[193] R. Vidhyapriya and P. Vanathi. Reliable energy-efficient routing with novel route update in wireless sensor networks. *Journal of Zhejiang University - Science A*, 9(8):1099–1110, 2008.

[194] D. Wang. An energy-efficient clusterhead assignment scheme for hierarchical wireless sensor networks. *International Journal of Wireless Information Networks*, 15(2):61–71, 2008.

[195] P. Wang and T. Wang. Adaptive routing for sensor networks using reinforcement learning. In *Proceedings of the 6th IEEE International Conference on Computer and Information Technology (CIT)*, pages 219–224, Bhubaneswar, India, 2006.

[196] W. Wang, W.-Z. Song, X.Y. Li, and K. Moaveni-Neja. Optimal cluster association in two-tiered wireless sensor networks. In *Proceedings of the 3rd IEEE International Conference on Distributed Computing in Sensor Systems (DCOSS)*, pages 110–123, Sante Fe, New Mexico, USA, 2007.

[197] Y. Wang, M. Martonosi, and L.-S. Peh. A supervised learning approach for routing optimizations in wireless sensor networks. In *Proceedings of the*

2nd International Workshop on Multi-hop ad hoc networks: from theory to reality (REALMAN), pages 79–86, Florence, Italy, 2006.

[198] C.J.C.H Watkins. *Learning from Delayed Rewards*. PhD thesis, Cambridge University, Cambridge, England, 1989.

[199] G. Werner-Allen, K. Lorincz, M. Ruiz, O. Marcillo, J. Johnson, J. Lees, and M. Welsh. Deploying a wireless sensor network on an active volcano. *IEEE Internet Computing*, 10(2):18–25, 2006.

[200] G. Wittenburg and J. Schiller. A quantitative evaluation of the simulation accuracy of wireless sensor networks. In *Proceedings of 6th Fachgespräch "Drahtlose Sensornetze" der GI/ITG-Fachgruppe "Kommunikation und Verteilte Systeme"*, pages 23–26, Aachen, Germany, 2007.

[201] G. Wittenburg, K. Terfloth, F. López Villafuerte, T. Naumowicz, H. Ritter, and J. Schiller. Fence monitoring – experimental evaluation of a use case for wireless sensor networks. In *Proceedings of the 4th European Conference on Wireless Sensor Networks (EWSN)*, pages 163–178, Delft, The Netherlands, 2007.

[202] A. Woo, T. Tong, and D. Culler. Taming the underlying challenges of reliable multihop routing in sensor networks. In *Proceedings of the 1st international conference on Embedded networked sensor systems (SenSys)*, pages 14–27, Los Angeles, CA, USA, 2003.

[203] C. W. Wu and Y. C. Tay. AMRIS: a multicast protocol for ad hoc wireless networks. In *Proceedings of the IEEE Military Communications Conference (MILCOM)*, volume 1, pages 25–29, Livingston, NJ, USA, 1999.

[204] Q. Wu, N.S.V. Rao, J. Barhen, S.S. Iyengar, V.K. Vaishnavi, H. Qi, and K. Chakrabarty. On computing mobile agent routes for data fusion in distributed sensor networks. *IEEE Transactions of Knowledge Data Engineering*, 16(6):740–753, 2004.

[205] Y. Wu, L. Zhang, Y. Wu, and Z. Niu. Interest dissemination with directional antennas for wireless sensor networks with mobile sinks. In *Proceedings of the 4th international conference on Embedded networked sensor systems (SenSys)*, pages 99–111, Boulder, CO, USA, 2006.

[206] D. Xia and N. Vlajic. Near-optimal node clustering in wireless sensor networks for environment monitoring. In *Proceedings of the 21st International Conference on Advanced Networking and Applications (AINA)*, pages 1825–1829, Niagara Falls, Canada, 2007.

[207] J. Xie, R. R. Talpade, A. Mcauley, and M. Liu. AMroute: Ad hoc multicast routing protocol. *Mobile Networks and Applications*, 7(6):429–439, 2002.

[208] P. Yalagandula and M. Dahlin. SDIMS: A scalable distributed information management system. In *Proceedings of the ACM SIGCOMM Conference*, pages 379–390, Portland, Oregon, 2004.

[209] M. Ye, C. Li, G. Chen, and J. Wu. EECS: an energy efficient clustering scheme in wireless sensor networks. In *Proceedings of the 24th IEEE International Conference on Performance, Computing, and Communications Conference (IPCCC)*, pages 535–540, Phoenix, AZ, USA, 2005.

[210] W. Ye, J. Heidemann, and D. Estrin. An energy-efficient MAC protocol for wireless sensor networks. In *Proceedings of the 21st Conference of the IEEE Computer and Communications Societies (INFOCOM)*, volume 3, pages 1567–1576, New York, NY, USA, 2002.

[211] O. Younis and S. Fahmy. HEED: a hybrid, energy-efficient, distributed clustering approach for ad hoc sensor networks. *IEEE Transactions on Mobile Computing*, 3(4):366–379, 2004.

[212] B. Yu, P. Scerri, K. Sycara, Y. Xu, and M. Lewis. Scalable and reliable data delivery in mobile ad hoc sensor networks. In *Proceedings of the 4th International Conference on Autonomous Agents and Multiagent Systems (AAMAS)*, pages 1071–1078, Hakodate, Japan, 2006.

[213] L. Yu, N. Wang, W Zhang, and C. Zheng. GROUP: A grid-clustering routing protocol for wireless sensor networks. In *Proceedings of the International Conference on Wireless Communications, Networking and Mobile Computing (WiCOM)*, pages 1–5, Wuhan, China, 2006.

[214] M. Yu, K.K. Leung, and A. Malvankar. A dynamic clustering and energy efficient routing technique for sensor networks. *IEEE Transactions on wireless communications*, 6(4):3069–3079, 2007.

[215] Y. Yu, R. Govindan, and D. Estrin. Geographical and Energy Aware Routing: A Recursive Data Dissemination Protocol for Wireless Sensor Networks. Technical Report UCLA/CSD-TR-01-0023, UCLA Computer Science Department, 2001.

[216] K. Yuen, B. Li, and B. Liang. Distributed data gathering in multi-sink sensor networks wth correlated sources sensor networks with correlated sources. In *Proceedings of the IFIP International Conference on Networking (Networking)*, pages 868–879, Coimbra, Portugal, 2006.

[217] Y. Yujie, W. Zhe, and J. Peng. An optimum mobile agent route for data fusion in wireless sensor network. In *Proceedings of the IEEE International Conference on Information Acquisition (AICA)*, pages 1502–1506, Weihai, China, 2006.

[218] L. A. Zadeh. Soft computing and fuzzy logic. *IEEE Transactions on Software Engineering*, 11(6):48–56, 1994.

[219] M.Z. Zamalloa, K. Seada, B. Krishnamachari, and A. Helmy. Efficient geographic routing over lossy links in wireless sensor networks. *ACM Transactions on Sensor Networks*, 4(3):1–33, 2008.

[220] K. Zawadzki and A. Förster. Simulating routing protocols for wireless sensor networks. Bachelor thesis at the University of Lugano, 2008.

[221] Q. Zhang, J. Huang, J. Wang, C. Jin, J. Ye, W. Zhang, and J. Hu. A two-phase localization algorithm for wireless sensor network. In *Proceed-*

ings of the International Conference on Information and Automation (ICIA), pages 59–64, Hunan, China, 2008.

[222] Y. Zhang and M. P. J. Fromherz. A robust and efficient flooding-based routing for wireless sensor networks. *Journal of Interconnection Networks*, 7(4):549–568, 2006.

[223] Y. Zhang, J. Wu, and P. J. M. Havinga. Implementation of an on-demand routing protocol for wireless sensor networks. In *Proceedings of the 13th International Conference on Telecommunications (ICT)*, pages 1–4, Madeira Island, Portugal, 2006. IEEE Portugal Section.

[224] L. Zhao and Q. Liang. Fuzzy deployment for wireless sensor networks. In *Proceedings of the IEEE International Conference on Computational Intelligence for Homeland Security and Personal Safety (CIHSPS)*, pages 79–83, Orlando, FL, USA, 2005.

[225] G. Zhou, T. He, S. Krishnamurthy, and J. A. Stankovic. Models and solutions for radio irregularity in wireless sensor networks. *ACM Transactions on Sensor Networks*, 2(2):221–262, 2006.

Die VDM Verlagsservicegesellschaft sucht für wissenschaftliche Verlage abgeschlossene und herausragende

Dissertationen, Habilitationen, Diplomarbeiten, Master Theses, Magisterarbeiten usw.

für die kostenlose Publikation als Fachbuch.

Sie verfügen über eine Arbeit, die hohen inhaltlichen und formalen Ansprüchen genügt, und haben Interesse an einer honorarvergüteten Publikation?

Dann senden Sie bitte erste Informationen über sich und Ihre Arbeit per Email an *info@vdm-vsg.de*.

Sie erhalten kurzfristig unser Feedback!

VDM Verlagsservicegesellschaft mbH
Dudweiler Landstr. 99
D - 66123 Saarbrücken
Telefon +49 681 3720 174
Fax +49 681 3720 1749
www.vdm-vsg.de

Die VDM Verlagsservicegesellschaft mbH vertritt

Printed by Books on Demand GmbH, Norderstedt / Germany